Patterns in History

A Christian View

D.W. Bebbington

InterVarsity Press
Downers Grove
Illinois 60515

Printed in America by InterVarsity Press, Downers Grove, Illinois, with permission from Universities and Colleges Christian Fellowship, Leicester, England.

InterVarsity Press is the book-publishing division of Inter-Varsity Christian Fellowship, a student movement active on campus at hundreds of universities, colleges and schools of nursing. For information about local and regional activities, write IVCF, 233 Langdon St., Madison, WI 53703.

Distributed in Canada through InterVarsity Press, 1875 Leslie St., Unit 10, Don Mills, Ontario M3B 2M5, Canada.

ISBN 0-87784-737-1
Library of Congress Catalog Card Number: 79-3062

Printed in the United States of America

---

16 15 14 13 12 11 10 9 8 7 6 5 4 3 2 1
93 92 91 90 89 88 87 86 85 84 83 82 81 80

'There are happily still people who ask what all the long and tragic train of history means, what great thing does it intend, what destiny is it moving to, where its close shall be . . . Do all its large lines converge on anything . . . do they all curve in some vast trend and draw together to a due close? . . . Do they all work together for good and love? What does man mean? Or are you so happy with the children, or so engrossed in your enterprises, that you can spare no attention to ask about the movement, the meaning, the fate of the race?'

P. T. Forsyth, *The Justification of God.*

Preface

The purpose of this book is to analyse historical thought. It examines beliefs about the meaning of the course of history. The subject is itself approached historically. How have societies and individuals down the ages conceived the historical process? The book ranges from ancient China down to the present day, but pays special attention to more recent developments in western civilization. It explores some of the ways in which understandings of the historical process have affected how history has been written. It also offers brief evaluations of some of the chief schools of thought. Its coverage cannot be exhaustive, but an attempt has been made to touch on most of the strands of historical thought that affect the English-speaking world of the late twentieth century.

The book's title, *Patterns in History*, is deliberately ambiguous. The significance of the historical process has usually been visualized as a pattern – a wheel, a straight line or something similar. These patterns form the central theme of the book. Beliefs about the course of history, however, have formed traditions of thought. Ideas have been transmitted from region to region and period to period. Schools of thought in this field therefore display a pattern. The idea that history should be seen as a revolving wheel, for example, has occurred repeatedly in eastern and western thought alike. The pattern of such beliefs in the history of ideas is equally the subject of this book.

The core of the book, chapters two to six, deals with the traditions of thought about history. Chapter two examines variations on the theme of history as a revolving wheel. Chapter three traces the course of an entirely different notion, the Christian conception of history as a straight line under the control of God. In chapter four the subject is the idea of progress that has dominated much of western thought over the last two centuries. Chapter five considers the historicist tradition that emerged in reaction against the idea of progress. And chapter six examines Marxism as a theory of history. The other chapters form a framework for these five. The first explains why an appreciation of alternative views of the historical process is important for those who read or write history. The seventh chapter argues that philosophical analysis of how history is written can be understood only in the light of the schools of thought about patterns in history. The final chapter builds a statement of the meaning of history on the earlier discussion.

The book as a whole is a study in historical thought. Some readers, however, may find that its argument has broader applications. The book may well serve as an index to large-scale trends of ideas in other fields such as politics, sociology and theology. Thinking about most disciplines concerned with man has been moulded by the same influences that have shaped historical thought. Theories of history – and in particular the idea of progress, historicism and Marxism – have themselves been responsible for the style of thinking in many adjacent areas. The pattern of schools of thought has therefore been similar in a variety of fields. That is why some light may be thrown incidentally on the development of other disciplines.

Two features of the book are intended to supplement the text. The booklist consists of a selection of items that deal in greater depth with topics considered in the book. It is hoped that the notes on the books and articles in the list will help the reader to discover the items that will best meet his needs. This booklist is a revision of part of a booklet issued in 1977 jointly with Dr R. J. Bauckham, now of the Faculty of Theology at the University of Manchester, to whom I am grateful for permission to re-use it. The other feature that may help the reader is the index. It includes a description and the date of birth and death for each individual discussed in the text. I am glad to express thanks to my wife for preparing it.

There are a few minor points to be noted. All footnote references (with only one exception) are to English language sources, and all phrases in foreign languages are translated. Classical quotations are taken from Penguin translations whenever they are available and biblical quotations are from the Revised Standard Version. It perhaps needs to be said that the words 'man' and 'men' are used comprehensively for all human beings without any 'sexist' intentions.

It remains to acknowledge the great help I have received from many quarters in the preparation of this book. A large number of friends have contributed ideas and references over a number of years; so have members of some groups and seminars where sections of the book have been read. Warm thanks go to the following, who read the draft of the book in whole or in part: Dr R. J. Bauckham, Dr A. C. Chitnis, Dr R. J. Holt, Dr M. C. W. Hunter, the Rev. R.

L. Kidd, Mr M. J. Lacey, Dr R. C. C. Law, Dr A. M. MacBeath, Dr J. S. Munro, Dr P. D. Stachura, the Rev. J. and Mrs H. G. Taylor, Dr D. Whitehead and Dr H. Willmer. The book has benefited a great deal from their critical comments, although I must apologize to several for the inadequacy of my attempts to meet their points. I am glad to thank Mrs D. H. Lacey, for her work on the proofs. I am also profoundly grateful to my wife Eileen for her help, advice and support.

Stirling, March 1979 D. W. Bebbington

1 What is history?

'I can read poetry and plays, and things of that sort, and do not dislike travels. But history, real solemn history, I cannot be interested in. Can you?'

Jane Austen, *Northanger Abbey*.[1]

History, some say, repeats itself. Others hotly deny it, arguing that history has a pattern that excludes repetition. Others again claim that history has no shape at all. The subject of this book is the shape, meaning or significance that people have seen in history. It offers a study of theories of history designed for those who may occasionally have been provoked into asking themselves whether there is a pattern in the past. What significance have others seen in history? Why have they held their opinions? How can we assess their viewpoints?

HISTORIOGRAPHY AND THE HISTORICAL PROCESS

First, however, an important distinction must be made. A visitor to the Tower of London may well buy a copy of its history. When 'history' is used in this way it means something different from 'history' in the claim that history repeats itself. A history of the Tower of London is its written history, a record of the past. The history that may or may not repeat itself, on the other hand, is the past itself, not a record but what really took place. In the English language the word 'history' can mean either what people write about time gone by, that is historiography; or else it can mean what people have done and suffered, that is the historical process. This book is about both these, about what the historian does as well as about what all men live through, about how such works as a history of the Tower are written as well as about the great configurations that have been discerned in the past.

1. Catherine Morland in Jane Austen, *Northanger Abbey*, 1/14, ed. John Davie (London, 1971), p. 97.

Historiography (what the historian attempts) and the historical process (what he writes about) are nevertheless related. The historian is bound to reflect the past itself in his books. Some of the most influential writers about the past, such as Sir Walter Scott, have created the atmosphere of long ago, but have then peopled it with men of their own invention. Even if some of their characters did really exist, many did not. The incidents that they relate seldom actually occurred. Such writers are classed not as historians, but as writers of historical novels. They avoid what is at once the discipline and the delight of historians, the responsibility of confining themselves to what took place. What historians write must correspond in some sense with the past itself.

The correspondence, nevertheless, can never be complete. A great deal of what took place in the past is omitted from history books. This is a point beloved by historical novelists, who sometimes take up their craft in preference to history because they are then free to describe and discuss much of the detail that historians leave out. Tolstoy frequently turns aside from his main plot in *War and Peace*, the greatest of historical novels, in order to belabour historians for their sins of omission. The historians, he contends, recount only the grand outline of the Napoleonic invasion of Russia, whereas the doings and remarks of obscure common soldiers, which he as a novelist can portray, were in reality as significant in contributing to the fate of armies and empires.[2] Tolstoy's accusation is valid. Historians certainly do omit much that contributed to the historical process. Edward Gibbon's study of *The Decline and Fall of the Roman Empire* is a massive work, but Gibbon does not pretend to incorporate every aspect of life in Rome's later years, let alone every individual. The experience of living in imperial Rome was far richer, far more varied, far more complex than even Gibbon could portray. There have always been gaps in the most thorough historical works, and there always will be. Even if he restricts himself to a tiny area and a narrow period, as Professor Richard Cobb characteristically does in his studies of revolutionary France, the historian cannot recapture the words and deeds of historical agents exactly as they were. Between the historian and the people about whom he writes there is a great gulf fixed.

2. Leo Tolstoy, *War and Peace* (1869: Harmondsworth, 1957), 2, pp. 715ff.

THE PROBLEM OF THE EVIDENCE

There are two reasons for this discrepancy between historiography and the historical process. One is the problem of the evidence; the other is the problem of the historian himself. Leaving aside the second for later consideration, let us concentrate on the problem of the evidence. The difficulty is that the historian does not have his subject-matter, the past, available for investigation. He is separated from his subject-matter by time. Most other disciplines do not normally experience this problem. The chemist can examine reactions in his test-tube, the literary critic can pore over his texts and the sociologist can investigate the views and behaviour of contemporary society. The historian, however, cannot conduct opinion polls on the dead. He shares this problem, admittedly, with the astronomer, who is separated from his objects of study by space – and often, exactly like the historian, by time too. The astronomer's knowledge of the stars is mediated by what his telescope picks up from them. Similarly, the historian has to rely on what is mediated. Between the historian and the past lies the evidence.

There would be no problem if the evidence were total and reliable, but in fact it is normally meagre and often misleading. Our knowledge of the earlier middle ages depends on a tiny number of written sources that can be eked out by such supplementary material as place-names and coinage. There is sufficient evidence to write full-length biographies of only half a dozen pre-Conquest Englishmen. Even for the period that is best documented, the late nineteenth century, when newspaper coverage was ample and letter-writing had not been supplanted by the telephone, we know far from everything about the greatest of men. Whole months of the doings of cabinet ministers in the 1880s are likely to remain a blank after every archive has been combed. The relative paucity of evidence dictates that historians will remain ignorant of a great deal about the best understood periods in the past.

Further, evidence is not necessarily reliable. Although a historian is guided by research done by his predecessors, he has to treat their conclusions with caution. They may have misinterpreted their sources. Only by examining the sources that they used can he be confident that their work was accurate. This axiom gives rise to the conventional division of source material into primary sources (original evidence from the period under scrutiny) and secondary sources (derivative evidence in the work of other historians). Primary sources are more likely to reflect the reality of the historical process than secondary sources. Yet primary material can itself be highly deceptive. Forgeries and misrepresentations, whether from good or bad motives, litter the world's archives. The so-called Donation of Constantine purported to be a grant to the papacy of imperial authority in the west by the fourth-century Christian emperor, but it was probably composed in the eighth century by some ingenious mind wishing to bolster growing papal claims.[3] For over 600 years, however, it was believed because its authenticity was not investigated. Evidence can achieve remarkable confidence tricks.

The historian, therefore, develops a sceptical turn of mind. Original documents may themselves mislead; and what books about the past claim is much more likely to be wrong. The 'textbook mentality', that an assertion is true because it is written down, is utterly alien to any historical outlook. History, on the contrary, entails investigation, questioning, inquiry: the word history is derived from the Greek for 'inquiry'. Where it is impossible to investigate whether an account of the past is firmly based on valid evidence, history in the strict sense of the word is not being done. Most school history and much undergraduate history do not entail actual historical investigation at all. Rather, they consist of learning about the discipline. An undergraduate is sometimes quite rightly described as 'reading' history. The discipline itself is not a matter of reading, but of researching. It entails calling accepted views into question on the basis of freshly discovered or freshly interpreted evidence. History demands a critical frame of mind.

This is the sense in which history is scientific. History, declared J. B. Bury in 1903, 'is a science, no less and no more.'[4] Reasons will shortly be offered for holding that history is more than a science;[5] and it is equally true that history is less than a science on the model of classical physics. History's distance from its subject-matter prevents the possibility of experimentation, a necessary element in the classical model of scientific method. The discipline is nevertheless scientific in that it is critical of received opinion, rigorous in examining evidence and systematic in the presentation of its discoveries.

3. Sir R. W. Southern, *Western Society and the Church in the Middle Ages* (Harmondsworth, 1970), pp. 91ff.
4. J. B. Bury, 'The Science of History' (1903), *Selected Essays of J. B. Bury*, ed. Harold Temperley (Cambridge, 1930), p. 4.
5. *Cf.* below, pp. 12–16.

That is not necessarily to suggest that history imitates the method of the natural sciences.[6] Rather it is to claim that history is a science if that word is given the force of its German equivalent, *Wissenschaft*, the systematic quest for ordered knowledge.

THE PROBLEM OF THE HISTORIAN HIMSELF

The other reason for the discrepancy between written history and the actual past, standing alongside the problem of the evidence, is the problem of the historian himself. He has the tasks of selecting and arranging the evidence. These tasks demand the exercise of the historian's judgment. He uses criteria by which, say, to include or omit reference to a society's mode of production in discussing the stance of its political leaders.[7] Those criteria are influenced by the cultural, political and religious values he may hold – not to mention his temperament. In this instance, the mode of production is likely to be included if he is a Marxist; it is less likely to be included if he is not. The historian's history is moulded by his values, his outlook, his worldview. It is never the evidence alone that dictates what is written. The attitudes that a historian brings to the evidence form an equally important element in the creation of history. The bias of a historian enters his history.

This is vividly illustrated by the various editions of *Leaders of Public Opinion in Ireland* by W. E. H. Lecky, a later nineteenth-century Irish-born historian who was on one occasion offered the Regius Professorship at Oxford. In one passage Lecky offered an estimate of the strength of the volunteer movement that provided backing for Irish demands for legislative independence in the early 1780s. In the first edition of 1861 he claimed that they numbered 80,000; in the 1871 edition he cut down the figure to 60,000; in the 1903 edition he further revised it to 40,000.[8] The change was not in the evidence but in Lecky's political opinions. He had begun with sympathy for Irish national aspirations, then grew lukewarm and finally after 1886 became an outspoken champion of the union between Britain and Ireland. The number of the volunteers is an

6. The question of whether historical method can be assimilated to that of the natural sciences is analysed in chapter seven.
7. On the 'mode of production', *cf.* below, pp. 122f.
8. Donal McCartney, 'Lecky's "Leaders of Public Opinion in Ireland"', *Irish Historical Studies*, 14 (1964), p. 134.

index of his national feeling. Lecky's views certainly moulded his history.

Although the case of Lecky is particularly striking, he is not an exception among historians in being influenced by his personal attitudes. He is remarkable only because the change in his views enables us to pinpoint one of the effects of his underlying convictions with special clarity. Bias may operate more subtly, but no historian can escape bias altogether. It is not only Marxists that allow their values to permeate their history. Even if the historian lacks definite political or religious views (which is a virtual impossibility, since not to be for a party or faith is in some measure to be against it), he will be moulded by his culture. A twentieth-century historian, for example, does not share the belief of a sixteenth-century chronicler that alchemy is a profitable activity. Value-neutrality is impossible. The unconscious assumptions of the historian's own age are inescapable. The historian himself is part of the historical process, powerfully influenced by his time and place.

It is true that the professionalization of history in the twentieth century has set up academic standards that a historian infringes at his peril. A historian has to observe the rules of the club, and so cannot, without loss of respect as a scholar, abandon the professional expectations of his fellows. This factor may counteract the influence of his culture, politics or religion.[9] But this is merely another influence to add to the other three, a novelty thrown up by a particular period, the twentieth century. It is as much of a bias in a historian to fulfil the expectation of his professional colleagues as to vindicate his political position. As it happens, the normal effect of the desire to win the approval of other historians in the Anglo-Saxon countries in the twentieth century is to restrain any bias thrown up by politics or religion. But this need not necessarily be so. In contemporary Russia, to take only one counter-example, professional expectations *encourage* the writing of history with a very definite political colouring. Professional sanctions do not always eliminate excesses of bias. Rather, they add a fresh bias to the historian, who is already – and necessarily – a bundle of biases.

It is often urged that although a historian may have an unfortunate tendency to entertain bias, he should try to suppress it so that he can

9. *Cf.* J. H. Hexter, 'The Historian and his Society: A Sociological Inquiry – Perhaps', *Doing History* (London, 1971).

make a dispassionate assessment of the past. This, however, is to assume that bias exercises a uniformly detrimental effect on his history. That is not necessarily so. It is true that a bias impervious to the evidence is an undesirable attribute of a historian. If, for instance, he accepts as genuine a document that is clearly spurious because it supports his case, he is guilty of being a poor historian – and he may be sure that his sin will find him out as historical research continues. Yet his bias need not make him compromise his integrity. He may admit that a particular item of evidence does not support his case, but claim that the balance of probability still lies in its favour. He may modify his case in the light of an accumulated weight of evidence. Or he may even change his fundamental political or religious views as a result of his research. A Marxist, for example, may discover that the mode of production did not apparently determine the political stance of a historical group that he has examined with great care, and so may shed his Marxism. Bias need not extinguish a historian's critical powers.

If a historian's personal attitudes do not necessarily harm his history, it is equally true that they can enhance it. Great history is commonly a consequence of a historian's pursuit of evidence to vindicate his previously formed beliefs. Gibbon, for instance, wrote his masterpiece, *The Decline and Fall*, because he conceived himself to be a champion of civilization and rationalism who could point out that Rome succumbed to 'the triumph of barbarism and religion'.[1] A pure love of scholarship is rare. Deeply held convictions are needed to drive people to major historical achievements. Again, bias can be used as a historical tool. R. R. Betts, a British scholar working on the Hussites of fifteenth-century Bohemia, was brought up a nonconformist. Hence, as a colleague pointed out after his death, he was particularly able to understand men who chose to be nonconformists from the established church of their day.[2] His background gave him the advantage of a certain imaginative sympathy which enabled him to illuminate a portion of the past. Bias can be treated not as a liability, but as an asset.

The problem of the historian himself nevertheless dictates that

1. Edward Gibbon, *The History of the Decline and Fall of the Roman Empire* (1776–88), ed. J. B. Bury, 7 (London, 1900), p. 308.
2. E. F. Jacob, Review of R. R. Betts, *Essays in Czech History*, *The Journal of Ecclesiastical History*, 22 (1971), p. 68.

two historians presented with the same evidence are likely to reach different conclusions. This is true of people living in the same period; it is more true of people living in different periods. That is why each age writes history that reflects its own concerns. A heightening of awareness of national identity – as in the Scotland of the 1970s – normally brings with it a flurry of studies of the nation's past. As social attitudes change over time, so what historians discern in the past changes. This ensures that finality is never attainable in history. It was supposed at the turn of the twentieth century that patient research would eventually discover all there was to be known about the past. The only limitation on knowledge was the extent of the evidence that survived. *The Cambridge Modern History* was to be a milestone on the road to that goal, a compendium of all the knowledge of any significance assembled so far. Its projectors reckoned without the problem presented to historical research by the historian himself. As historians began to ask fresh questions dictated by new interests *The Cambridge Modern History* seemed increasingly dated and had to be superseded by a fresh version, *The New Cambridge Modern History*. The vision of definitive history has faded. There can be no universally accepted story of the past.

THE PROBABILITY OF HISTORY

The two problems of the evidence and of the historian himself ensure that written history cannot correspond precisely with the actual past. It may seem to follow that nothing can be known about the past. 'History', commented Tolstoy drily, 'would be an excellent thing if only it were true.'[3] Since we possess records of only a tiny fraction of human activities in the past, there is endless room for misinterpretation; and misinterpretation by those holding partisan views may seem unavoidable. This was in fact the conclusion of many in the late seventeenth century. The weakness of history as a means of acquiring knowledge appeared obvious by contrast with the power of the newly emerging natural sciences. A French writer, La Mothe le Vayer, in an essay of 1668, was one of the first to systematize this view as historical Pyrrhonism, the belief that all historical assertions

3. N. N. Gusev, *Dva goda s Tolstym* (Moscow, 1912), p. 175, cited by Sir Isaiah Berlin, *The Hedgehog and the Fox* (London, 1953), p. 13.

are too dubious to be given credence.[4] The past was dismissed as unknowable.

The late seventeenth-century climate of opinion that depreciated history also provoked its most cogent vindication. Pierre Bayle, perhaps the most learned European of his day, rejected historical Pyrrhonism. 'No valid objection', he wrote, 'will ever be raised to the fact that Caesar defeated Pompey. On whatever grounds we may choose to argue it, there is hardly anything more unshakeable than this proposition: Caesar and Pompey existed.'[5] There are some statements about the past which we cannot bring ourselves to doubt. A logical train of thought might compel us to acknowledge the possibility that all our evidence about Caesar and Pompey was fabricated five centuries after their time, in the manner of the Donation of Constantine, at a time when historians found contemporary history too gloomy to record. But how unlikely this would be! A wide range of sources, supported by non-documentary evidence such as coins, tells us of Caesar and Pompey. 'They were not merely', as Bayle continued, 'in the minds of those who wrote their lives.'[6] The probabilities of the case guide us, where strict logic does not, to believe that Caesar and Pompey did exist. The technical possibility that they were figments in the imagination of a later generation we reject on the grounds of its total improbability.

This instance reveals the status of historical knowledge. It is always probable rather than certain. There are matters, like the existence of Caesar and Pompey, that for all practical purposes we can take for granted; yet even these matters are technically not certainties. They are extremely strong probabilities. An early nineteenth-century writer brought the point powerfully to the attention of his generation.

In 1819, two years before the death of Napoleon but four years after his disappearance from the European scene, Richard Whately, a Fellow of Oriel College, Oxford, published a slim volume entitled *Historic Doubts relative to Napoleon Buonaparte*. In all the controversies over Napoleon, he observed, the preliminary question of his existence had been ignored. But what had been unquestioned was

4. A. D. Momigliano, 'Ancient History and the Antiquarian', *Studies in Historiography* (London, 1969), p. 10.
5. Quoted by Marc Bloch, *The Historian's Craft* (Manchester, 1954), p. 103.
6. *Ibid*

not unquestionable. The British newspapers had been full of Napoleon, but their sources, vaguely specified as other journals or unknown correspondents, could not be checked by British readers. The newspaper proprietors had an interest in circulating reports of Napoleon in order to promote their sales. And there was disagreement over important incidents in his career, such as whether he had won or lost the battle of Borodino. It might be objected that some had actually seen Napoleon at Plymouth as he was being taken to exile in St Helena. No, declared Whately, they merely saw a figure whom they were *told* was Napoleon. Altogether, he concluded, the evidence for Napoleon's existence was highly suspect.[7]

The whole argument was an exercise in satire. Whately's target was the eighteenth-century Scottish freethinking philosopher, David Hume. Hume had contended that belief in remarkable events like miracles should be suspended until the reliability of the evidence for them had been investigated. Whately was arguing that the evidence for the extraordinary career of Napoleon was technically no less doubtful than the evidence for miracles. Whately's point is surely valid. Any historical account is, in strict logic, open to doubt. It is not just remarkable events of long ago like biblical miracles that are not logically certain. Even events of the recent past, such as (we might say) the Watergate affair in America, are not logically certain. We accept that events took place if the balance of probabilities is in their favour. Probability, wrote Bishop Butler, 'is the very guide of life'.[8] Probability is the guide of history also.

THE FACTUAL IN HISTORY

Since certainty is technically unattainable in history, the popular idea that a good historian tells us the facts about the past must be rejected. A fact is normally taken to be a statement that is incontrovertibly true. Facts are supposed to form a reservoir of ascertained historical knowledge. 'Great abilities', once remarked Dr Johnson, 'are not requisite for an Historian.' Why? 'He has the facts ready to his hand.'[9] All the historian has to do, Johnson believed, is to

7. Richard Whately, *Historic Doubts relative to Napoleon Buonaparte* (London, 1819).
8. Joseph Butler, *The Analogy of Religion . . .* (1736), ed. Joseph Angus (London, n.d.), p. 5.
9. James Boswell, *Life of Johnson* (1791: London, 1970), p. 301.

draw out a few facts from his stock and assemble them in an intelligible order. Johnson had no doubt of the availability of pure facts. But such a view of historical facts will not withstand scrutiny.

The first consideration is a consequence of the problem of the evidence. The historian has no direct access to the past. He stands beyond a barrier of time. Facts, however, belong to the past. Strictly speaking they have no existence in the historian's present. Facts – the deeds or *facta* of men like Caesar or Pompey – took place long ago. A complete account of their deeds is irrecoverable. Even the recent past is beyond our reach. Uncertainty surrounds events near to us in time that have taken place in the full glare of public attention. The assassination of President Kennedy, for instance, occurred when a large number of witnesses was within sight and sound. Security men from several agencies who were on the spot attempted to discover who was responsible. Millions of dollars have since been spent in an intensive effort to establish whether or not there was a conspiracy to murder the president. Yet the broad outline of what happened and even such basic 'facts' as how many bullets were fired remain topics of debate. Investigation may have led to convergence of view on some aspects of the assassination, but it has multiplied disagreements over others. Even eye-witness testimony does not end discussion. That is why when the press calls for a public enquiry 'to get at the facts' in order to settle some controversy it is crying for the moon. Facts take place once for all and cannot be recovered afterwards in their full integrity.

A second factor that prevents the historian from presenting pure facts is a corollary of the problem of himself. The historian's judgment enters into his account of the past. He imposes order on his evidence by concepts drawn from the stock-in-trade that he keeps in his own mind. There is nothing in the evidence, for example, that tells him that something called 'the industrial revolution' took place in Britain between the mid-eighteenth and the mid-nineteenth centuries. The very phrase did not come into currency until the 1880s. Yet such concepts are essential if the historian is to write intelligibly. It might be thought that the use of phrases like 'the industrial revolution' is a matter of interpretation entirely different from the task of finding facts. It has often been supposed that interpretation and fact are clearly distinguishable and should be kept apart. According to C. P. Scott, editor of *The Manchester Guardian* in the early twentieth century, editorial commentary may represent a point of view, but news reporting must be strictly factual. 'Comment is free', he declared in 1921, 'but facts are sacred'.[1] The difficulty is that interpretation and fact interpenetrate. Our concepts determine which 'facts' we single out for attention. The invention of the spinning jenny, for instance, is important not so much in itself as because it contributed to the industrial revolution. Our concepts even determine the language in which we state our facts. To call certain central European towns by their German or by their Slavonic names is to take sides in territorial disputes that have stoked the fires of enmity in central Europe for a millennium. Interpretation unavoidably enters our very terminology. We can hardly make a significant historical statement without it being coloured by our point of view. To write a value-free account of the past is beyond the historian's power.

We may conclude that the historian cannot be expected to record indubitable facts. Yet that does not mean that he has licence to create interpretations totally divorced from the events of the past. He is necessarily concerned with the factual. The past itself, when Caesar and Pompey were alive, is inescapably his subject-matter. The evidence must discipline his history. His writing is consequently the result of an interaction between the givenness of the past and the creativeness of the historian. It would be difficult fully to disentangle what reflects the factual from what reflects the historian's mind in any particular historical statement. In his statements of detail there is, no doubt, more of the factual, and in his general statements more of himself. Thus a comment on the manoeuvres at the battle of Edge Hill is likely to be more factual than an assessment of which side won. It might be possible to locate a particular statement along a continuum that stretches between the poles of the factual and the subjective. No passage, however, could consist solely of fact – or of the subjective. The factual enters into what a historian writes, but so does the mind of the historian.

ARGUMENT IN HISTORY

History, then, can never be definitive. It can attain only probability. The historian does not deal with pure facts. It follows that there is always scope for discussion in history. The evidence can be construed

1. Quoted by Francis Williams, *Dangerous Estate: The Anatomy of Newspapers* (London, 1957), p. 134.

in different ways. Historians of equal integrity can persist in holding opposite interpretations of what actually happened. This is why the discipline is so marked by long-lived controversies. The Pirenne thesis that the Middle Ages began only with Mohammed and Charlemagne continues to provoke debate fifty years after its first enunciation; the still-raging controversy over the relations of Protestantism and capitalism has a longer history; and the discussion of the reasons for the fall of Rome goes back beyond Gibbon to writers like Augustine who were alive when the city was first taken by the barbarians. None of these controversies seems to be nearing resolution. In view of the nature of history it would be surprising if their end were in sight. There is perennial opportunity to adduce fresh evidence, to raise questions over the nature and reliability of the existing evidence, and (though this is probably done to a lesser extent) to debate the influence of a historian's personal views on the case he has presented. A distinguished historian can write of 'the endless discussion that is history'.[2]

Historical writing is therefore structured in the form of argument. Even when an area of the past is explored for the first time, its historian (whether or not he recognizes it) is arguing a case. That is why a research dissertation in history, as in other subjects, is called a thesis – a contention that is set up and maintained against possible attack. Argument with real or imagined opponents is of the essence of history. The historians whose names are remembered are those who argue a striking case with marked ability. Gibbon is once more a good example; and, in our own day, A. J. P. Taylor is a historian who never puts pen to paper (or appears on television) without a case to press home. As a general rule, the more cogent the argument, the greater the historian.

Some have believed that the essence of history lies elsewhere – usually in some form of narrative. G. J. Renier, a distinguished Dutch historian, for example, has written of history as 'the story of the experiences of men living in civilized societies' – no different in kind, though no doubt different in degree, from the yarn-spinning of a returned sailor or the recitation of traditions by the elderly in non-literate societies.[3] There is an important element missing from

2. Pieter Geyl, 'Historical Appreciations of the Holland Regent Regime', *History of the Low Countries: Episodes and Problems* (London, 1964), p. 169.
3. G. J. Renier, *History: Its Purpose and Methods* (London, 1961), p. 38.

such a description: the teller of a story need not be telling a story that is true. We should be inclined to caution before accepting either the yarns of a sailor or the legends of a non-literate society. A story may not represent the factual quality of the past. History, however, does reflect, albeit in a limited sense, what actually happened. The historian wants to convince the reader that his account of the past is the most probable. He therefore adduces evidence for his account, tries to show that his examples are fair ones and discounts alternative interpretations – in a word, he argues. He may do so either at length in the text or else simply by citing his sources in footnotes. This is what a historical novel need never do, for it has no obligation to show its foundation in a real past. History is a matter of argument because, by contrast with fiction, it is concerned with the factual.[4]

A historian, then, characteristically argues, presenting reasons for adopting a particular version of the past. He is trying to persuade his reader to adopt his own view. The historian brings forward, as La Popelinière (a sixteenth-century Huguenot who reflected on historical method) put it, 'arguments so probable as to persuade the reader that the historian's version of the events is at least the most plausible'.[5] The historian, that is to say, employs rhetoric, the art of persuasion. Rhetoric is not restricted, as La Popelinière and his contemporaries of the Renaissance well knew, to the spoken word. The term equally applies to the written word. Whenever someone gives reasons to others for holding a point of view he is employing rhetoric. The historian, as someone who argues a case, is a user of rhetoric.

The word 'rhetoric' has come to have adverse connotations. The 'rhetorical' in everyday usage is the flowery, the highblown, the pretentious: rhetoric needs puncturing. But rhetoric ought to be rescued from use as a term of contempt. It originally meant the technique of argumentation. In antiquity and from the Renaissance into the eighteenth century the art of rhetoric was treated with a

4. The view here taken of history as argumentation also entails rejecting the contention that explanation in history is ancillary to narrative, for which *cf.* W. B. Gallie, *Philosophy and the Historical Understanding* (London, 1964), pp. 105–25.
5. La Popelinière, *The Idea of Perfect History*, p. 317, quoted by George Huppert, *The Idea of Perfect History: Historical Erudition and Historical Philosophy in Renaissance France* (Urbana, Illinois, 1970), p. 146.

proper respect. Cicero used rhetoric when addressing the Roman senate (and also wrote the most influential treatise on rhetoric); and equally, Sir Walter Ralegh consciously used rhetoric in his *History of the World*. Rhetoric is not necessarily flowery, even if convention frequently dictated that it should be. It is a method as capable of systematization as logic. And it is intrinsically rational, for it suggests the most cogent ways of presenting *reasons* for a point of view.[6] To point out that history uses rhetorical technique is in no way to treat history as either pretentious or imprecise.

It is the rhetorical character of history that makes the subject a branch of literature. Rhetoric not only provides rules about the nature of arguments. It also concerns itself with the presentation of arguments. Rhetoric demands that the medium should befit the message, that the prose composed by a writer should be calculated to enlist the reader on the writer's side. A book is more likely to persuade if it is well written. This was the rediscovery that did most to stimulate the Renaissance on its literary side. Historians, like other prose writers, noticed that their predecessors in the ancient world had taken pains in the choice of words and illustrations.[7] The sixteenth-century Florentine historian, Guicciardini, for instance, was at least as concerned to turn a polished phrase as to reflect faithfully what had happened in the past. Since the Renaissance historians have commonly been expected to write well, even after the fading of the awareness that historians were in principle bound to the task as a consequence of using the techniques of rhetoric.

It is no accident that some of the greatest achievements of English prose have been the work of historians – of Clarendon and Gibbon, of Macaulay and Trevelyan. The last of these, G. M. Trevelyan, Bury's successor as Regius Professor of Modern History at Cambridge, was the champion of history as a literary activity over against Bury's assertion that it was solely scientific. Bury had been intending to banish rhetoric from history.[8] Trevelyan was trying to reinstate it. History, according to Trevelyan, is like poetry in being an art-form: it has a presiding muse, Clio. It should therefore be treated as a branch of literature that the reading public in general can

6. On rhetoric as the method of argumentation *cf.* Charles Perelman, *The Idea of Justice and the Problem of Argument* (London, 1963).
7. *Cf.* N. S. Struever, *The Language of History in the Renaissance* (Princeton, New Jersey, 1970).
8. Bury, *Selected Essays of J. B. Bury*, ed. Temperley, p. xvi.

enjoy.[9] It has already been suggested that history is properly called a science, so long as that word is understood in the sense of a systematic quest for ordered knowledge.[1] We must now add, with Trevelyan, that it is a form of literature. History departments in some British universities are affiliated to the faculty of arts as well as to the faculty of social sciences. That surely represents a just view of the place of history in the range of human knowledge.

THE ASSUMPTIONS OF HISTORIANS

What has been said so far would suggest that an appreciation of the views of historians is of great importance to the study of history. If all historians confronted by the same evidence came to an identical conclusion; if the historian could put his own views into abeyance when working on the evidence; if history could produce certain knowledge, a catalogue of ascertained facts, a story of the past that was beyond argument – if all this were possible, then the attitudes and techniques of historians would be of little interest. Historiography would be dictated by the past itself. Historians would be machines for registering advances in human knowledge. Their assumptions could be safely ignored.

In reality, however, historians are like others in sharing the convictions and prejudices of their time and place. Their outlook affects what they write far more strongly than is normally supposed. Objectivity in one sense is within their capacity, for they can treat all the evidence at their disposal with scrupulous fairness and allow it to call their prejudices and even their convictions into question. But the evidence is unlikely to modify more than a few of their assumptions. Their basic beliefs about the past, about its shape and meaning, are likely to remain and are certain to influence what they write. Objectivity in the sense of detachment is beyond the historian's power. 'Even the will to be objective', the early twentieth-century American historian Carl Becker pointed out, 'is itself a purpose, becoming not infrequently a passion, creating the facts in its own image.'[2] The historian's outlook, whatever it may be, plays a major

9. G. M. Trevelyan, 'Clio, a Muse' (1904, revised 1913), *Clio, a Muse, and Other Essays* (London, 1930), p. 175.
1. *Cf.* above, pp. 4f.
2. C. L. Becker, 'Detachment and the Writing of History' (1910), *Detachment and the Writing of History: Essays and Letters of Carl L. Becker*, ed. P. L. Snyder (Ithaca, New York, 1958), p. 14.

role in shaping the history read by his contemporaries and sometimes by posterity. This is why the underlying assumptions of historians are so worthy of scrutiny.

Perhaps most important is what historians believe about the historical process itself. It is sometimes suggested that opinions about the grand patterns of history, 'philosophies of history', can be dismissed as mere speculation. They seem undemonstrable, contradictory and a diversion from real history, whether for its reader or for its writer. 'Philosophies of History are many', wrote G. M. Young, 'and all of them are wrecked on the truth that in the career of mankind the illuminated passages are so brief, so infrequent, and still for the most part so imperfectly known, that we have not the materials for a valid induction.'[3] The study of philosophies of history, it might appear, has no value. Yet views about history, even if they are invalid, cannot but affect historians. They will be influenced more by their attitude to where history is going or what the past is about, than by most (perhaps any) of their other convictions. Their society's understanding of the historical process will colour their history even if they personally lack a fully-articulated philosophy of history. Their history, impregnated with views about the significance of the past, will in turn contribute to their society's worldview. Philosophies of history can drastically affect, for good or ill, the self-understanding of individuals, nations and civilizations.

It might seem that the variety of philosophies of history is so great that to analyse and evaluate them all would be impossible within a single book. But philosophies of history themselves fall into patterns. Five broad categories can be distinguished. Each embraces a variety of views, but each is a definite tradition of thought. Some who write about the meaning of the historical process have come under a variety of influences, so that their views are an amalgam. In these cases the influences can nevertheless be assigned to one or other of the five schools of thought. With only this small qualification, philosophies of history can be divided into groups, each of which will form the subject of one of the next five chapters.

PHILOSOPHIES OF HISTORY

A brief survey of these five schools is appropriate here. The first is the cyclical school, typical of both the oriental world and the ancient

3. G. M. Young, *Victorian England: Portrait of an Age* (London, 1953), p. 184.

world. This theory holds history to be a pattern of cycles, perhaps on the analogy of the cycle of seasons in nature. It conceives of a rhythm in the rise and fall of nations, of civilizations, or even, in its most epic forms, of the universe as a whole. It is clearly expressed in the second-century Stoic philosophy of Marcus Aurelius. The 'rational soul', he wrote, can comprehend 'the great cyclic renewals of creation' and therefore recognizes

> that future generations will have nothing new to witness, even as our forefathers beheld nothing more than we of today, but that if a man comes to his fortieth year, and has any understanding at all, he has virtually seen – thanks to their similarity – all possible happenings, both past and to come.[4]

Such views tend to be pessimistic. Affairs can never improve much, says Marcus Aurelius; decline is all that can be expected, say other representatives of this school. These views were not confined to the east and antiquity, but also exercised a fascination over many Renaissance humanists, and appeared in modern thinkers such as Nietzsche, with his doctrine of eternal recurrence, and Toynbee, with his panorama of the emergence and decay of civilizations.

The second school of thought is that especially associated with the Judaeo-Christian tradition. History is seen not as a cycle, but as a straight line. The historical process begins at a particular point, creation; and it continues under providential guidance to its goal, the last things. In between there are divine interventions, most notably (in the Christian view) in the coming of Christ. The guaranteed future makes this view characteristically optimistic, although not without reservations. Augustine's *City of God* gives classic expression to confidence in divine superintendence of earthly affairs, at least for the good of the church. Joachim of Fiore, a twelfth-century abbot, was to have almost as much influence on men who wrote history within a Christian framework in subsequent generations. Christian assumptions remained persistent in western culture, even after thinkers had set out in the eighteenth century either to demolish or to modify a Christian worldview. The twentieth century has produced a number of Christian interpretations of

4. Marcus Aurelius Antoninus, *Meditations*, 11/1, trans. Maxwell Staniforth (Harmondsworth, 1964), p. 165.

history, whether by theologians such as Reinhold Niebuhr or by historians like Sir Herbert Butterfield.

The Enlightenment of the eighteenth century was responsible for the emergence of a third school of thought about the historical process, the school whose central concept is progress. The straight line of the Christian pattern is preserved, but the theological rationale is removed. Instead of seeing God as the guide of history, thinkers of this school normally see people as its sole agents. Progress can be made in morality as much as in technology until in the future each human being will be, as Condorcet, one of the school's leading exponents, put it, 'emancipated from his shackles, released from the empire of fate and from that of the enemies of progress, advancing with a firm and sure step along the path of truth, virtue and happiness.'[5] This decidedly optimistic belief became widespread as the nineteenth century gave evidence of material progress. Systematized by Comte and other French theorists, it laid a groundwork for the development of sociology. This 'idea of progress' continues to attract the loyalty of historians like J. H. Plumb and Sidney Pollard.

The fourth school, historicism, also began its development in the eighteenth century. It was in large measure a German reaction against the idea of progress that had grown up in France and Britain. Historicism abandons the belief that history is linear. Instead, its central motif is the idea that each nation enjoys a distinctive culture. History is the story of the growth of the various cultures. The historian's task is to understand cultures different from his own by a technique of empathy. Most of these views were held by a forerunner of the historicist school in early eighteenth-century Italy, Giambattista Vico, but the whole body of thought was elaborated only as romanticism came to dominate Germany in the years after about 1780. Herder was its first great spokesman; B. G. Niebuhr applied its premises to the history of Rome; and Ranke refined its methods in a number of monumental works of scholarship. Historicism continued to mould most aspects of German intellectual life into the later twentieth century. The tradition is also represented by that apparently enigmatic work, R. G. Collingwood's *Idea of History*.

Marxism constitutes the fifth school of thought about history. The

5. Antoine-Nicolas de Condorcet, *Sketch for a Historical Picture of the Progress of the Human Mind* (1795), trans. June Barraclough (London, 1955), p. 201.

premise of all the thinking of Karl Marx was the conviction that the historical process is created by man as he labours to satisfy his basic needs. Marxism is therefore in essence an outlook on history, 'historical materialism'. Marx worked out his views in relation to those of Hegel, who blended ideas drawn from the Enlightenment and from historicism. Consequently Marxism owes a great deal to these other two traditions of historical thought. As it has developed inside and outside Russia down to the present, Marxism has tended to veer towards one or the other of the two traditions. Certainly it has not remained a static body of thought. Marxism of one type or another provides the framework for a great deal of the historiography of the modern world. Even when historians have passed through and beyond orthodox Marxism, as in the cases of Christopher Hill and E. P. Thompson, their history is strongly marked by elements drawn from the tradition of Marxist thinking.

Each of these five schools of the philosophy of history has continuing influence, not least on historians themselves. Different standpoints about the significance of history also affect discussion in the philosophy of historiography, the analysis of how historians write, which is the subject of chapter seven. The debate over how far history should use the methods of the social sciences is an instance of the issues to be explored there. The conclusions of chapter seven offer guidance for trying to resolve the problems that have emerged in the rest of the book. By that stage a mental map of the relations between the various viewpoints should have been plotted. The map can help us to approach the question of the meaning of history in the final chapter. There we should be in a position to outline the pattern that can legitimately be discerned in history.

2 Cyclical history

'Times glorie is to ... turne the giddy round of Fortunes wheele.'

William Shakespeare, *The Rape of Lucrece.*

A sense of history is not natural to man. Societies have existed, and continue to exist, where there is little awareness of the ongoing historical process and no desire to find out what happened in the past. In archaic Greece and in many non-literate societies of today, people are content to position themselves *vis-à-vis* the past by recounting the stories of gods, demigods and heroes. There is no question of establishing when great events took place. It all merely happened 'long ago'. Nor is there any question of argument about what story of the past is likely to be accurate. Entirely different versions can coexist without causing offence. Such tales are myth, not history.[1]

Where history has taken the place of myth, people have normally attributed the same type of pattern to the past. They have seen the historical process as being like a revolving wheel. Unless, as some have believed, the wheel has only one revolution, history repeats itself. Such a cyclical interpretation has been widely diffused in China, India, the Middle East and the Graeco-Roman world. There are probably two main explanations of its popularity. First, the life of any individual follows a pattern of growth to maturity followed eventually by decrepitude and death. The same schema was projected on to the historical process. Secondly, societies that were predominantly agricultural tended to conceive of history as part of nature. They came to think that the yearly rhythm of the seasons was reproduced on a grander scale in the world of men. On the basis of either of these obvious analogies, people concluded that history should be understood as a cyclical pattern.

There have been three main variations on the theme. In the first,

1. Sir M. I Finley, 'Myth, Memory and History', *The Use and Abuse of History* (London, 1975), esp. p. 15.

the circular pattern is restricted to particular dynasties or civilizations. Each in turn rises to prosperity before falling to defeat, disaster or decay. The second variation holds that the whole inhabited earth or even the universe is passing through a cycle, which usually extends over a vast period of time. The conclusion of a cycle may mean the end of all things, or else be the prelude to a fresh cycle of a new earth and sometimes a new heaven. In the third, the past is a time of steady decline from a lost golden age to the decadence of the present. This view, often called primitivism because it idealizes primitive times, concentrates on only a section of a cycle, its downward curve.[2] The three variations interacted with each other, but it is broadly true to say that, while the third has coloured thought throughout the world, the first was specially characteristic of China and the second of India.

CHINESE DYNASTIC CYCLES

Traditional Chinese historiography was organized in terms of dynasties. Copious records were kept to illustrate the rise of new dynasties, their tenure of power and their final collapse. The central concept was the 'mandate of heaven', given to the first ruler of a dynasty and forfeited by the last. The idea was by no means fatalist, since the mandate was a reward for good behaviour. Each dynasty ended with a 'bad-last ruler' whose moral irresponsibility explained the subsequent transfer of power. His reign was a time of troubles for himself and his people, reflected as much in bad harvests as in governmental follies. What heaven had decreed cast its shadow over all departments of life, even down to poetry, painting and drama. Adversity, like prosperity before it, was thought to affect the whole of society. The cyclical pattern was much more strongly marked than if politics alone had been concerned.[3]

History written on this schematic model was thought to serve a

2. Primitivism is sometimes treated as a pattern of linear decline rather than as a form of cyclical theory. But primitivism has normally been bound up with the downswing of a cycle. At its origin belief in decline was rooted in a cyclical view (*cf.* below, pp. 24ff., 27f.), and subsequently it was frequently thought that another golden age might follow contemporary decadence (*cf.* below, pp. 28, 34f.).
3. A. F. Wright, 'On the Uses of Generalization in the Study of Chinese History', *Generalization in the Writing of History*, ed. Louis Gottschalk (Chicago, 1963), pp. 41f.

practical purpose. People turned to history to discover examples of how to live upright lives and warnings of what errors to avoid. Those aspiring to public office, the normal destiny of successful educated men, would read the Confucian classics for general principles of ethics and government, but would read history to find concrete illustrations. Many of the popular texts were written for this readership – books like *The Comprehensive Mirror for Aid in Government* by Ssu-ma Kuang and *The Outlines and Details based on the Comprehensive Mirror* by Chu Hsi.[4] It was common for a later digest like *The Outlines and Details* to derive much of its material from an earlier one like *The Comprehensive Mirror*. Since the aim was to produce object lessons in ethics, the overriding need was for the best example rather than for an accurate account. Good examples could often be derived not from fresh sources but from old handbooks. Popular history therefore tended to consist of uncritical compilations.

Behind the popular history for aspiring bureaucrats were the state archives compiled by bureaucrats who had reached high office. State historians enjoyed great prestige in China, for from early times their records provided guidance not just for potential officials but also for rulers. Scribes seem to have been appointed for the first time to record events in the state of Ch'in as early as 753 BC, by coincidence the legendary year of the foundation of Rome.[5] They were responsible not just for keeping records but also for performing divination. The combination may appear less strange when it is noticed that such officials were experts in the past and the future – the whole historical process. The first comprehensive history of China, *Records of the Historian* by Ssu-ma Ch'ien, was not written until about 100 BC. It provided a model for the *Standard Histories* of the imperial dynasties, a voluminous series that continued down to the twentieth century. There was some privately composed history, but it, too, was written by bureaucrats.[6] The dominant mode of historiography was therefore

4. Lien-Sheng Yang, 'The Organization of Chinese Official Historiography: Principles and Methods from the Standard Histories from the T'ang through the Ming Dynasty', *Historians of China and Japan*, ed. W. G. Beasley and E. G. Pulleyblank (London, 1961), p. 49.
5. P. van der Loon, 'The Ancient Chinese Chronicles and the Growth of Historical Ideas', *Historians of China and Japan*, ed. Beasley and Pulleyblank, p. 24.
6. *Historians of China and Japan*, ed. Beasley and Pulleyblank, pp. 3, 6.

the compilation of state archives – what might be the result if keepers of the Public Record Office were trained as civil servants but not as historians and endowed with the prestige of advisers on all government policy-making, and then were to write all the history of Britain over two millennia. Chinese historiography is bulky and stereotyped and concentrates on subjects related to state policy. It is natural that rulers should appear in the foreground of history written by public officials, and equally natural that the *Standard Histories* should analyse the rise and fall of dynasties.

Chinese historiography is also studded with maxims. 'Officials oppress,' runs one of the soundest, 'the people rebel.'[7] Here was condensed wisdom for the future. But every incident set down in the public records had a similar purpose. It would supply a case-history of behaviour that could be adopted or shunned in subsequent generations. History was seen as a body of precedents. This conception of history was the result of two fundamental assumptions. First was the belief that there was a stable moral order. Similar behaviour led to similar consequences: a ruler's misgovernment, for instance, would always lead to the withdrawal of the mandate of heaven. Such a belief was a premise of the teaching of the sages of China, and supremely of Confucius. The second assumption was that patterns of behaviour did recur. This was a result of a disposition to see the historical process as a series of cycles. People could learn from a history that repeated itself.

INDIAN COSMIC CYCLES

Indian thought has attributed a bolder pattern to history. The chief sources, the *Puranas* composed by Brahmans of the first millennium AD, reflect earlier material in agreeing that the universe is passing through a cycle of enormous proportions.[8] The cycle normally consists of four *yugas* or ages, each of which is preceded by dawn and followed by twilight. The first *yuga* is of 4,000 years, preceded by 400 of dawn and followed by 400 of twilight; the second is of 3,000, with 300 of dawn and 300 of twilight; the third of 2,000, with two 200-year periods; the fourth of 1,000, with two 100-year periods.

7. Wright, 'Study of Chinese History', *Generalization*, ed. Gottschalk, p. 44.
8. *Historians of India, Pakistan and Ceylon*, ed. C. H. Philips (London, 1961), p. 4.

Each *yuga* is marked by a decrease in human longevity, morality and happiness. The present is the fourth *yuga*, a time of decadence. After the whole cycle of 12,000 years, a *Mahayuga*, the universe dissolves into chaos and a new cycle begins. Sometimes speculation suggested larger patterns of the *Mahayugas*, but the main point of agreement was that the process is endless.[9] It followed that people must resign themselves to a pattern of perpetual recurrence. Human activity is in the last resort futile, since all will take place exactly as it did before. What matters is not to perform great or good deeds within the historical process, but to escape from it. Only beyond history, in an eternal sphere, is there meaning. There was therefore no point in seeking guidance about the future from the past, as the Chinese attempted to do. In any case, the *yugas* were too long for any records to have survived from a comparable time in the past. Although Indian thought included a definite attitude to the historical process, it held the world of men – especially in the decadent present – to be unworthy of detailed consideration. The people of early India wrote little history.[1]

Buddhism and Jainism took over the traditional Indian view of the historical process. Buddhist writers, for instance, would compare a *Mahayuga* to a wheel with twelve spokes.[2] The Indian distaste for history was overcome in some measure by the need of the early Buddhist sects to justify themselves by composing biographies of their founders. Political history in a connected form, however, did not appear until the twelfth century, when a Kashmiri writer, Kalhana, argued that benevolent despotism is preferable to feudal rivalries. There remains in Kalhana's work a strong sense of the impermanence of all earthly things.[3] Resignation in the face of the transience of the world is the prescription even of the historian in India. Cosmic cycles breed passivity.

THE ANCIENT MIDDLE EAST

Elements that appear in Indian thought can also be detected in beliefs about history in the ancient Middle East. There was a Persian conception of four successive ages that clearly had affinities with the

9. Mircea Eliade, *The Myth of the Eternal Return* (London, 1955), pp. 113ff.
1. *Historians of India, Pakistan and Ceylon*, ed. Philips, p. 4.
2. Eliade, *Eternal Return*, p. 115.
3. *Historians of India, Pakistan and Ceylon*, ed. Philips, pp. 4f.

Indian pattern of four *yugas*. A lost text of the Zoroastrian religion of ancient Persia, for instance, referred to four successive ages of gold, silver, steel and a mixture including iron.[4] The metals were intended to symbolize a progressive decadence. This element of primitivism, the belief that history was taking a downward course from a golden age, was, however, far stronger in the Persian than in the Indian view. The thought that the times are steadily growing worse, though present in the Indian conception, is overshadowed by an awareness that fresh cycles will take place. In Persia, by contrast, there was no doctrine of eternal recurrence. There would be only one cycle of four ages, each worse than the last. The process would lead inexorably to a time of judgment when there would be a universal cataclysm.[5] Far from resigning themselves to passivity, according to Zoroastrianism, people must prepare for judgment by ranging themselves with the forces of good against the forces of evil. The sense that decadence was growing led to a pessimism about what it was possible to achieve within history; but the belief that decadence would eventually be terminated encouraged a heroic activism.

Ancient Mesopotamia and ancient Egypt seem to have entertained a less precise idea of history. Among the Sumerians and Akkadians, the Babylonians and the Assyrians, there was held to be a multiplicity of gods, each with very limited authority. The course of history was determined in divine councils where any one of many points of view might prevail. In ancient Mesopotamia, it has been concluded, 'history ruled the gods more than the gods ruled history'.[6] People could have no confidence in a long-term future, but could merely attempt to penetrate the mystery of what was immediately to come by seeking omens. In the earlier Babylonian empire of the second millennium BC, the past began to be seen as a cyclical pattern of happiness and disaster as dynasties rose and fell – much on the Chinese model.[7] The future, however, remained obscure and likely to be erratic. Egyptians had an advantage over Mesopotamians in believing that their ruler was divine. Although they, too, had to suffer the caprice of the gods, the pharaoh was able to guarantee a

4. Eliade, *Eternal Return*, pp. 124f.
5. *Ibid.*
6. E. A. Speiser, 'Ancient Mesopotamia', *The Idea of History in the Ancient Near East*, ed. R. C. Dentan (New Haven, Conn., 1955), p. 55n.
7. *Ibid.*, p. 56.

greater measure of order and continuity in Egyptian life. History had no particular pattern because it was always essentially the same.[8] In both Mesopotamia and Egypt, therefore, history was an indistinct notion: neither civilisation had a word for it.[9] It is not surprising that Persia, despite the greater distance of its heartland, exercised a stronger influence over Greek views on history than either Mesopotamia or Egypt.

CLASSICAL ANTIQUITY

The influence of Persia is betrayed by the earliest ancient Greek writer to expound something like a philosophy of history. The writer was not himself a philosopher or historian, but the poet Hesiod, who probably lived at the end of the eighth century BC – some fifty years, apparently, after the Homeric poems reached their final form. He writes of a sequence of races beginning with one of gold and ending with the present race of iron. The golden race experienced the joys of paradise:

> *The gods, who live on Mount Olympus, first*
> *Fashioned a golden race of mortal men;*
> *These lived in the reign of Kronos, king of heaven,*
> *And like the gods they lived with happy hearts*
> *Untouched by work or sorrow.*[1]

A silver race followed, less gifted with years and wisdom, yet great by later standards. Then there was a bronze race, next (rather oddly) a race of heroes, and finally the fifth race of iron, already feeble and wicked and destined to grow worse:

> *Now, by day,*
> *Men work and grieve unceasingly; by night,*
> *They waste away and die . . .*
> *The just, the good, the man who keeps his word*
> *Will be despised, but men will praise the bad*

8. Ludlow Bull, 'Ancient Egypt', *The Idea of History in the Ancient Near East*, ed. Dentan, p. 32.
9. Ludlow Bull, 'Ancient Egypt' and E. A. Speiser, 'Ancient Mesopotamia', *The Idea of History in the Ancient Near East*, ed. Dentan, pp. 3, 38.
1. Hesiod, 'Works and Days', lines 110–13, *Hesiod and Theognis*, trans. Dorothea Wender (Harmondsworth, 1973), p. 62.

And insolent. Might will be Right, and shame
Will cease to be.[2]

The overall pattern of increasing decadence symbolized by metals of decreasing worth is clearly akin to the Persian pattern; so is the detail that there are four different metals, three of which are the same as their Persian counterparts. Hesiod strikes out on a different course by inserting the race of heroes in the series of metallic races. This, it seems, is his attempt to provide a slot in his scheme for inherited Greek myths about the deeds of heroes like Heracles and Jason. Everybody supposed that they lived just before the present age of men, so there they must be fitted. The odd insertion is a sign that Hesiod was integrating two bodies of thought: Greek myth was incorporated in a Persian worldview.

Most ancient poets who touched on the pattern of history followed Hesiod in describing happier times in the past that contrasted with the dismal contemporary state of affairs. Aratus of Soli, for instance, a Hellenistic poet of the third century BC, wrote of a golden age of justice that had been succeeded by eras of silver and bronze.[3] It was not until Virgil that a poet expounded a longer cyclical view that gave grounds for optimism. Spurred on by the desire to provide literary sanction for the new regime of Augustus, Virgil wrote in his fourth *Eclogue* of the imminent return of a golden age.[4] This was not a consistent theme of Virgil, for in his *Georgics* he wrote of a decline from an idyllic period when the earth yielded produce without human effort.[5] He was rare in believing that better times would come at all; he was unique in supposing that they were at hand.[6] As far as the poets are concerned, a cryptic generalization by Lord Acton is broadly correct: 'The Ancients looked back to a Golden Age. How very general the belief was. Things getting worse and worse.'[7] As in Persia, primitivism was dominant and encouraged pessimism.

2. Hesiod, lines 176–78, 190–93, *ibid.*, p. 64.
3. Aratus, 'Phaenomena', lines 114–36, *The Oxford Book of Greek Verse in Translation*, ed. T. F. Higham and C. M. Bowra (Oxford, 1938), pp. 572f.
4. Virgil, 'The Eclogues', 4, *The Pastoral Poems*, trans. E. V. Rieu (Harmondsworth, 1954), pp. 53–57.
5. Virgil, 'The Georgics', lines 125–28, *Virgil*, trans. H. Rushton Fairclough (London, 1967), p. 89.
6. E. R. Dodds, 'The Ancient Concept of Progress', *The Ancient Concept of Progress and other Essays on Greek Literature and Belief* (Oxford, 1973), p. 21.
7. Acton Collection, Cambridge University Library, MS Add. 4916, f. 57.

ANCIENT PHILOSOPHERS

What of the ancient philosophers? They had little time for historiography. The reason is given in one of the rare mentions of the subject by a philosopher, when Aristotle compares unfavourably the particular facts that the historian can discover with the universal truths that the poet can present. Poetry is like philosophy, concerned with what is always valid; historiography is concerned merely with the contingent, with 'what, say, Alcibiades did, or what happened to him'.[8] Even the historical process was of far less interest to philosophers than the permanent features of the universe. What was real in the strongest sense lay beyond the bounds of time. This was axiomatic in the thought of Plato, and the principle was taken over, though in modified form, by the other towering figure of ancient philosophy, Aristotle. The flux of history was therefore unimportant. As much as in Indian thought, eternity was what mattered. There was in ancient Greece, as Collingwood put it, 'a rigorously anti-historical metaphysics'.[9]

Yet there are traces in the philosophers of an acquaintance with oriental conceptions of history as cyclical. Plato, in the *Timaeus*, the work in which he ventured most fully on an analysis of the universe, mentions the notion of a Great Year.[1] This was conceived to be the period taken by all the heavenly bodies to return to the same position in relation to each other as they had occupied at its beginning. The idea of a Great Year was probably held by Heraclitus, a philosophical predecessor of Plato, as well as by a number of Plato's successors.[2] It seems to have been transmitted to Greece by the Pythagorean school of philosophy. There are persistent traditions in ancient literature that Pythagoras, who probably lived in the mid-sixth century, visited the wise men of Persia and even Zoroaster himself.[3] The Pythagoreans seem to have imagined the Great Year to be a cycle in the historical process that would end in catastrophe but then be repeated in identical form.[4] Alternatively the Great Year could

8. Aristotle, 'The Poetics', 9/4, *Classical Literary Criticism*, trans. T. S. Dorsch (Harmondsworth, 1965), p. 44.
9. R. G. Collingwood, *The Idea of History* (Oxford, 1946), p. 20.
1. Plato, *Timaeus*, 39D, trans. H. D. P. Lee (Harmondsworth, 1965), p. 54.
2. W. K. C. Guthrie, *A History of Greek Philosophy*, 1 (Cambridge, 1967), p. 458.
3. *Ibid.*, pp. 146, 252–55.
4. *Ibid.*, pp. 281f.

be treated as a cycle of civilization, separated from other cycles by a partial world disaster that ruined culture but permitted the continuity of the human race. This was the view of Aristotle.[5] The cyclical interpretation of history left its mark on the earlier philosophers.

The more drastic belief that the world was periodically destroyed and renewed was taken over as a primary doctrine by the Stoics.[6] Chrysippus, who taught at Athens in the late third century BC, held that, after fire had consumed the earth, there would be a new world:

> There will again be a Socrates, a Plato, and each man with the same friends and the same fellow-citizens . . . and this restoration will not take place once but many times; or rather, all things will be restored eternally.[7]

This was the background to the belief of Marcus Aurelius, emperor and Stoic, that nothing in the world could be truly new.[8] Everything was a repetition of what had passed in a previous age of the world. Eternal recurrence encouraged the attitude for which Stoics are best remembered, the self-disciplined acceptance of all that happened in a spirit of resignation – what has come to be called, because Stoics have been taken to be typical of philosophers, a 'philosophical' attitude. Both the teaching about history and the spirit of resignation resemble, though they do not duplicate, Indian views. Seneca, whose writings form the fullest repository of Stoic philosophy, cites a Babylonian source for his version of the cycle theory, and there can be little doubt that its roots lie further east.[9]

Seneca, however, is one of the ancient writers who can be cited in support of the contention that a pattern in history entirely different from any form of cycle, the idea of progress, was held in antiquity.[1] Seneca wrote of adding to the store of human knowledge in a thousand years' time.[2] But he certainly did not hold every aspect of

5. Dodds, *Ancient Concept of Progress*, p. 14.
6. F. H. Sandbach, *The Stoics* (London, 1975), pp. 78f.
7. Cited by Bishop Nemesius of Emesa, *On Human Nature*, 38, J. von Arnim, *Stoicorum Veterum Fragmenta*, 2 (Leipzig, 1903), no. 625, p. 190.
8. *Cf.* above, p. 18.
9. F. E. Manuel, *Shapes of Philosophical History* (London, 1965), p. 10.
1. This view is developed in Ludwig Edelstein, *The Idea of Progress in Classical Antiquity* (Baltimore, 1967). For discussion of the idea of progress, *cf.* below, chapter four.
2. Seneca, *The Letters*, 64/7, trans. R. M. Gummere (London, 1925), p. 441.

what was to emerge in the eighteenth century as the idea of progress: he did not entertain an optimism about the potential of all things human; nor did he think of the historical process as anything like a straight line, moving towards a goal.[3] It is equally true that the Stoics' rivals, the Epicureans, cannot be enlisted as recruits to the cause of progress. In the fullest statement of their philosophy, Lucretius' *On the Nature of the Universe*, there is, to be sure, an extended account of social development from a time before people wore animal skins to the stage of the emergence of art, but, according to Lucretius, there has been a simultaneous moral decline.[4] 'Skins yesterday', he writes, 'purple and gold to-day – such are the baubles that embitter human life with resentment and waste it with war.'[5] Better conditions encourage people to behave worse. Again, there are traces of the idea of progress in earlier non-philosophical writers, especially playwrights of the age of Pericles, but the allusions are to material or technological progress.[6] The notion of moral progress, central to the modern belief, can hardly be discerned at all in the writers of antiquity.[7]

ANCIENT HISTORIANS

It has been argued that the Greek historians, by contrast with the ancient philosophers, conceived history to be, if not a pattern of progress, then at least a straight line of successive events. The historians, it is claimed, did not share the philosophers' view that this world has little meaning, and certainly did not go so far as to see history as a weary round of cycles.[8] It is true that Herodotus, 'the father of history', shows no sign of discerning any cyclical rhythm in the past. His aim, he says at the beginning of his work, is to present 'the result of my inquiries into history', to explain the achievements of the Greeks and the Asiatics and to show why they

3. Georges Sorel, *The Illusions of Progress* (1908), introd. R. A. Nisbet (Berkeley, Calif., 1969), pp. xviif.
4. Lucretius, *On the Nature of the Universe*, 5, lines 925–1457, trans. R. E. Latham (Harmondsworth, 1951), pp. 199–216.
5. *Ibid.*, lines 1423f. (p. 215).
6. J. H. Finley, *Thucydides* (Cambridge, Mass., 1942), p. 83.
7. Dodds, *Ancient Concept of Progress*, pp. 24f.
8. C. G. Starr, 'Historical and Philosophical Time', *History and Theory*, Beiheft 6 (1966)

came into conflict in the Persian War.[9] He offers no fuller explanation relating his purpose to the broader sweep of the historical process. Just as there is no concrete evidence to show that he held a cyclical view of history, so there is nothing suggesting that he wished to break with the conception of history that dominated his civilization. Herodotus was an innovator in technique, the inventor of systematic historical research, rather than an innovator in theory.

Thucydides, the other eminent historian of ancient Greece, further refined technique. He devised an ingenious method for checking the validity of evidence. This was to write the history of what lay in the future, for he determined to be the historian of the Peloponnesian War at its outbreak.[1] He would have the advantage of living through the events he recorded. He displays no strong sense of a grand pattern in the historical process. But he does make his purpose explicit. He tells us that he is writing for 'those who want to understand clearly the events which happened in the past and which (human nature being what it is) will, at some time or other and in much the same ways be repeated in the future'.[2] This could possibly refer to a fully-developed cyclical view of history;[3] or it could merely be a comment that the irrationality of men might well lead to fresh wars.[4] Perhaps it is most likely to be the remark of a man who has unconsciously imbibed the common supposition of his culture that, in some sense, history repeats itself. Thucydides, at any rate, betrays his assumption that some human affairs will go on much as before. History, he implies, throws up nothing that is drastically new. It is one of the characteristics of a linear view to hold, on the contrary, that history as it moves onward reveals novelty.[5] Thucydides must be ranged on the side of the ancient philosophers rather than as an exponent of an alternative, linear view of history.

In other ancient historians there is evidence of a more fully articulated cyclical view. Pompeius Trogus, a historian of Augustus' time whose work does not survive, is known to have written according

9. Herodotus, *The Histories*, 1/1, trans. Aubrey de Sélincourt (Harmondsworth, 1954), p. 13.
1. Sir M. I Finley, ed., *The Greek Historians* (London, 1959), p. 7.
2. Thucydides, *The History of the Peloponnesian War*, 1/22, trans. Rex Warner (Harmondsworth, 1954), p. 24.
3. Finley, *Thucydides*, p. 83.
4. Dodds, *Ancient Concept of Progress*, p. 12.
5. *Cf.* below, chapters three and four.

to a scheme of monarchies whose rise and fall reflect the dynastic version of the cyclical pattern.[6] Polybius, part of whose account of Roman history has come down to us, recounts that when the general Scipio put Carthage to the flames in 146 BC he wept at the thought that the same fate must lie in store for Rome herself.[7] And the belief that history must recur is developed by Polybius as a constitutional theory. Rome, like all other states, must grow and then decay in a 'cycle of political revolution'.[8] In Livy there is a similar, though far less schematic, sense of how the early Romans acquired and expanded their power and of how their successors have entered on a protracted moral decline.[9] Tacitus, the other great Latin historian, is eager to record instances of virtue and vice for posterity's benefit, clearly supposing that circumstances will recur in which the one can be imitated and the other shunned. He is prepared to speculate on the pattern in history. 'Or perhaps', he muses, 'not only the seasons but everything else, social history included, moves in cycles.'[1] The rhythm of the natural world continued to be a reason for seeing the past as a process of recurrence.

REJECTION AND REVIVAL OF THE CYCLICAL THEORY

The cyclical theory was thus widely diffused in the ancient world. Poetry, philosophy and even history were coloured by the doctrine. It appears in ancient literature in all the three forms that it took in the east. The Chinese dynastic pattern is there; the recurrent world cycle of Indian thought emerges; and the Persian pattern of an unrepeated decline from an age of gold occurs. This is perhaps a sign of the existence of a shared heritage of ways of understanding the world. Certainly in some instances it is a sign of the influence of oriental thought over antiquity. But this widespread belief was challenged by an entirely different view of the historical process that sprang from Palestine. The Judaeo-Christian view of history as

6. Starr, 'Historical and Philosophical Time', *History and Theory*, Beiheft 6 (1966), p. 27.
7. Polybius, *The Histories*, 38/22, trans. W. R. Paton (London, 1922), 6, p. 439.
8. *Ibid.*, 6/9/10 (3, p. 289).
9. Livy, *The History of Rome from its Foundation*, 1/1, *The Early History of Rome*, trans. Aubrey de Sélincourt (Harmondsworth, 1971), p. 34.
1. Tacitus, *Annals*, 3/55, trans. Michael Grant (Harmondsworth, 1971) p. 146.

moving towards a goal, the subject of the next chapter, supplanted the cyclical view. Christian faith, Augustine protested, could have nothing to do with the belief that 'the same ages and the same temporal events recur in rotation'.[2] The prestige of Augustine's thought in the succeeding millennium had no parallel, and helped ensure that a cyclical view was no longer a respectable opinion in Christian Europe. It was not entirely banished, for it appears from time to time, in Chaucer for instance, under the guise of the wheel of fortune.[3] It seems to have been a common element in popular culture to think of people or nations as rising on the upward turn of the wheel to prosperity, only to fall again into adversity. Yet this was but a faint echo of the bolder statements of the past. Western civilization had taken a decisive turn away from conceiving the historical process as cyclical.

At the Renaissance the Christian worldview remained dominant, but the renewed study of the writers of the ancient world encouraged a corresponding renewal of interest in all forms of the cyclical view. Machiavelli, for instance, developed a theory of constitutional cycles reflecting those of Aristotle and Polybius.[4] The great prestige of Cicero, a Stoic by philosophy, during the Renaissance encouraged particular attention to the Stoic idea that a world cycle would end in a great conflagration.[5] And there was a powerful strain of variations on the theme of a golden age, often identified with the great art and literature of classical antiquity, whose passing might be lamented or whose return in the revival of letters might be celebrated. This can be illustrated not just in literature but also by a tableau carried round Florence in a chariot to mark the election of the Florentine humanist, Giovanni de' Medici, to the papacy in 1513:

> In the midst of the car was a great globe, upon which lay a man, as if dead, his arms all rusted, his back open and emerging therefrom a naked gilded child, representing the

2. Augustine, *Concerning the City of God against the Pagans*, 12/14, trans. Henry Bettenson (Harmondsworth, 1972), p. 488.
3. *E.g.* 'The Knightes Tale', *The Complete Works of Geoffrey Chaucer*, ed. W. W. Skeat (Oxford, 1900), 4, p. 28.
4. Niccolo Machiavelli, *The Discourses*, 1/2, trans. L. J. Walker and Brian Richardson and ed. Bernard Crick (Harmondsworth, 1974), pp. 106–09.
5. Manuel, *Shapes*, p. 71.

> Golden Age revived by the creation of the Pope and the end of the Iron Age from which it issued.[6]

The small boy at the centre of this display unfortunately died of the after-effects. But the message was plain: the Florentine electoral triumph would usher in a time whose splendours would match those of the poets' distant past.

Cyclical views were held by historians in these years. Among them were men like Leonardo Bruni, another Florentine, who in the fifteenth century wrote of the past as the story of the rise and fall of human achievement;[7] and Louis Le Roy, a French humanist, who in the sixteenth century composed a discourse to show 'the vicissitude of all human affairs – arms, letters, languages, arts, states, laws, morals – and how they never cease rising and falling, growing better and worse alternately'.[8] One of Le Roy's circle of historically-minded humanists, La Popelinière, pressed the cyclical principle towards its logical conclusion. 'Each past event', he wrote, 'recurs.'[9] All that La Popelinière seems to have meant is that motives and circumstances do not change drastically over time. But, as much as Marcus Aurelius, La Popelinière was concluding that the historical process, because it is cyclical, is doomed to a certain sameness.

Yet optimism was sometimes associated with a cyclical view in the Renaissance period. People could feel that they were participating in one of the periodic upswings of civilization. Jean Bodin, Huguenot and humanist, tried to refute two contemporary philosophies of history, the four monarchies and golden age theories (themselves cyclical in origin), because he disliked their implication that the present was a time of decay. He could point to such evidence as advances in astronomy and the discoveries of travellers in support of the contention that his age was one of increasing realization of human potential.[1] The combination of a cyclical view with confidence

6. Giorgio Vasari, 'Jacopo da Pontormo', *The Lives of the Painters, Sculptors and Architects*, trans. A. B. Hinds and ed. William Gaunt (London, 1963), 3, p. 239.
7. J. A. Mazzeo, *Renaissance and Revolution: The Remaking of European Thought* (London, 1969), p. 42.
8. Louis Le Roy, *On the Vicissitude of Affairs* (Paris, 1579), f. 112, quoted by Peter Burke, *The Renaissance Sense of the Past* (London, 1969), p. 88.
9. La Popelinière, *History of Histories* (1599), p. 39, quoted by Manuel, *Shapes*, p. 53.
1. E. L. Tuveson, *Millennium and Utopia: a Study in the Background of the Idea of Progress* (1949: Gloucester, Mass., 1972), pp. 56f.

in the future, however, was possible only because the cyclical view was tempered by the Christian framework within which it was set. The goodness of God, it was held, forbade one to think that a downswing of the cycle was imminent. The best-known English writer of the Bodin school, George Hakewill, spelt out this argument in his work *An Apologie of the Power and Providence of God in the Government of the World* (1627). The world was not in a state of advancing degeneration, he claimed, since God wanted to ensure the continued well-being of man.[2] In antiquity cyclical theories had almost always encouraged pessimism or resignation. The Renaissance could root optimism in a cyclical theory only because it was incorporated into a providential pattern.

It was equally possible to combine elements of the cyclical and Christian views to produce a pessimistic interpretation of the historical process. A Christian expectation that the world would soon come to an end could foster the belief, as the next chapter will show, that history was running down. The degeneration of the world was leading inexorably to the day of judgment. Such attitudes could readily blend with the ancient beliefs that there had been nobler, better days in the past, that there had been a declining curve of civilization and morality and that the result in the present was decadence. The mixture produced the common theme in Renaissance literature of 'the decay of nature'. Among its apologists in England was the man who provoked George Hakewill into asserting an optimistic view. This was Godfrey Goodman, chaplain to the Queen, who wrote *The Fall of Man, or the Corruption of Nature, Proved by the Light of our Natural Reason* (1616). Goodman's work is a classic of primitivism, drumming up evidence from all available quarters to demonstrate the steady decline of man and his environment.[3] Reinforced by the favourite poetic theme of the mutability of all things, Goodman's point of view was widespread in his age.

There can be little doubt, in fact, that Goodman enjoyed more support than Hakewill in the seventeenth century. What is more, pessimism continued to outbalance optimism in popular thinking about history even into the eighteenth century – the age when *avant-garde* thinkers were turning to the idea of progress. 'People', wrote Voltaire in 1744, 'are always crying that this world is in the process

2. Mazzeo, *Renaissance and Revolution*, pp. 295ff.
3. *Ibid.*, pp. 294f.

of degeneration'.[4] To lament that the times are growing worse and worse is a common human trait, but in the eighteenth century the attitude was still grounded in the Renaissance assimilation of the cyclical theory to the Christian worldview. Eighteenth century titles of history books commonly use the word 'revolutions' – meaning not crises in which one regime supplants another, but the rise and fall of nations. Gibbon's title, *The Decline and Fall of the Roman Empire*, alludes to the unavoidable downswing of a curve. The decline of Rome, he explains, was 'the natural and inevitable effect of immoderate greatness'.[5] Gibbon even portrays a golden age, the idealized rule of the Antonines, at the beginning of the process. Cyclical thinking about history had been subsumed once more into western culture. In weak and diffused forms, it had become a commonplace.

NIETZSCHE, SPENGLER AND TOYNBEE

Isolated thinkers, however, continued to seize on some fully elaborated type of cyclical theory as a means of challenging established ways of looking at the past. Giambattista Vico argued in early eighteenth-century Italy that the history of non-Jewish nations conformed to the cyclical pattern with the aim of defending the uniqueness of Jewish history as a linear pattern.[6] In the nineteenth century the German philosopher Ernst von Lasaulx wrote a *Philosophy of History* (1856) to express his belief that western civilization was nearing the end of its appointed cycle.[7] Arthur de Gobineau, the French writer of an *Essay on the Inequality of the Human Races* (1853–55) that was the source of much subsequent racialist theory,

4. Voltaire, 'Nouvelles Considérations sur l'Histoire', *Oeuvres Complètes*, 16, p. 140, quoted by Henry Vyverberg, *Historical Pessimism in the French Enlightenment* (Cambridge, Mass., 1958), p. 75.
5. Edward Gibbon, *The History of the Decline and Fall of the Roman Empire* (1776–88), ed. J. B. Bury, 4 (London, 1898), p. 161. On Gibbon's place in the literature of decline, *cf.* Peter Burke, 'Tradition and Experience: The Idea of Decline from Bruni to Gibbon,' *Edward Gibbon and the Decline and Fall of the Roman Empire*, ed. G. W. Bowersock, John Clive and S. R. Graubard (Cambridge, Mass., 1977), esp. pp. 98ff.
6. *Cf.* below, pp. 95ff.
7. G. G. Iggers, *The German Conception of History: The National Tradition of Historical Thought from Herder to the Present* (Middletown, Conn., 1968), p. 129.

adapted the cyclical pattern to the history of races.[8] And Friedrich Nietzsche, particularly in *Thus Spake Zarathustra* (1883–92), whose title alludes to Zoroaster, set out in flashes of eccentric genius a belief in eternal recurrence. His explicit object was to dismiss the Christian view that history was guided towards a specific goal by the divine will – and indeed any system of belief setting its hope on the future.[9] Cycles remained for the adventurous an alternative to the dominant linear view.

Nietzsche was probably the strongest intellectual influence over Oswald Spengler, whose background was historicist but who composed one of the most striking twentieth-century expositions of cyclical thought. Spengler treated human societies as organisms that necessarily pass through the same life-cycle. The earlier, creative phase (its period of 'culture') takes place when the society derives strength from its roots in the countryside; its later, decadent phase (its 'civilization') comes when urbanization brings ossification in its train. The distinction between 'culture' and 'civilization' was drawn from Nietzsche, but the application was Spengler's own.[1] The nineteenth century was the time of 'civilization' for western society, and so the end of its cycle of existence was at hand. The work in which he set out these views, *The Decline of the West*, was published in the summer of 1918, shortly before Germany suffered defeat in the First World War.[2] In the soul-searching that ensued his book became a best-seller. The gloomy message fitted the public mood. It could also exercise a strange fascination over other minds. Lord Bullock, the biographer of Hitler and master of St Catherine's College, Oxford, recounts that when he first read Spengler's bold generalizations, he was 'bowled over' by them.[3] But Spengler's impact, on Lord Bullock as well as on Germany, was transient. His writing has more force than durability.

A thinker often coupled with Spengler is the Oxford historian Arnold Toynbee, whose massive work *A Study of History* was conceived during the First World War even if it was not completed

8. *Gobineau: Selected Political Writings*, ed. M. D. Biddiss (London, 1970), p. 25.
9. Walter Kaufmann, *Nietzsche: Philosopher, Psychologist, Antichrist* (Princeton, New Jersey, 1968), pp. 316–28.
1. H. S. Hughes, *Oswald Spengler: A Critical Estimate* (New York, 1952), p. 72.
2. *Ibid.*, p. 1.
3. Lord Bullock, 'The Historian's Purpose: History and Metahistory', *History Today* (Feb. 1951), p. 10.

until the 1950s. Like Spengler, Toynbee compared the fortunes of whole societies larger than nations. Toynbee, however, was more careful in formulating his list of civilizations and far more detailed in his comparisons. He also claimed to use the ordinary methods of historical inquiry rather than to rely wholly on intuition as Spengler did. Toynbee was therefore not satisfied when he had identified a rhythm in the rise and fall of his twenty-one civilizations. He wanted to go further by examining the periods of chaos that intervened between civilizations. He was interested not only in cycles, but in how cycles fitted together. This concern led him to a drastic revision of his point of view between the publication of his first batch of volumes in 1934 and the appearance of the final batch in 1954.

What happened was this. In 1934 Toynbee set out a cyclical pattern according to which the disintegration of any civilization is marked by the emergence of a universal state, a universal church and barbarian war-bands.[4] By the 1939 volumes he could no longer tolerate the thought that there is no more to history than an eternally revolving pattern.[5] He hinted that each cycle might be creative. 'The perpetual turning of a wheel', he wrote, 'is not a vain repetition if, at each revolution, it is carrying a vehicle that much nearer its goal'.[6] The vehicle, he suggested, is the succession of universal churches that fill the gaps between civilizations.[7] In 1954 he announced that he now saw the civilizations as secondary elements in the pattern of history. Their place as the central protagonists had been taken by universal churches.[8] Religion emerges from the downswing of a cycle of civilization, he explained, because spiritual progress depends on suffering.[9] With the rise and fall of each civilization, man's knowledge of God increases. This belief bordered on orthodox Christianity, but did not quite correspond to it because Toynbee did not see any religion as final. But what Toynbee did do was to superimpose on a cyclical view of history a Christian view of history. All things are moving, he came to believe, towards a goal. Cycles by themselves could not be endured.

4. A. J. Toynbee, *A Study of History*, 1 (London, 1934), pp. 51–64.
5. *Ibid.*, 4 (London, 1939), p. 33.
6. *Ibid.*, 6 (London, 1939), p. 324.
7. *Ibid.*, p. 326.
8. *Ibid.*, 7 (London, 1954), p. 420.
9. *Ibid.*, p. 423.

ASSESSMENT OF THE CYCLICAL THEORY

No fully articulated cyclical theory is popular in the West today. Toynbee's achievement created a stir, but his earlier volumes were ignored in British historical journals and his last batch was treated by and large with deep-seated scepticism.[1] He was accused of indulging in speculation. Yet cyclical theory in its various forms made such considerable inroads into western thought in the past that it can still be detected in unexpected places; and it remains a powerful influence in other parts of the world. Thus Christian congregations sing with little sense of anomaly in a Christmas hymn of the time when 'with the ever-circling years comes round the age of gold'.[2] Cosmic cycles continue to be assumed in much Buddhist thought. And dynastic cycle patterns persist in post-Second World War Chinese historiography, despite western influence.[3] Cyclical theory is not dead.

There are, however, serious problems in any form of the theory. The idea of a decline from a golden age can muster very little evidence. People have not grown puny in comparison with their ancestors. On the contrary, as anyone who has struck his head on a lintel while visiting a mediaeval castle will testify, average height has considerably increased. Nor do moral standards seem to have degenerated from any recorded point in the past: the earliest tales of most societies commonly dwell on butchery and revenge. But primitivism has flourished despite the lack of evidence in its favour. This would suggest that the notion of degeneration from an idyllic past is closely allied with myth. A golden age is conjured up by minds eager to escape, if only in imagination, to a better world. In this view the past forms a striking contrast with the present, and so permits people to indulge in one of the most common of pastimes, the criticism of what goes on today. Primitivism is a form of idealization of the past impervious to the existence or absence of evidence. It is not surprising that, of all philosophies of history, this is the one that has least often commanded the allegiance of historians.

There is also a problem of evidence about any theory of repeated cosmic cycles. How, we might ask, can we know that we are living

1. E. T. Gargan, ed., *The Intent of Toynbee's 'History'* (Chicago, 1961), pp. 11–14.
2. E. H. Sears, 'It came upon the midnight clear', *That Glorious Song of Old* (London, 1886).
3. Wright, 'Study of Chinese History', *Generalization*, ed. Gottschalk, p. 50.

in a cycle that has taken place before and will take place again? To know such a thing there would have to be some memory of the previous turn of the circle. But the theory itself usually suggests that there is a total break between separate cycles that excludes any such memory. Even if a version of the theory did not posit a total break, a problem would remain. If anyone did remember a previous occurrence, that very act of memory would be a factor differentiating the later from the earlier occurrence. The two sets of circumstances that the theory supposes to be identical would not then prove to be so. The idea seems to have contradictions at its heart. The only way of avoiding the contradictions would be to hold that belief in eternal recurrence is based not on any evidence like memory, but on some special form of enlightenment. This many Buddhists would hold. But it seems necessary to embrace a whole Buddhist worldview if one is to have any sympathy for a theory of cosmic cycles. The apparent evidence that once attracted men to the theory was derived from the astronomical observations of the ancient East and Mediterranean worlds. Plato was mistaken about the existence of a Great Year of the heavenly bodies. It seems fair to suggest that he and others were equally mistaken about the existence of equivalent cycles in world history.

The most plausible form of cyclical theory is that which postulates a pattern in the rise and fall of dynasties, nations, or civilizations. There is an inescapable kernel of truth here. Nations do become more powerful and then grow weak once more. But it is difficult to suggest any consistent similarities between the various instances that would establish a regular pattern. The reasons that led Britain to concede independence to her colonies in the twentieth century, for example, were not the same as those that induced Portugal to part reluctantly from hers. Nations lose power for particular, distinctive reasons as well as for reasons that can be generalized. It is easiest to attempt generalizations about the fate of the largest of units, as when Toynbee selected whole civilizations for study. But even then it is possible, as Toynbee's critics found, to fault an analyst for misrepresenting the history of civilizations by trying to fit them into a preconceived mould. The rises and falls of history show no consistent pattern.

This, perhaps, is just as well, for cyclical theory has an almost unavoidable consequence for anyone who works out its implications. A belief that history has declined from a golden age, a belief that the cosmos will be destroyed without any better replacement, and a belief that the chief teaching of history is that any ruling house or society is bound to come to nothing have this in common: the prospect is dark. In all these visions of a long-term process there is no reason for entertaining high expectations of the future. If decline were merely a short-term affair, its effect might be to stir people to action that would reverse the trend. But on any cyclical view decline seems so deeply ingrained in the fabric of history as to be irreversible. Upswings are ephemeral. Necessary decay is a gloomy outlook. People either give themselves up to pessimism, as did (for instance) Hesiod and Spengler, or else they cultivate an attitude of stern resignation, as did the Stoics and the earlier Toynbee. Of all those touched by the cyclical theory, only Virgil, a number of Renaissance thinkers and the later Toynbee saw in it grounds for confidence in the future. Virgil did so because Rome's politics seemed at last to be stable; the Renaissance writers and the later Toynbee were prepared to hope only because their cyclical view was modified by a belief in the divine superintendence of history. With only a solitary exception, then, unmodified cyclical theory led to a sense of the ultimate futility of human existence. It was the Christian view of history that gave western civilization its remarkably widespread conviction that the future offers hope.

3 Christian history

> 'O God, our help in ages past,
> Our hope for years to come . . .'
>
> Isaac Watts, *Psalms of David Imitated.*

The Christian understanding of history is markedly different from any version of the cyclical theory. Even if in the development of western thought the two have sometimes been blended together, in their original forms they show hardly any similarity to each other. Whereas the cyclical view has no necessary bond with theism of any kind, the Christian idea of history is derived from belief in a God who intervenes in the world. Again, circular patterns are excluded by the Christian assumption that the historical process is linear. Furthermore, cyclical theories, despite their variety, usually place little stress on what happens at the end of a cycle, but Christianity holds that the goal of history is all-important. Christians, then, have normally adhered to these three convictions about history: that God intervenes in it; that he guides it in a straight line; and that he will bring it to the conclusion that he has planned. The three beliefs together form the core of the Christian doctrine of providence.

Such views, however, did not emerge for the first time when Christianity was born. They form part of the legacy to Christians of the Jews, and remain as deeply implanted in Judaism today as in Christian thought. The Judaeo-Christian idea of history has been moulded by the convictions about God shared in common by the two religions. To believe in one God who is sovereign and shows steadfast love is to believe in one who participates in history, guides the whole process and will bring it to a triumphant conclusion. Christianity reinforced these Jewish beliefs rather than supplanting or modifying them. The roots of the Christian idea of history are therefore to be found in the Old Testament.

THE OLD TESTAMENT

The God of the Old Testament is one who is so great that he stands outside history, yet who is so concerned for his world that he is active within history. Jewish writers recorded that their God, Yahweh, had directed the travels of their ancestors, had engaged himself by covenant to be their God and had brought them to Palestine. Very often Yahweh is described as participating in person, in summoning a patriarch or winning a battle. Perhaps most characteristically he is represented as overruling human intentions. Thus, for instance, when Joseph has been sold by his resentful brothers to a band of desert merchants but has nevertheless risen to become the right-hand man of the pharaoh of Egypt, he eventually explains to the brothers that 'it was not you who sent me here, but God'.[1] The brothers had intended harm, but God had been active to ensure unexpected benefits. Again, during the rebellion of Absalom against King David, the capable strategy devised by Absalom's adviser Ahithophel was surprisingly rejected. 'For the LORD', comments the writer of 2 Samuel, 'had ordained to defeat the good counsel of Ahithophel, so that the LORD might bring evil on Absalom.'[2] Yahweh had been at work to frustrate another human scheme that ran contrary to his will. Divine participation, the Jews believed, was part of the ordinary stuff of history.

The interventions had a purpose. They were commonly designed to bring judgment or mercy. The rejection of Ahithophel's advice was a divine act of judgment; the elevation of Joseph was one of mercy. Some kind of wrongdoing was normally the reason for divine judgment. Sodom and Gomorrah are destroyed in one of the archetypal acts of divine judgment recounted in the Old Testament because 'their sin is very grave'.[3] Turning from the worship of Yahweh to other gods is repeatedly given as the explanation of other judgments. This type of divine intervention was therefore understood as a sanction for the morality and worship that God had ordained. Divine acts of mercy, on the other hand, were not so much rewards for doing right as the result of Yahweh's disposition to bless the undeserving if only they would trust him. Thus Jacob, for one, is prepared to acknowledge to Yahweh at one point in his career, 'I am not worthy of the least of all the steadfast love and all the faithfulness which thou hast shown to thy servant.'[4] Divine mercy

1. Genesis 45:8.
2. 2 Samuel 17:14.
3. Genesis 18:20.
4. Genesis 32:10.

was unmerited. God's interventions were a reflection of his character as it was revealed to Moses:

> The LORD, the LORD, a God merciful and gracious, slow to anger, and abounding in steadfast love and faithfulness, keeping steadfast love for thousands, forgiving iniquity and transgression and sin, but who will by no means clear the guilty, visiting the iniquity of the fathers upon the children and the children's children, to the third and fourth generation.[5]

Yahweh, the Jews believed, was at once 'merciful and gracious' and one who would 'by no means clear the guilty'. His acts in history were therefore supremely ones of mercy or judgment – or both. Events could be simultaneous demonstrations of the two divine qualities. Israel's greatest memory as a people, of the exodus from Egypt, was of an event at once big with mercy for the Israelites and with judgment for the Egyptians. Here was an epitome of what historical events were like.

In some measure Israel shared this view with the surrounding nations. The Canaanites whom they dispossessed of Palestine worshipped gods that were expected to intervene in human life. Yet there were two major differences between Israelite faith and the religion of their neighbours. The gods of the other peoples were first and foremost nature deities. Their chief function was to guarantee the fertility of the seed and the abundance of the harvest.[6] Yahweh, by contrast, showed himself less in the seasonal round of agriculture than in his mighty acts in history. Yahweh did ensure growth in nature,[7] but he revealed more of his power and his character in the events of the past. Again, whereas the other gods were confined in their scope, either to one people or to one sphere of life, Yahweh was increasingly believed to be the true God of all men. Yahweh asks Israel:

> *Did I not bring up Israel from the land of Egypt,*
> *and the Philistines from Caphtor and the Syrians from Kir?*[8]

The one God exercised himself on behalf of other peoples, even

5. Exodus 34:6f.
6. Gerhard von Rad, *Old Testament Theology*, 2 (Edinburgh, 1965), p. 111.
7. Psalm 65:9ff.
8. Amos 9:7.

Israel's traditional enemies. No part of history was beyond Yahweh's capacity to intervene.

Israel came to believe not only that God acted at particular points in time, but also that the whole historical process was under his guidance. Events in the past were seen not as isolated occurrences but as successive items in the working out of a divine plan. There emerged catalogues of happenings in 'sacred history' like that in Psalm 136, which traces God's consistent purpose for Israel from the plagues of Egypt down to the settlement in Palestine. A belief in Yahweh as creator supported some such view; a God who made the world would also care for his people in it. There is no incongruity in the fact that immediately before the catalogue of events in Psalm 136 there is an account of God's work in creation. Although there was an awareness that other nations had a place within the world created by the one God,[9] Israel's chief interest was in her own past rather than in universal history. As Samuel succinctly put it, 'Hitherto the LORD has helped us.'[1] Israel was steadily moving forward under God's direction. History was conceived as linear.

It has been argued that, on the contrary, the Old Testament philosophy of history is cyclical.[2] Of the variety of evidence adduced for the presence of a cyclical view of history, some instances, like the predictions of a messianic reign similar to David's, are merely analogies, and do not reflect an expectation of repetition. The pattern of history in the book of Judges, which admittedly does follow a cycle of apostasy, deliverance through a judge, prosperity and decline to apostasy, is something the writer bemoans as the result of disobedience to the divine will rather than the working out of God's own purpose in history.[3] The most serious point advanced on behalf of the presence of the cyclical theory in the Old Testament is the suggestion that Israel's recurring weekly and annual festivals provided the framework of her historical experience. These cyclical commemorations, however, derived their meaning from past events. The sabbath recalled God's rest following creation, the passover the deliverance from Egypt.[4] Far from providing an alternative philos-

9. *E.g.* Genesis 10.
1. 1 Samuel 7:12.
2. Most thoroughly by J. B. Curtis, 'A Suggested Interpretation of the Biblical Philosophy of History,' *Hebrew Union College Annual*, 34 (1963).
3. *E.g.* Judges 4:1ff.
4. Exodus 20:11; 12:21–27.

ophy of history, the festivals pointed to the reality of God's acts in the past. They reminded Israel of the linear development of their history under God.

In addition to the ideas that history is marked by divine interventions and that it is linear rather than cyclical, the Old Testament contains the idea that it is moving towards a goal. Like the other two elements, this conviction is as much about Yahweh as about history: in essence, it is the belief that God will bring history to a climax rather than let it take its ordinary course indefinitely. The reason is that he will not tolerate the wickedness of human beings for ever. The minor acts of judgment that mark the course of the past will have a counterpart in a decisive act of judgment in the future. Isaiah predicts the awesome event:

> *Behold, the day of the* Lord *comes,*
> *cruel, with wrath and fierce anger,*
> *to make the earth a desolation*
> *and to destroy its sinners from it.*[5]

Belief in a 'day of the Lord' when injustice will be ended is common in the prophets of the Old Testament. There had been expectations of divine blessing, an orientation towards the future, from early times in Israel: Abraham's journeyings were undertaken in the confidence that God would create a great nation out of his descendants.[6] But the belief in a future divine intervention that would be decisive crystallized only among the prophets of a later period, the eighth to sixth centuries BC. This was the birth of eschatology, an expectation of the 'last things'. History was moving towards this climax.

The goal of history was given greater precision in the type of literature known as apocalyptic. In apocalyptic, of which the second half of the book of Daniel is the clearest Old Testament example, vivid pictures are used to portray events leading up to 'the time of the end'.[7] Apocalyptic steps beyond prophecy in predicting not only that God will intervene decisively, but also that history will be brought to a conclusion. The view that judgment is to come is reinforced in apocalyptic, but 'the day of the Lord' often also inau-

5. Isaiah 13:9.
6. Genesis 12:1f.
7. Daniel 12:4.

gurates a new age, not subject to the conditions of the present.[8] The 'last things' are put outside history. This was to add a further facet to the Old Testament view of history. The straight line guided by God would lead to something beyond itself: history would find its end and significance in the new age that would succeed it. The Old Testament therefore encompasses the belief that history is teleological, its content determined by its goal or *telos*. The historical process, the Jews came to believe, could be understood only in the light of what was to happen at the end of the world. God was guiding history towards a new age.

THE NEW TESTAMENT

The earliest Christians retained the attitude to history found in the Old Testament. They continued to believe in divine intervention, to conceive of the historical process as a straight line and to see the panorama of world events as moving towards a goal. Each of these aspects of their faith was deepened by their understanding of Jesus. Primary was their belief that Jesus was himself a divine intervention in the world: 'God was in Christ reconciling the world to himself.'[9] What Jesus had said, done and suffered was in reality God at work. And God was continuing to act through the followers of Jesus as they bore witness to what God had achieved for man's salvation. 'So we are ambassadors for Christ, God making his appeal through us.'[1] Through Christian preaching, and also through remarkable events such as healings in the name of Jesus,[2] God contrived to take a part in human affairs.

Just as in the Old Testament, the interventions were characteristically acts of judgment or mercy. The coming of Jesus was to bring mercy, but had judgment as a corollary:

> For God sent the Son into the world, not to condemn the world, but that the world might be saved through him. He who believes in him is not condemned; he who does not believe is condemned already, because he has not believed in the name of the only Son of God.[3]

8. *E.g.* Zechariah 14.
9. 2 Corinthians 5:19.
1. *Ibid.*, 5:20.
2. *E.g.* Acts 3:1–10.
3. John 3:17f.

Mercy and judgment were thought to be mingled in God's work through Jesus, although one was in the foreground, the other in the background. The gospel of Luke includes a comment by Jesus on acts of judgment in a wider sense. Jesus explains that a number of Galileans whose blood was mixed in their sacrifices by the Roman governor were not being punished by God as though they were worse sinners than their neighbours; and, taking an instance where no human agency was directly responsible for death, goes on to say that eighteen people killed by a falling tower were not receiving their due as if they were the worst element in Jerusalem.[4] This has sometimes been understood as a rejection of the popular Jewish opinion that God undertakes particular acts of judgment. Jesus, however, goes on to warn that 'unless you repent you will all likewise perish'.[5] That is far from a denial that God sometimes brings judgment on sin. On the contrary, it implies that, since all deserve judgment now and will receive it in the end unless they turn from their sins, God is merciful in not bringing immediate judgment on all. Judgment, according to Jesus, is not an automatic divine response to the most heinous offences, but an occasional intervention that is a merciful warning to all. Judgment and mercy are intertwined. This is a view of judgments in history at once more developed than any to be found in the Old Testament and yet fully consonant with it.

Christians also took over the Old Testament's vision of history as linear. Jesus was seen as unique, yet as part of the succession of Israel's prophets:

> In many and various ways God spoke of old to our fathers by the prophets; but in these last days he has spoken to us by a Son . . .[6]

It was part of the burden of the apostles' preaching that Jesus fulfilled Old Testament predictions.[7] There was therefore continuity with the sacred history of God's people. Paul, although the apostle to the Gentiles, was concerned to stress that non-Jews were grafted on to the stock of the Jews.[8] Despite the novelty of Christianity,

4. Luke 13: 1–5.
5. *Ibid.*, 13:5.
6. Hebrews 1:1f.
7. *E.g.* Acts 2: 25–31.
8. Romans 11:17.

there was a straight line of God's purpose running from creation through his chosen people to the present. History was moving forward, and would continue to do so as the Christians proclaimed their faith to widening circles – 'in Jerusalem and in all Judea and Samaria and to the end of the earth'.[9]

The third element in the view that the early Christians inherited from Judaism was their eschatology. The historical process would come to an end. Like the Old Testament prophets, Christians expected judgment to come. Their ideas were more precisely focused, however, because their expectations centred on Jesus. At the end of time Jesus would return to judge the nations.[1] This last judgment would divide men into those receiving eternal punishment and those receiving eternal life. There was a sense, admittedly, in which early Christians believed that these eschatological events were already taking place in their own day. The coming of Jesus had inaugurated the last days; there was already the opportunity to embrace eternal life; the continuing historical process was therefore charged with something of the heightened drama that the prophets had attributed to the end of time alone.[2] Yet, even if eschatological events had begun, they had not reached a climax. There was still to come 'the end, when he [Jesus] delivers the kingdom to God the Father after destroying every rule and every authority and power'.[3] The future would bring victory for Jesus and for those who believed in him.

Confidence in the future was therefore a characteristic Christian attitude. Apocalyptic literature anticipating the final triumph finds a place in the New Testament as well as in the Old. The book of Revelation, using imagery drawn especially from Daniel and Zechariah, depicts the appearance of the new Jerusalem. There in a deathless, painless community, people will live with God.[4] Even before the descent of the new Jerusalem, according to the book of Revelation, the course of history is guaranteed by divine sovereignty. Christian confidence in the future helps to explain why hope is given comparable status with faith and love in the New Testament. Hope was not an airy matter, but a certain expectation. The future was

9. Acts 1:8.
1. Matthew 25:31f.
2. *E.g.* Acts 2: 16–21.
3. 1 Corinthians 15:24.
4. Revelation 21:2ff.

sure to be good because it was in the hands of God. History had a goal.

Christian optimism, however, was not unqualified. Despite God's control of history, troubled times will precede the coming of the new Jerusalem. There will, for instance, be an eruption of evil associated with the mysterious Old Testament figures of Gog and Magog.[5] Again the gospels contain predictions by Jesus of wars, sufferings and convulsions that will take place before the end.[6] Christians had to take these into account when looking to the future. Both their experience of persecution and their belief in the power of Satan confirmed their view that ultimate victory did not necessarily ensure security in this life. 'Your adversary the devil prowls around like a roaring lion,' says Peter, 'seeking some one to devour.'[7] Christians suffering for their faith could hardly fail to reckon that the forces of evil were extensive and dangerous. History was a battle-ground between good and evil where evil might sometimes win an engagement. Christians therefore avoided any facile optimism about the future. Their hope was tempered by realism.

THE EARLY CHURCH

Each of the three elements in the Christian idea of history – interventions, linearity and eschatology – was the subject of discussion in the early church. The greatest approach to unanimity was over linearity. Christian writers customarily branded as pagan the notion that history was in any sense cyclical. Justin Martyr in the second century, for instance, rejected the view that people would go through a second life.[8] History, on the Christian view, did not repeat itself. There seems to have been only one thinker in the early church who toyed with cyclical theories: Origen, the third-century scholar who was the greatest figure in the Alexandrian school of theologians. The original text of what he composed is lost to us because it was edited out by his translator Rufinus, but Origen, according to his critic Jerome, 'in his desire to confirm the most impious dogma of the Stoics through the authority of the Divine Scriptures, dared to write

5. *Ibid.*, 20:8.
6. *E.g.* Mark 13.
7. 1 Peter 5:8.
8. Justin Martyr, *The Dialogue with Trypho*, 1/5, trans. A. L. Williams (London, 1930), p. 3.

that man dies over and over again'.[9] Yet Origen himself protests elsewhere against implications of the cyclical view such as that the work of Jesus will be repeated indefinitely.[1] It seems clear that, as on other issues, Origen had unconsciously assimilated Stoic thinking about cycles even though his conscious purpose was to rebut the arguments of pagan scholarship.[2] In the following century both Rufinus and Jerome, despite divergence over the value of Origen, were aware that on this matter he had erred from the Christian consensus. Even had not Jerome's contemporary Augustine delivered his weighty condemnation of the cyclical theory,[3] the Christian church would have endorsed the conviction that history proceeds in a straight line according to the will of God.

There was a wider range of speculation around the subject of eschatology. Various strands of biblical thought seemed to suggest that even before the end of time there would be a bright future for believers. There was the promise of Jesus that the Spirit would guide his followers into all the truth,[4] which could be interpreted to mean that there would be in the future a qualitatively different period of history. There was the statement in the letter to the Hebrews that 'there remains a sabbath rest for the people of God',[5] which could be similarly glossed. And supremely there was the prediction in Revelation that Satan would be prevented from doing harm for a period of a thousand years.[6] Here was the germ of an idea that was to prove fertile in the Christian imagination over succeeding centuries – the belief that there would be, in the future but before the end of time, a millennium of peace and plenty. All three passages were drawn upon by the Montanists of late second-century Phrygia whose prophecy, full of millennial expectation, was too ecstatic for the leaders of the church to tolerate. The hope of a millennium appears also in the thought of second-century theologians like Justin and Irenaeus. It was one of Origen's aims to discredit the

9. Jerome, *Letters*, 96/9, quoted by T. E. Mommsen, 'St Augustine and the Christian Idea of Progress: the Background of the City of God', *Journal of the History of Ideas*, 12 (1951), p. 355.
1. Origen, *Against Celsus*, 4/67, trans. Henry Chadwick (Cambridge, 1953), p. 238.
2. *Cf.* Henry Chadwick, *The Early Church* (Harmondsworth, 1967), p. 101.
3. *Cf.* above, p. 34f.
4. John 16:13.
5. Hebrews 4:9.
6. Revelation 20:3.

idea, and partly through his influence millenarianism waned in the East.[7] The tendency of such millennial expectation was to fan Christian optimism about the future to a white heat. A protracted time of divine blessing could be looked for within history. This was to expand on the standard view of the early church that God's richest blessing would be dispensed when history had reached its goal.

But what of God's blessings in the present? Did God intervene to bless in response to human obedience? This was the nub of an issue raised when the Roman Empire showed toleration or even encouragement to Christianity. Christians had to decide whether the empire was upheld by God because true worship flourished within its bounds. In the first century there was no thought that the authorities which were responsible for persecution could be specially favoured by God, but by the later second century when the empire seemed at least potentially friendly the suggestion began to be advanced. In a petition to Marcus Aurelius against the treatment of Christians in Asia Minor, Bishop Melito of Sardis wrote:

> . . . the greatest proof that the establishment of our religion at the very time when the Empire began so auspiciously was an unmixed blessing lies in this fact – from the reign of Augustus the Empire has suffered no damage, on the contrary everything has gone splendidly and gloriously, and every prayer has been answered.[8]

Melito was contending that imperial prosperity was God's reward for the rise of Christianity. The tendency to link the fortunes of church and empire grew steadily. When Constantine embraced Christianity as the official imperial religion what had been a tendency became the norm. Constantine himself appears to have believed that respect for the Christian God 'conferred the greatest good fortune on the Roman name'.[9] Christians began to assume that a Christian empire had earned God's favour.

This was the foundation of the 'imperial theology' of the fourth century. Its greatest exponent was Constantine's contemporary, the

7. Chadwick, *The Early Church*, p. 78.
8. Eusebius, *The History of the Church from Christ to Constantine*, 4/26/7f., trans. G. A. Williamson (Harmondsworth, 1965), p. 188.
9. Imperial letter from Constantine to Anulinus. *Ibid.*, 10/7/1 (p. 407).

church historian Eusebius. He dilated on God's response to human merit:

> God, that God . . . who is the common Saviour of all, having treasured up with himself, for those who love godliness, greater blessings than human thought has conceived, gives the earnest and first-fruits of future rewards even here, assuring in some sort immortal hopes to mortal eyes.[1]

Eusebius was responsible for historiographical innovations like careful attention to doctrinal controversies and the copious use of documents,[2] but his chief importance lies in his singling out of Constantine as the supreme example of a ruler who had deserved and received God's blessing. The authority of the emperor in the world, he claimed, was a reflection of the authority of the Word of God in the universe.[3] The description of peace and righteousness under an ideal king in Psalm 72, traditionally applied to the rule of Messiah, was used by Eusebius of the reign of Constantine.[4] Similar confidence that a Christian emperor was a guarantee of the security and prosperity of Rome can be found in many fourth-century Christian writers of East and West like Jerome, Lactantius, Ambrose and Prudentius.[5]

This was the prevailing pattern of thought in the Christianity to which Augustine was converted in 386. As a bishop nine years later he shared with his contemporaries a vision of the extension of the Christian faith with the assistance of imperial authority. Augustine, however, underwent a change of mind. In about 397 he referred to Psalm 72 as a description of the Christian empire in the Eusebian manner; some eighteen years later his exposition avoided any such

1. Eusebius, *Life of Constantine*, 1/3/3, trans. E. C. Richardson, *A Select Library of Nicene and Post-Nicene Fathers of the Christian Church*, 1, ed. Henry Wace and Philip Schaff (Oxford, 1890), p. 482.
2. A. D. Momigliano, 'Pagan and Christian Historiography in the Fourth Century AD.', *Essays in Ancient and Modern Historiography* (Oxford, 1977), pp. 115–17.
3. Eusebius, *In Praise of Constantine*, 1/6, trans. H. A. Drake (Berkeley, Calif., 1976), p. 85.
4. *Ibid.*, 16/7f. (p. 121).
5. Mommsen, 'St. Augustine and the Christian Idea of Progress', *Journal of the History of Ideas*, 12 (1951), p. 363. L. G. Patterson, *God and History in Early Christian Thought* (London, 1967), pp. 83–93.

identification.[6] He abandoned the 'imperial theology'. The change was related to the transformation of Augustine's views on grace. He came to reject the assumption of the Eusebian view that God treated the empire according to the merit of the emperors. God, he increasingly felt from the late 390s, deals with nobody according to merit. God's blessings are free gifts to the undeserving, a matter of grace.[7] There is therefore no exact correlation between human deserts and divine intervention in history. Even before the fall of Rome in 410 he had abandoned the view that the city's profession of Christian faith would ensure its permanence.

Other Christians, however, adhered to the Eusebian view. For them the fall of Rome came as a disturbing blow. The pagan argument that the desertion of Rome's traditional religion would bring retribution seemed to have been vindicated. It was chiefly to rebut this pagan argument and so to encourage such Christians that Augustine wrote *The City of God*, a magisterial contrast between 'the city of this world', all those arrayed against God, and the City of God, the community of believers in every age. The City of God, he contends, unlike the city of this world, does not depend on power. Augustine points out, in repudiation of the imperial theology, that some Christian emperors had not lasted long, so that there is no constant correlation between the profession of Christianity and divine blessing.[8] More generally, God's mercy extends to the undeserving; and his judgment is not inevitable for any particular sin.

> For if punishment were obviously inflicted on every wrongdoing in this life, it would be supposed that nothing was reserved for the last judgment; on the other hand, if God's power never openly punished any sin in this world, there would be an end to belief in providence.[9]

Augustine was propounding the normal Christian belief in divine

6. Augustine, *Against Faustus the Manichaean*, 13/7, trans. Richard Stothert, *A Select Library of the Nicene and Post-Nicene Fathers of the Christian Church*, 4, ed. Philip Schaff (1887: Grand Rapids, Mich., 1974), p. 202. Augustine, *Enarration on Psalm 71:10*, trans. A. C. Cox, *A Select Library of the Nicene and Post-Nicene Fathers of the Christian Church*, 8, ed. Philip Schaff (1888: Grand Rapids, Mich., 1974), p. 330.
7. Peter Brown, *Augustine of Hippo: A Biography* (London, 1967), p. 154.
8. Augustine, *Concerning the City of God against the Pagans*, 5/25, trans. Henry Bettenson (Harmondsworth, 1972), p. 221.
9. *Ibid.*, 1/8 (p. 14).

judgment and mercy in history, but at the same time modifying the over-simple form of this belief that had emerged following the imperial recognition of Christianity.

CHRISTIANITY IN THE MIDDLE AGES

The ascendancy of Augustine over the Latin West in the Middle Ages did much to determine the way in which people thought of their position in history.[1] In the twelfth century Bishop Otto of Freising still entitled his history of the world *A Chronicle or History of the Two Cities* in imitation of Augustine.[2] It was not, however, Augustine's careful treatment of God's judgment and mercy that was remembered. On the contrary, mediaeval writers were often influenced by Augustine's pupil Orosius, whose *Seven Books of History against the Pagans* had drawn close correlations between obedience to God and earthly blessings in the fashion of the fourth-century writers whose views Augustine had repudiated.[3] It was a mediaeval commonplace to explain how God consistently blessed the good but punished the wicked. But the Augustinian influence is particularly marked in two other areas, in the reformulation of eschatological expectation and in periodization.

Much of Book 20 of *The City of God* is directed against millenarianism. Augustine had once believed, he explains, that there would be a spiritual rest of a thousand years for the saints on earth,[4] but had come to reject the view as an erroneous interpretation of Scripture. The thousand years should be understood instead as 'the period beginning with Christ's first coming'.[5] This was to become the most orthodox mediaeval view.[6] Augustine went further. Not only did he identify the millennium with the present history of the church. He also applied biblical predictions that were normally taken to describe what would happen at the end of time to the period

1. Sir R. W. Southern, 'Aspects of the European Tradition of Historical Writing: 2. Hugh of St Victor and the Idea of Historical Development', *Transactions of the Royal Historical Society*, 5th Series, 21 (1971), pp. 160f.
2. *Ibid.*, p. 176.
3. Patterson, *God and History*, pp. 127–32.
4. Augustine, *City of God*, 20/7 (p. 907).
5. *Ibid.*, 20/9 (p. 914).
6. Marjorie Reeves, *The Influence of Prophecy in the Later Middle Ages: A Study in Joachimism* (Oxford, 1969), p. 298.

of the church. The new Jerusalem would not suddenly descend in the future, but had been coming down in the form of grace to create the church in 'this present age'.[7] Augustine himself never relaxed his grip on the belief that the Christian hope is to be fulfilled in the next world. Subsequent interpreters of Augustine's teaching, however, can be excused for shifting attention from future hope to present realization, from eschatology to ecclesiology. The institutionalization of the church over the centuries accentuated the tendency. The result was to decrease the awareness that history is moving towards a goal. Little except the last judgment remained in man's future. The mediaeval Christian world-view was remarkably static. Clerical chroniclers of the thirteenth century, for instance, markedly lacked a feeling for time.[8] The teleological dimension of Christian history was neglected.

Augustine was more directly responsible for the most popular mediaeval method of dividing history into periods. In the final chapter of *The City of God* he propounds a scheme of seven epochs. The first five epochs stretched from Adam to Jesus: the first from Adam to the flood, the second from then till Abraham, the third to David, the fourth to the Babylonian exile, and the fifth to the incarnation. The sixth epoch, according to Augustine, is the age of the church militant, and the seventh, corresponding to God's rest after the six days of creation, is a time of rest for the church.[9] The pattern draws inspiration not only from the days of creation but also from the seven seals of the book of Revelation,[1] and had already become a patristic commonplace.[2] There were alternative schemes for interpreting world history, especially the series of four monarchies described in the book of Daniel and taken up by Jerome, which was to enjoy renewed attention after the Reformation, particularly in Germany.[3] In the Middle Ages, however, the preponderant scheme was that of seven epochs. It bore witness to the continuing belief

7. Augustine, *City of God*, 20/17 (p. 928).
8. W. J. Brandt, *The Shape of Medieval History: Studies in Modes of Perception* (New Haven, 1966), p. 170.
9. Augustine, *City of God*, 22/30 (p. 1091).
1. Revelation 5:1.
2. R. A. Markus, *Saeculum: History and Society in the Theology of St Augustine* (Cambridge, 1970), p. 18.
3. Sir Herbert Butterfield, *Man on his Past: The Study of the History of Historical Scholarship* (Cambridge, 1955), pp. 45f.

that from time to time God undertakes epoch-making interventions in human history.

The early Middle Ages saw an offshoot from the Judaeo-Christian tradition that shared much of its view of history: Islam. The passionate monotheism of the early Muslims ensured that they would concur in the Christian conviction that God is responsible for beginning, participating in and guiding world history to its goal. There was only one substantial difference. In the face of the success of pagan barbarians, Christians had lost something of the optimism characteristic of biblical writers. Mohammed, by contrast, had such an unshakeable confidence in the capacity of true believers to fulfil God's purposes in history that he placed less emphasis than the Bible on human sin and divine judgment in history.[4] So optimistic was Muslim historiography in consequence that it tended to lack the realistic sense of the weaknesses and sufferings of God's servants displayed by the biblical writers. Yet when, in the fourteenth century, a Muslim composed a full-scale philosophy of history, it did not describe the historical process as a straight line fulfilling God's will. Ibn Khaldun in his *Introduction to History* presented the normal pattern as a cycle that is only rarely disturbed by supernatural interference, which edges it in the divinely willed direction. Aristotelian influence was partly responsible for Ibn Khaldun's treatment of history, and especially dynasties, as essentially cyclical.[5] Muslim history proved to be less committed to a linear pattern than might have been expected.

The most significant mediaeval Christian theorist of history, second only to Augustine in influence among post-biblical writers, was Joachim of Fiore, a Cistercian abbot of the twelfth century. He was celebrated in his own day for his prophetic gifts and was summoned, for instance, by Richard Coeur de Lion to Messina in 1190/91 to deliver an interpretation of the seven heads of the dragon in the twelfth chapter of Revelation. The sixth head he dutifully identified as Richard's enemy Saladin.[6] He was gifted with a visual imagination that revelled in enigmatic deliverances. It is perhaps no

4. Franz Rosenthal, 'The Influence of the Biblical Tradition on Muslim Historiography', *Historians of the Middle East*, ed. Bernard Lewis and P. M. Holt (London, 1962), p. 38.
5. Ibn Khaldun, *An Introduction to History: The Muqaddimah*, esp. 3/12–15, trans. Franz Rosenthal, ed. N. J. Dawood (London, 1967), pp. 136–42.
6. Reeves, *The Influence of Prophecy*, pp. 6ff.

wonder that an official church investigation of his works in 1255 discovered *plurima curiosa, inutilia et inepta.*[7] His purpose, however, was to discern in the Bible the structure of world history. His starting point, like Augustine's, seems to have been the seven seals of Revelation.[8] He suggested that seven times of conflict could be discovered in both the Old Testament and the New Testament. The Old Testament conflicts and the New Testament conflicts paralleled each other. In this twofold pattern the final conflict was in both cases the worst: the tribulation of Antiochus Epiphanes in the time of the Maccabees and the tribulation of Gog and Magog in the future. Here was the element of stern realism traditionally found in the Christian view of history.

Joachim, however, took a crucial step by combining his twofold pattern with a threefold pattern. He divided the divine plan of history not only into the two dispensations of the Old and New Testaments but also into three ages or 'states' which corresponded to the three persons of the Trinity. The first 'state' was from Adam to Isaiah; the second, the period of Christ, began with the messianic prophecies of Isaiah; and the third, the period of the Spirit, began with Benedict, the creator of the spiritual life of monasticism.[9] This third 'state' was therefore simultaneous with the second, or post-Benedict, stage of the New Testament dispensation. But the third 'state' of history also overlapped beyond the period of the New Testament dispensation and carried on to the consummation of the age. This was to reintroduce into Christian thinking an expectation of a blessed period following the tribulation of Gog and Magog but before the end of time.[1] It was to restate a strong form of the Christian hope. Attention was directed back from a preoccupation with the church as the realization of God's promises to what God would do in the future. Where Joachim's influence was felt, history began to be seen again as moving towards a goal, and so as dynamic rather than static. Joachim's thought was repeatedly taken up, often in an exaggerated form, by heralds of a new age like the Spiritual Franciscans of the thirteenth century and Thomas Müntzer in the

7. 'Many things that are strange, useless and absurd'. Marjorie Reeves and Beatrice Hirsch-Reich, *The 'Figurae' of Joachim of Fiore* (Oxford, 1972), p. 56.
8. *Ibid.*, p. 5.
9. The interrelation of the twofold and threefold patterns is represented diagrammatically in *ibid.*, p. 9.
1. Reeves, *The Influence of Prophecy*, p. 303.

German radical Reformation of the sixteenth.[2] Although himself fully aware of the realistic strand in the biblical outlook, Joachim represents a decisive recovery of optimism in Christian historical thought.

CHRISTIANITY IN THE MODERN PERIOD

Joachim of Fiore constituted more of a turning-point in historical thought than did the Renaissance or the Reformation. In so far as the age of the Renaissance modified the received body of ideas about history, it was either to develop the optimistic trend inaugurated by Joachim or to graft cyclical theories on to a Christian stock as described in the last chapter. And the framework for men's conception of history remained remarkably consistent with what had gone before. Sir Walter Ralegh, that representative Renaissance man, for instance, wrote in his *History of the World* that the doctrine of creation implied providential care of the historical process, 'for what Father,' he asks, 'forsaketh the child that he hath begotten?'[3] Ralegh was equally convinced of God's judgments, which, he believed, ensured that 'ill doing hath always been attended with ill success'.[4] Thus the breach of faith and seizure of the crown by Henry IV of England was rewarded by the murder and dispossession of Henry VI.[5] Belief in the linearity of history and divine interventions was still general.

There was greater disagreement over eschatology. Luther, following Augustine, treated Revelation as an account of church history. His own time was the reign of antichrist, which he identified closely with the papacy.[6] Encouraged by anticipations of the fall of papal power, Luther differed from Augustine only in believing that the end of the world was imminent.[7] The other major reformers shared Luther's view. The effect was to extinguish high expectations of the course of history before the consummation of the age. Hope was restricted to what God would do at the end of time. Human

2. *Ibid.*, pp. 59ff., 490. *Cf.* Norman Cohn, *The Pursuit of the Millennium* (London, 1970).
3. Sir Walter Ralegh, *The History of the World*, ed. C. A. Patrides (London, 1971), p. 71.
4. *Ibid.*, p. 51.
5. *Ibid.*, p. 52.
6. J. M. Headley, *Luther's View of Church History* (New Haven, 1963), p. 224.
7. *Ibid.*, p. 267.

wickedness could be expected only to increase until then. The Puritan preacher John Dove declared in a sermon at Paul's Cross in London during 1594 that the world

> is not onely in the staggering and declining age, but, which exceedeth dotage, at the very vpshot, and like a sicke man which lyeth at deaths doore, ready to breath out the laste ghaspe.[8]

Apocalyptic bred pessimism. Yet the tradition of optimism stemming from Joachim lived on, especially among some of the radical groups on the left wing of the Reformation.[9] Here it was customary to take Revelation as the story of things still to come when God would vindicate his saints. The eager expectations of the radical groups formed one of the reasons why they seemed so dangerous to the sixteenth-century social order. By the early seventeenth century, however, such hopes began to be entertained by widely respected scholars. Joseph Mede, Fellow of Christ's College, Cambridge, embraced a fully-fledged millenarianism in his *Clavis Apocalyptica* of 1627.[1] Mede's thought was to be the starting-point of a trend that did much to foster the idea of progress.[2] Despite the influence of the reformers, eschatology continued to sustain Christian confidence in the course of history.

As the seventeenth century advanced the Christian understanding of history persisted, but the western European technique of historiography was transformed. The Renaissance ideal of combining moral instruction with literary excellence in historical narrative was steadily supplanted by a fresh ideal of 'erudition'. In the new phase of scholarship, which was to run on into the mid-eighteenth century, rhetoric was discounted and accuracy in historical research was exalted. By the turn of the eighteenth century William Wotton could explain in the preface to his *History of Rome* that

> Affectation of Eloquence becomes History the least of anything, especially such an History as this, which like Mosaic Work

8. John Dove, *A Sermon Preached at Pauls Crosse the 3 of November 1594* ... (London, 1594), f. A3r, quoted by E. L. Tuveson, *Millennium and Utopia: A Study in the Background of the Idea of Progress* (Gloucester, Mass., 1972), p. 50.
9. G. H. Williams, *The Radical Reformation* (Philadelphia, 1962), p. 684.
1. Tuveson, *Millennium and Utopia*, pp. 76–85.
2. *Cf.* below, pp. 70f.

> must be made up and interwoven with the Thought and Sentences of other Men, and where to add to, or diminish from ones Authors, may be of ill consequence.[3]

It was thought essential to cite authorities copiously in order to carry conviction. Consequently treatises of the period were normally bulky and often marked by digression and repetition. This was an age of historical scholarship that valued content far above form. George Hickes, a friend of Wotton's, for example, issued in 1703–05 an important composite work called the *Thesaurus of the Northern Tongues* which included a series of Latin treatises on the languages and cultures of northern Europe in the early Middle Ages, separate grammars of Anglo-Saxon, Gothic and Icelandic, a treatise on Saxon coins and a catalogue of Saxon manuscripts.[4] The passionate quest for fuller and more accurate knowledge drove scholars both to draw freshly on non-literary sources and to assess critically the authenticity of texts. This was therefore the period of the germination of the 'auxiliary sciences' of history – archaeology and numismatics, palaeography and diplomatic. If history was tending towards antiquarianism, it was towards a thorough and fruitful antiquarianism.

This was not, as it might appear, a period of 'history for history's sake'. The preference of scholars of the time for argument rather than narrative is a sign that a polemical purpose normally underlay this phase of historiography. They were trying to justify the shape – or to modify the details – of the settled order in western Europe that had emerged from the wars of religion of the previous hundred years. The Earl of Clarendon's *History of the Rebellion and Civil Wars in England*, published posthumously in 1702–04, for instance, was intended to display the chaotic consequences of revolt against the established order in church and state.[5] The delving into the more

3. William Wotton, *The History of Rome from the Death of Antoninus Pius to the Death of Severus Alexander* (1701), quoted by J. M. Levine, 'Ancients, Moderns, and History: The Continuity of English Historical Writing in the Later Seventeenth Century', *Studies in Change and Revolution: Aspects of English Intellectual History, 1640–1800*, ed. P. J. Korshin (Menston, W. Yorks., 1972), p. 64.
4. Levine, 'Ancients, Moderns, and History', *Studies in Change and Revolution*, ed. Korshin, p. 67.
5. Edward, Earl of Clarendon, *The History of the Rebellion and Civil Wars in England Begun in the Year 1641*, ed. W. D. Macray (Oxford, 1888).

distant past, the desire for completeness and the care for accuracy were all designed to bolster a distinctly partisan case. In England this motive is very evident in the study by William Wake, later Archbishop of Canterbury, of mediaeval church councils, the *State of the Church and Clergy of England* (1703): it was written to justify from past precedents the existing control by the crown of the clerical convocation of the Church of England.[6] But the greatest achievements of the age were the launching by the Belgian Roman Catholic community of Bollandists of a project that still continues, the application of critical techniques to the lives of the saints; and the composition by Mabillon, the leading scholar of the French Maurist community, of a textbook on methods for authenticating documents, *De Re Diplomatica* (1681).[7] It was quite characteristic of the men of this age to be motivated by zeal for religion, and especially for the institutional church that formed the greatest guarantee of stability in a potentially insecure world. They thought of themselves as Christian historians.

This does not mean that the historical scholarship of the period went out of its way to emphasize that history was a linear pattern in which God intervened and which led on to the last things. On the contrary, the bold outlines of the Christian theory could still be taken for granted. The concern of scholars of the age of erudition was typically not with overall patterns at all, but with minutiae. Yet the age did produce a theology of history in the grand manner that won widespread acclaim. Jacques-Bénigne Bossuet, appointed Bishop of Meaux in 1681, published in the same year his *Discourse on Universal History*. Taking *The City of God* as his chief model, he composed a history of man from the creation to the time of Charlemagne organized around the theme of the expanding community of the faithful.[8] Bossuet, however, shows traces in his *Discourse* of thinking in ways alien to traditional Christian understandings of history. In particular he betrays the influence of Descartes in seeing God as working not directly in history through miracle but indirectly

6. D. C. Douglas, *English Scholars, 1660–1730* (London, 1951), p. 213.
7. M. D. Knowles, 'Great Historical Enterprises: 1. The Bollandists; 2. The Maurists', *Transactions of the Royal Historical Society*, 5th Series, 8 (1958) and 9 (1959).
8. Jacques-Bénigne Bossuet, *Discourse on Universal History*, ed. Orest Ranum (Chicago, 1976).

through men's minds.[9] This was an anticipation of a stress on human reason that was to come into its own in the following century.

The traditional framework of the Christian view of history could be assumed by scholars at the beginning of the eighteenth century but not by writers at its end. The challenge to Christian beliefs posed by the Enlightenment intervened and forms the subject of the next chapter. When scholarship tried to reassert aspects of Christian thought about history, it did so within the rationalist framework erected by the Enlightenment; or else, in reacting against Enlightenment values, it gave rise to a new approach to historical understanding, the historicism that is the subject of the fifth chapter. Thus, for example, Lord Acton tried to identify a Christian view of history with the idea of progress stemming largely from the Enlightenment;[1] and Thomas Arnold, with Christian aims in view, embraced a historicist worldview.[2] There were still men of the second rank who composed history on traditional Christian principles. There was, for instance, Joseph Milner's *History of the Church of Christ*, written from an evangelical standpoint in the 1790s.[3] Such writers, however, tended to confine themselves to church history, leaving secular history to others. A sense of providence decayed, even at a popular level. In 1862 the magazine of the Primitive Methodist denomination discontinued its section recording acts of providence.[4] By the mid-twentieth century the inclusion of providential elements in historical writing by professing Christians was rare, even though Roman Catholic theory still upheld the view that history should be written in the light of man's ultimate destiny.[5] W. den Boer's *Between Quay and Ship*, published in 1957 by a Dutch Calvinist, was an isolated instance.[6] There was a phase following the shock of the Second World War when several writers, of whom Reinhold Niebuhr and

9. J. H. Brumfitt, *Voltaire: Historian* (London, 1958), p. 31.
1. *Cf.* below, pp. 88f.
2. *Cf.* below, pp. 106f.
3. J. D. Walsh, 'Joseph Milner's Evangelical Church History', *The Journal of Ecclesiastical History*, 10 (1959).
4. James Obelkevich, *Religion and Rural Society: South Lindsey, 1825–1875* (Oxford, 1976), p. 254n.
5. H. F. Kearney, 'Christianity and the Study of History', *The Downside Review*, 67 (1949), pp. 73–75. The more traditional theory is here upheld in an anonymous note appended to a liberalizing article by Kearney.
6. Cited by A. D. Momigliano, 'Historicism in Contemporary Thought', *Studies in Historiography* (London, 1966), p. 238.

Sir Herbert Butterfield were the most eminent, propounded afresh a providentialist understanding of history.[7] But western civilization had ceased to be dominated by the Christian view of history long before.

ASSESSMENT OF THE CHRISTIAN VIEW

Of the elements in the Christian understanding of history some have more appeal for modern man than others. Belief that history is linear accords closely with modern assumptions. As we shall see in the next chapter, the idea of progress that has coloured so much popular thinking shares the Christian view of history as linear. The accelerated pace of change in the modern world also encourages us to agree that history is moving forward. This feature of the Christian view secures widespread assent. Belief that history is moving towards a goal is less popular. Yet it must be admitted to be a reasonable corollary of monotheism. A God who guides the course of history but who is opposed on the way will surely bring the process to a triumphant conclusion. That is why the essence of Christian eschatology is shared with Judaism and Islam, the other monotheistic world religions. Monotheism creates hope. A question does arise over the specific reasons for hope in the Christian scheme. Millenarianism has in practice fostered confidence in the future – among groups in the early church, among those influenced by Joachimism and among thinkers following in the wake of Joseph Mede. Within Christianity itself, however, Augustine, the classical reformers and many biblical commentators have come to the opinion that there are inadequate grounds for taking the thousand years mentioned in the book of Revelation as a period of blessing before the end of time. It is a symbol, they argue with some cogency, of the history of the church.[8] The note of hope retains its prominent place in the Christian view, because it is based on confidence in continuing divine control and expectation of ultimate divine victory. The millenarian stimulus to hope, however, appears to have been unjustified. One of the chief reasons for Christian optimism seems groundless even on Christian terms.

7. Reinhold Niebuhr, *Faith and History* (London, 1949). Sir Herbert Butterfield, *Christianity and History* (London, 1949). On these, *cf.* below, pp. 176–80.
8. Mathias Rissi, *The Future of the World: An Exegetical Study of Revelation 19:11–22:15* (London, 1972), pp. 30–34.

More acute problems for the Christian view arise over the idea that God intervenes at specific points in history. Why is such intervention necessary if he controls the whole process? Belief in particular providences seems incompatible with a conviction that there is a general providence. A medal struck by Elizabeth I to commemorate the victory over the Armada supplies a typical instance of the belief that God takes part directly in events. The inscription runs, *Afflavit Deus et dissipati sunt.* God's breath dispersed the hostile fleet. If God rules over all events, why should this one be interpreted as more particularly God's doing than others? After all, the Spaniards undoubtedly discerned the hand of God in the assembling of the fleet for the conquest of heretical England. It seems difficult to hold that God was at work in both cases. The whole subject of particular providences appears to be fit only for satire. Dickens has Mr Podsnap in *Our Mutual Friend* declare that 'this island was blest, Sir, to the Direct Exclusion of such Other Countries as – as there may happen to be'.[9] The harnessing of providential interference to national interests suggests that the idea may be dangerous as well as an apparent contradiction of the notion of divine sovereignty.

A further problem attaches to the same belief in particular providences. If God does intervene in specific events, how can we discern what is happening? God's way must be complex, and human beings are fallible. Claims to understand God's dealings with men seem bold or even ridiculous. As it was put in the eighteenth century:

> To deny the exercise of a particular providence in the Deity's government of the world is certainly impious: yet nothing serves the cause of the scorner more than an incautious forward zeal in determining the particular instances of it.[1]

The problem is accentuated by the difficulty that if cases of God's interventions cannot be put forward, the claim that he does intervene seems to become vacuous. This element in the Christian view risks turning into a formal assertion without content. If no instances are cited, the whole idea of providence is robbed of plausibility. The American Christian historian E. H. Harbison formulates the prob-

9. Charles Dickens, *Our Mutual Friend*, 1/11, introd. E. S. Davies (London, 1952), p. 133.
1. Dr Abernethy's Life in *Biographia Britannica* quoted by James Boswell, *Life of Johnson* (London, 1970), p. 1276n.

lem as one of how to see history 'as governed by a predestinating Providence, without falling into the sin of playing God and saying "Lo, here – lo, there"'.[2] Either providence disappears from history or else human beings make extravagant claims. Belief in particular providences creates a dilemma.

The other serious objections to the Christian view of history concern particular interventions in judgment and the doctrine of providence overall. They revolve around the problem of suffering. Divine judgments can cause suffering; general providence permits it. In both ways God seems responsible, on the Christian view, for a world where human beings go through pain and trouble. Should not God's love ensure that pain and trouble are excluded from a world he controls? The Lisbon earthquake of 1755 that caused extensive loss of life brought similar questions to the lips of many in Europe.[3] The issue becomes most acute when the victims of disasters seem in no way to deserve their fate. The French novelist Albert Camus portrays exactly such an instance, the death anguish of an innocent child suffering from the plague. A Jesuit priest who witnesses the scene finds his faith in providence called into question.[4] The problem is not just that any suffering seems incompatible with Christian beliefs about God, but also that the distribution of suffering seems unfair. To this and the other problems posed by providence we shall return in the final chapter. Here it suffices to note that, as the biblical book of Job recognizes, the problem of suffering sets a question mark against the Christian view of history, the world and God.

2. E. H. Harbison, *Christianity and History* (Princeton, 1964), p. 288.
3. T. D. Kendrick, *The Lisbon Earthquake* (London, 1956), p. 149.
4. Albert Camus, *The Plague* (1947), trans. Stuart Gilbert (Harmondsworth, 1960), pp. 173–91.

4 The idea of progress

> 'In two or three hundred years, or maybe a thousand years . . . life will be different. It will be happy. Of course, we shan't be able to enjoy that future life, but all the same, what we're living for now is to create it, we work and . . . yes, we suffer in order to create it. That's the goal of our life, and you might say that's the only happiness we shall ever achieve.'
>
> Vershinin in Anton Chekhov, *Three Sisters.*

The idea of progress that emerged in the Enlightenment of the eighteenth century was a secularization of the Christian view of history. Belief in divine intervention was eliminated, but otherwise the structure of the idea of progress betrays its Christian origins. It is linear, offers confidence in the future and entails acceptance of unchanging moral values. The linearity is to be found in the pattern of progress attributed to the past. Man, according to the idea of progress, has advanced not just in matters like technology and the improvement of material conditions. There has been progress also in the use of man's intellect and, in many versions, in his moral capacity. Human history is therefore the account of the improvement of the human condition from barbarism to civilization. There is a striking similarity to the Christian story of man's pilgrimage between two points, but the starting-place is no longer creation and the finishing-place is no longer judgment. Different presentations of the idea of progress vary in the degree to which they admit that there have been periods of regression within the process. Many eighteenth-century writers treated the Middle Ages, an era of superstition in their view, as a temporary triumph for the forces opposed to human improvement. But it was only a matter of time before the steady advance of mankind was resumed. Despite certain deviations, the pattern in the past is essentially a straight line.

The second characteristic feature of the idea of progress is its high expectation of the future. If the past has witnessed the gradual improvement of man, then it is reasonable to suppose that the future offers a similar prospect. Thus the idea of progress shares the optimism of the Christian view, even if there are usually no divine sanctions for a happy future. In the eighteenth century and sometimes afterwards there was nevertheless a strong conviction that the course of history was predetermined. Progress would certainly continue, and eventually, according to many versions, man would attain a state of unparalleled happiness. There would be a form of utopia at the climax of history. Here is a close analogy to the hope of Christian eschatology.[1] Whether or not such a goal of history was expected, theorists of progress agreed that the improvement discerned in the past can be projected into the future.

The third element in the idea of progress is that there exists a criterion for assessing what is progress and what is not. The criterion has to be a set of values that does not change over time. In some versions, for instance, it is human happiness; in others it is rationality. These or similar qualities are traced as they develop over time so that progress can be identified. As much as on the Christian understanding of history, values are held to be absolute. When a state of perfection was looked for in the future it was believed that the chosen values – happiness, rationality or something similar – would be fully realized there. Even when no specific goal of history was posited and an expectation of indefinite progress replaced it, theorists assumed that improvement would be in qualities already known to be good in themselves. By contrast with historicism, which is to be discussed in the next chapter, the idea of progress entails a rejection of any belief that values are relative to different cultures.

ORIGINS OF THE IDEA OF PROGRESS

The idea of progress has often been seen as an outgrowth of the debate between the ancients and the moderns in the seventeenth century.[2] This was the controversy whose English episode was satirized in Swift's *The Battle of the Books* (1704) over whether or not modern scholarship surpassed that of the ancients. At the beginning of the seventeenth century the superiority of the ancients

1. This and other similarities between the Christian view and the idea of progress received classic treatment in C. L. Becker, *The Heavenly City of the Eighteenth-Century Philosophers* (New Haven, Conn., 1932).
2. Notably by Georges Sorel, *The Illusions of Progress* (1908: Berkeley, Calif., 1969); and J. B. Bury, *The Idea of Progress* (London, 1920).

had been taken for granted so that, for instance, the first Camden Praelector of History appointed at Oxford in 1622 had the statutory duty not of lecturing but merely of adding comments to Florus and other ancient historians.[3] Even in the course of the controversy at the end of the century the champion of the moderns, William Wotton, would go no further than to allege that in history *some* modern practitioners had come up to the standard of the ancients.[4] In France the cultural triumphs of the court of Louis XIV encouraged grander claims for modern learning. Perrault in his *Comparison of the Ancients and the Moderns* (1688-96) and Fontenelle in his *Digression on the Ancients and Moderns* (1688) formulated the argument that knowledge cannot but accumulate over time.[5] This contention did help prepare the way for the eighteenth-century belief in the inexorable advance of civilization, but the opinion of the moderns was more a symptom than a cause of an increasing tendency for optimism to triumph over pessimism in thinking about the course of history.[6] The debate between the ancients and the moderns was after all only about literature, not about society as a whole. The prime movers in the tendency to optimism were philosophically-minded theologians.

The transition from the Christian view to the idea of progress may be taken as having started when Joseph Mede drew scholarly attention afresh to millenarianism.[7] Belief in a future blessed state within history became a standard element in the schemes worked out by late seventeenth-century theologians. Thomas Burnet, Master of Charterhouse, for example, incorporated an eventual millennium in his *Sacred Theory of the Earth* (1684-90). How, though, is man to reach that state when the debilitating consequences of the fall are taken into account? Burnet's answer was that man steadily advances in knowledge so that he is ready for the millennium.[8] Burnet still incorporated in his scheme of the future a catastrophe preceding the

3. A. D. Momigliano, 'Ancient History and the Antiquarian', *Studies in Historiography* (London, 1966), p. 6.
4. J. M. Levine, 'Ancients, Moderns and History: The Continuity of English Historical Writing in the Later Seventeenth Century,' *Studies in Change and Revolution: Aspects of English Intellectual History, 1640–1800*, ed. P. J. Korshin (Menston, W. Yorks., 1972), pp. 50f.
5. Bury, *The Idea of Progress*, pp. 83–88, 98–125.
6. For these alternatives in the scholarship of the time, *cf.* above, pp. 35ff.
7. *Cf.* above, p. 61.
8. E. L. Tuveson, *Millennium and Utopia: A Study in the Background of the Idea of Progress* (1949: Gloucester, Mass., 1972), p. 117.

millennium, but gradually that disappeared from the pages of eighteenth-century theologians. William Worthington, a Canon of York, could argue by 1773 that nothing but gradual human improvement stood between the present and the millennial state.[9] Worthington rejected what he called in an earlier book

> the Prejudice which Men in all Ages have against their own Times, and the vulgar Opinion, that the World grows worse and worse, Mankind more degenerate, and the Seasons more unfavourable.[1]

Presenting human improvement as not only intellectual but also moral, Worthington had embraced a full-blooded version of the idea of progress. His optimism owes something to the cyclical theory, for he writes of the future state as the restoration of Virgil's golden age,[2] but the overriding debt was to Christian millenarianism. Worthington, like many of his contemporaries in the church, was turning the Christian view of history into the story of the development of human culture.

Why was it that churchmen were responsible for dissolving the Christian view? It was partly because the germ of the idea of progress, the argument that there had been continuous intellectual improvement, had attractions as a potent weapon in the armoury of Christian apologetic. In the seventeenth century critics of Christian orthodoxy used classical sources to assert the eternity of the world and so to deny the doctrine of creation. If knowledge was advancing, the orthodox could reply, then it must have had a beginning at some point in the past.[3] Again, in the eighteenth century deists argued that natural religion rather than revealed religion must be true, since a faith necessary for salvation must have been known always and everywhere. Edmund Law, later Bishop of Carlisle, supplied a popular answer by claiming that revealed religion was available to all men, but that their understanding of it had gradually improved.[4]

9. William Worthington, *The Scripture Theory of the Earth* (1773), cited by Tuveson, *Millennium and Utopia*, p. 142.
1. William Worthington, *An Essay on ... Man's Redemption ...* (1743), quoted by R. S. Crane, 'Anglican Apologetics and the Idea of Progress, 1699–1745' (1934), *The Idea of the Humanities and other Essays Critical and Historical* (Chicago, 1967), 1, p. 240.
2. *Ibid.*, p. 250.
3. *Ibid.*, p. 215.
4. *Ibid.*, pp. 265–74.

Both lines of argument asserted that knowledge is advancing. But the birth of the idea of progress among churchmen was also due to a respect for reason that they shared with their opponents. Their views were decreasingly derived from the repository of Christian convictions in the Bible, and increasingly from what enlightened men of the age held to be rational. 'There is a great difference', wrote Burnet, 'betwixt Scripture with Philosophy on its side, and Scripture with Philosophy against it.'[5] He believed that parts of the Bible were intended only for previous unenlightened times. Reason could now dispense with ideas out of harmony with the age.

On that ground the element of intervention in the Christian idea of history was discarded. Providence was not denied, but it was commonly reduced to a natural sequence of cause and effect. Burnet, for example, explained:

> If we would have a fair view and right apprehensions of Natural Providence, we must not cut the chains of it too short, by having recourse, without necessity, either to First Cause, in explaining the Origins of things, or to Miracles, in explaining particular effects.[6]

There was no need to posit divine interference in a well-ordered universe. This was not far from the main claim of the deists that God remained apart from his world after its creation. Edmund Law, in opposing the deists, came perilously close to them by denying the need for divine intervention. God's care for the world was a matter of 'superintendence' only.[7] In attempting to defend a Christian position, broad-minded men in the Church of England therefore deprived it of one of its most salient features.

A similar process was at work in France. There, too, men like Joseph Adrien Le Large, the Abbé de Lignac, propounded a doctrine of progress from the standpoint of the church.[8] The greatest of them was the Prior Anne Robert Jacques Turgot, Baron de L'Aulne, who was to become an earnestly reforming chief minister to Louis XVI

5. Thomas Burnet, *Theory of the Earth*, 2 (London, 1690), p. 46, quoted by Tuveson, *Millennium and Utopia*, p. 118.
6. Burnet, *Theory of the Earth*, 2, p. 11, quoted by Tuveson, *Millennium and Utopia*, p. 119.
7. Edmund Law quoted by Tuveson, *Millennium and Utopia*, p. 151.
8. Henry Vyverberg, *Historical Pessimism in the French Enlightenment* (Cambridge, Mass., 1958), p. 51.

in 1775-76. Although Turgot had abandoned a clerical vocation and with it attendance at mass,[9] he delivered at the Sorbonne, in 1750 when he was twenty-three, a series of orations extolling Christianity as a progressive force in history. He dwelt on the theme that the church had been responsible for the improvements in knowledge and material conditions that had marked the Christian era. Evil and ignorance had been overruled by providence, as Bossuet had written; but, unlike Bossuet, Turgot speaks of providence acting according to uniform laws in the manner of Edmund Law's 'superintendence'. The 'designs of providence' are equated with the 'progress of enlightenment'.[1] Turgot writes only of the past, but his providential belief that error contributes to truth leads him to present human advance as inevitable. A well-developed idea of progress had grown on Christian soil.

PHILOSOPHICAL HISTORY

Changes in the discipline of history also promoted the belief that the past should be read as the story of man's rise towards civilization. As the eighteenth century advanced there arose a dissatisfaction with the quest for detail that marked the age of erudition.[2] In fashionable literary circles such scholarship was held in contempt. Henry St John, Viscount Bolingbroke, describes how he had met a historian of the school:

> The man was communicative enough; but nothing was distinct in his mind. How could it be otherwise? He had never spared time to think, all was employed in reading.[3]

The remedy was to infuse thinking into historical scholarship, to make history philosophical. The story is told that an early composition of the new genre was the result of a complaint to Voltaire by the Marquise du Châtelet that history was unpalatable:

> A confused mass of unrelated facts, a thousand accounts of

9. F. E. Manuel, *The Prophets of Paris* (Cambridge, Mass., 1962), p. 307.
1. Turgot, *Oeuvres*, 1, p. 283, quoted by R. V. Sampson, *Progress in the Age of Reason: The Seventeenth Century to the Present Day* (London, 1956), p. 167.
2. On the age of erudition, *cf.* above, pp. 61ff.
3. Henry St John, Viscount Bolingbroke, 'Letters on the Study and Use of History', 4, *The Works of the late Right Honourable Henry St John, Lord Viscount Bolingbroke* (London, 1809), 3, p. 404.

> battles which have decided nothing. What is the point for a Frenchwoman like myself of knowing that in Sweden Egli succeeded Haquin and that Ottoman was the son of Ortogul?[4]

Voltaire concurred in the criticism. He therefore set to work on his *Essay on the Manners and the Spirit of the Nations* (1756) which reduced facts to a minimum and concentrated on broad cultural patterns. The practice of history was changing.

Criticism of the age of erudition went deeper. Perhaps the hard-working scholars were wasting the time spent on researching the past. The opinion that history could yield no credible knowledge, the historical Pyrrhonism first mooted in the later seventeenth century,[5] gained ground in France during the early eighteenth century. A central figure in the debate on the subject was Father Jean Hardouin, a Jesuit and himself a devotee of painstaking scholarship, who contended that all the writings of classical antiquity except the Bible and six authors had been forged in the thirteenth and fourteenth centuries. When asked why he was thinking up such extraordinary theories, he is alleged to have replied, 'Do you think I get up at four o'clock every morning in order to say the same as everyone else has said before me?'[6] If the authenticity of Aristotle or Livy could not be assumed, it was doubtful if anything could be known about the past. A fierce controversy on this theme racked the Academy of Inscriptions, the headquarters of French historical scholarship, for a number of years after 1720.[7] The work of pure antiquarians on coins, inscriptions and other material remains which, unlike literary sources, could hardly be forged was eventually to restore academic confidence in the viability of historical knowledge.[8] In the meantime, however, traditional history was seriously devalued. Philosophical history alone seemed worthwhile.

Writers of this new style of history were concerned to avoid

4. Quoted by Paul Sakman, 'The Problems of Historical Method and of Philosophy of History in Voltaire' (1906), *History and Theory*, Beiheft 11 (1971), p. 24.
5. *Cf.* above, pp. 8f.
6. W. O. Chadwick, *From Bossuet to Newman: The Idea of Doctrinal Development* (Cambridge, 1957), p. 51.
7. Robert Flint, *Historical Philosophy in France and French Belgium and Switzerland* (Edinburgh, 1893), pp. 254–61.
8. Momigliano, 'Ancient History and the Antiquarian', *Studies in Historiography*, p. 27.

catalogues of details. 'Malheur aux détails', wrote Voltaire to a correspondent: 'c'est une vermine qui tue les grands ouvrages.'[9] William Robertson, whose *History of the Reign of the Emperor Charles V* (1769) is a classic Scottish example of this mode of historiography, put his details, what he called 'Proofs and Illustrations', in a separate appendix lest they should mar his narrative.[1] This distaste for the particular has given rise to the notion that the Enlightenment took little interest in history. Analysis of a cross-section of French private libraries of the period 1750 to 1780 shows, however, that over a quarter of the items were works of history.[2] It was simply that contemporaries wanted history of a certain kind. 'Historical science when not enlightened by philosophy', wrote the philosopher D'Alembert, 'is the lowest ranking of all realms of knowledge.'[3] History when enlightened by philosophy was very much in fashion.

The programme of the new history was succinctly stated by Voltaire in the introduction to his essay on the age of Louis XIV:

> In this history we shall confine ourselves only to what is deserving the attention of all ages, what paints the genius and manners of mankind, contributes to instruction, and prompts to love of virtue, of the arts, and of our country.[4]

There was, in a word, to be an emphasis on culture. The leading ideas and attitudes of an age were depicted on a broad canvas. Similarly in Britain the philosopher David Hume, in his popular *History of Great Britain*, concentrated on civilization. This was not to neglect politics, for Hume interpreted civilization as having at its

9. 'A plague on detail. It is a pest that destroys great works.' Voltaire to M. l'Abbé Dubos, 1738, 'Correspondence', *Oeuvres Complètes* (1880), 3, p. 30, quoted by A. D. Momigliano, 'Gibbon's Contribution to Historical Method' (1954), *Studies in Historiography*, p. 43.
1. Momigliano, 'Gibbon's Contribution to Historical Method,' *Studies in Historiography*, p. 46.
2. Daniel Mornet, 'Les Enseignements des bibliothèques privées (1750–1780)', *Revue d'histoire littéraire de la France*, 17 (1910), p. 456.
3. D'Alembert, 'Mémoires et Réflexions sur Christine, Reine de Suède', *Oeuvres*, 2, p. 119, quoted by Vyverberg, *Historical Pessimism*, pp. 106f.
4. Voltaire, 'Age of Louis XIV', *Works* (1761), 6, p. 168, quoted by Charles Frankel, *The Faith of Reason: The Idea of Progress in the French Enlightenment* (New York, 1948), pp. 110f.

centre the law and order essential to a stable society.[5] If the subject was culture in its broadest sense, the method was explanatory. Writers of history wished not only to recount, but to show why developments had taken place. Montesquieu was a major influence here. His *The Spirit of the Laws* (1748) attempted to explain the varying characteristics of peoples and their governments by reference to their environment, especially soil and climate. His environmentalism found little favour, but his capacity to explain differences over space and time was taken as a model. The publication of *The Spirit of the Laws* was, for instance, the spur that finally set Hume to writing his *History*.[6] Explanation of cultural change was therefore the keynote of the new history.

Cultural change, it was generally believed, had been for the better. The refined manners, the tolerance, the reasonableness of the late eighteenth century were signs that mankind had improved. Voltaire's *Essay on the Manners and the Spirit of the Nations*, for instance, censures past ages for their barbarity, bigotry and superstition, and although he hints that their residue remains he is sure that they are being superseded.[7] Similarly Hume traces how liberty, to him the supreme civilized value, had emerged from the struggles of the Stuart period.[8] There had been progress. Neither Voltaire nor Hume makes explicit any theory of how improvement would continue, but this was to be the work of their successors. The germ of the idea of progress was present in the new history.

Both Voltaire and Hume reveal how belief in progress, despite its Christian background, was not always generated by defenders of orthodoxy. Voltaire the deist was permanently embroiled in a bitter onslaught on the church. He consistently treats the Christian religion as a form of irrational superstition, the polar opposite of enlightenment, and so, for instance, holds up Bossuet to ridicule for writing a 'universal history' that makes no reference to China.[9] Hume the

5. David Hume, *The History of Great Britain: The Reigns of James I and Charles I* (1754), ed. Duncan Forbes (Harmondsworth, 1970), p. 15.
6. H. R. Trevor-Roper, 'The Historical Philosophy of the Enlightenment', *Studies on Voltaire and the Eighteenth Century*, ed. Theodore Besterman, 27 (1963), p. 1673.
7. J. H. Brumfitt, *Voltaire: Historian* (London, 1958), p. 127.
8. Hume, *The History of Great Britain*, p. 52.
9. Trevor-Roper, 'The Historical Philosophy of the Enlightenment', *Studies on Voltaire and the Eighteenth Century*, 27 (1963), p. 1670.

agnostic also brings out the less admirable qualities of religion. He clearly enjoys recounting how those in England who followed Arminius in turning away from Calvinism, 'finding more encouragement from the superstitious spirit of the church than from the fanaticism of the puritans, gradually incorporated themselves with the former'.[1] It is not surprising that divine intervention was far from the thoughts of Voltaire and Hume as they wrote. These men, like Gibbon after them, were using history as a vehicle for anti-Christian propaganda. Man's cultural improvement could be seen not as an ally but as an alternative to the Christian view of history.

THE SCIENCE OF MAN

A further set of influences helped to mould the thinkers of the late eighteenth century who elaborated the idea of progress. Sir Isaac Newton was generally revered as the creator of modern science. What was taken to be his method, the careful examination of phenomena without preliminary reasoning or recourse to authority with a view to discovering regular laws, enjoyed great prestige. Such empiricism, it was widely held, was also the method that the philosopher John Locke had begun to apply to the study of man. Knowledge, according to Locke, is gained through the reception of sense impressions by the human mind. On this view, often called sensationalism, the mind plays no active part in the acquisition of knowledge, but passively accepts whatever is presented to it. Newtonian empiricism and Lockean sensationalism formed the premises of late eighteenth-century theorists.

The implications for an understanding of history were considerable. If (following Newton) the external world is subject to consistent laws and if (following Locke) human knowledge is given by the external world, then people will everywhere and always be formed by experience of a single order. The result was belief that human nature is constant. As David Hume puts it:

> Would you know the sentiments, inclinations, and course of life of the Greeks and Romans? Study well the temper and actions of the French and English . . . Mankind are so much the same, in all times and places, that history informs of nothing new or strange in this particular. Its chief use is only to discover the

1. Hume, *The History of Great Britain*, pp. 319f.

> constant and universal principles of human nature, by showing men in all varieties of circumstances and situations, and furnishing us with materials from which we may form our observations and become acquainted with the regular springs of human action and behaviour.[2]

History, Hume tells us, allows us to apply empirical investigation to man over time and so to establish psychological laws. It is assumed, on this view, that man as an object of study is no different from nature. Laws remain to be discovered in the human world that have as much validity as those already established by Newton and his successors in the natural world. The aim of history is to create a science of man.

This was the intellectual framework of the Scottish Enlightenment. History was examined by men like William Robertson, Principal of Edinburgh University, and his colleague there, Adam Ferguson, with a view to elucidating the psychology behind human action. These writers found no difficulty in reconciling the idea that human nature is constant with the belief that man is advancing. On the contrary, as Ferguson writes, it seemed that progress is natural for man:

> If we admit that man is susceptible of improvement, and has in himself a principle of progression, and a desire of perfection, it appears improper to say, that he has quitted the state of his nature, when he has begun to proceed . . .[3]

The pattern for investigation in any field of human endeavour was therefore one of progress. Thus Adam Smith's *Inquiry into the Nature and Causes of the Wealth of Nations* (1776) was a systematic analysis of the cause of 'the greatest improvement in the productive powers of Labour', which he identified as the division of labour.[4] So convinced was Smith that there was a definite scheme of economic development that when his evidence and his scheme came into conflict he felt bound to explain the divergence rather than to modify the

2. David Hume, 'An Enquiry concerning Human Understanding' (1748), *Enquiries concerning the Human Understanding and concerning the Principles of Morals*, ed. L. A. Selby-Bigge (Oxford, 1962), p. 83.
3. Adam Ferguson, *Essay on the History of Civil Society* (Edinburgh, 1767), p. 14, quoted by Tuveson, *Millennium and Utopia*, p. 191.
4. Adam Smith, *An Inquiry into the Nature and Causes of the Wealth of Nations*, ed. R. H. Campbell, A. S. Skinner and W. B. Todd (Oxford, 1976), 1, p. 13.

scheme.[5] There was confidence that the laws of progress were being laid bare.

It was not doubted in the late eighteenth century that steps could be taken to ensure that human improvement would continue. Locke's position provided the basis for this conviction. If people's opinions are the result of their experience of the world, then to release them from bondage to error it is necessary only to manipulate their experience. Rousseau's *Emile* (1762), for example, is a tract explaining how experience of the benign influences of nature would form the ideal upbringing. This type of attitude soon took on a political colouring. It was felt that the work of reformers was being frustrated by the caution of corrupt and self-interested rulers. 'The progress of reason is never retarded save by the vices of government,' writes Condillac, an extreme French disciple of Locke.[6] The need for the purging or even the overthrow of government became a frequent theme among French theorists like Diderot, the *philosophes* who were the heroes of the revolution. Political reform was also to be a recurring goal among those in later periods who held in the manner of the *philosophes* that the human constitution is itself an encouragement to progress.

Once the obstacles posed by government had been surmounted or circumvented, the future seemed to offer boundless opportunities to those steeped in the philosophy of the Enlightenment. If the pattern of the past is progress and human nature does not change, then progress will certainly continue. The laws of human improvement will not be suspended. Posterity will achieve undreamt-of happiness. Man need not stop short of something like perfection. There will be a time when liberty will be fully realized – even liberty and economic equality too, if the most advanced thinkers like William Godwin are to be believed.[7] History is moving towards a goal, 'glorious and paradisaical, beyond what our imagi[n]ations can now conceive'.[8] The phraseology of this description by Joseph Priestley, English dissenting minister as well as chemist, reveals the debt of such

5. *Ibid.*, pp. *55f.*
6. Condillac, 'Histoire Ancienne', *Oeuvres*, 10, p. 72, quoted by Vyverberg, *Historical Pessimism*, p. 126.
7. William Godwin, *Enquiry concerning Political Justice* (1793), ed. K. C. Carter (Oxford, 1971), p. 297.
8. Joseph Priestley, *An Essay on the First Principles of Government; and on the Nature of Political, Civil, and Religious Liberty* (London, 1768), p. 8.

teleology to its Christian background. But by the last years of the eighteenth century the millennium had been shorn of its Christian overtones and firmly incorporated in a body of thought that was often militantly secular.

Of such a body of thought the Marquis de Condorcet is the most complete exponent. Condorcet drew inspiration for his vision of the perfectibility of man from Turgot, whose biographer he was, and from Priestley, but differed from them in adopting atheism.[9] He wrote of 'that confidence in one's own reason which is the bane of all religious beliefs'.[1] Condorcet was the martyr of the creed of progress. He died while under detention during a Jacobin purge in 1793. His profession of faith, a *Sketch for a Historical Picture of the Progress of the Human Mind*, was composed shortly before while in hiding.[2] It asserts his conviction that nothing had resisted the march of progress, not even the Middle Ages, of which he took a dim view:

> Man's only achievements were theological day-dreaming and superstitious imposture, his only morality religious intolerance. In blood and tears, crushed between priestly tyranny and military despotism, Europe awaited the moment when a new enlightenment would allow her to be reborn free, heiress to humanity and virtue.[3]

New enlightenment had inevitably appeared, and improvement had returned. Permanent arrest was inconceivable. There was consolation for the philosopher confronted by the wrongs of the present in the thought that the future would have no place for slavery or prejudice.[4] Human destiny is guaranteed by the laws of nature, and so history is the foundation of 'a science for predicting the progress of the human race'.[5] Here was confidence that the past was marked by human improvement, confidence that the process would be sustained into the indefinite future and supreme confidence in the chosen

9. Manuel, *The Prophets of Paris*, pp. 61, 63n.
1. Antoine-Nicolas de Condorcet, *Sketch for a Historical Picture of the Progress of the Human Mind* (1795), trans. June Barraclough (London, 1955), p. 72.
2. Manuel, *The Prophets of Paris*, p. 59.
3. Condorcet, *Sketch*, p. 77.
4. *Ibid.*, pp. 201f.
5. *Ibid.*, p. 11.

values of liberty, humanity and virtue. Condorcet's *Sketch* is the classic statement of the idea of progress.

THE SPREAD OF THE IDEA

Condorcet's mantle was taken up by Henri de Saint-Simon, whose heterogeneous life had included fighting for American independence and large-scale financial speculation at home in France. In a succession of diffuse works published in the first quarter of the nineteenth century, Saint-Simon tried to popularize various schemes for the realization of his dream:

> The Golden Age of mankind does not lie behind us, but before; it lies in the perfection of the social order. Our fore-fathers did not see it; one day our children will reach it. It is for us to clear the way.[6]

Science was to be the means to the end. Condorcet had insisted that mankind had developed according to laws, but had not attempted to discover them. This was Saint-Simon's programme: the working out of what he calls 'the science of man'.[7] The new body of knowledge will permit the proper planning of the final age of history which is about to dawn, the 'industrial age'. Saint-Simon regularly tricked out his proposals with a variety of details such as a cult of Newton and a Nicaraguan canal linking the Atlantic and Pacific,[8] but their essence could always be distilled in a notion with a long future ahead of it: the potency of social science.

Although Saint-Simon drew heavily on Condorcet and the commonplaces of the *philosophes* of the previous century, his thought also included elements of a different character. A key to the novel element is Saint-Simon's attitude to the Middle Ages. He shows none of Condorcet's distaste for everything mediaeval. He showers praise on every period of the past on the ground that each was necessary for the achievement of the present. This was to move towards cultural relativism, the idea that every culture is valuable in itself, which marked nineteenth-century historicism.[9] There is a

6. Henri de Saint-Simon, 'On the Reorganization of European Society' (1814), *The Political Thought of Saint-Simon*, ed. Ghita Ionescu (London, 1976), p. 98.
7. D. G. Charlton, *Secular Religions in France, 1815–1870* (London, 1963), p. 45.
8. Manuel, *The Prophets of Paris*, p. 105.
9. *Cf.* below, pp. 92ff.

shift away from the eighteenth century's preoccupation with reason as the only faculty that man should cultivate. Saint-Simon holds that will and feeling should be developed too. Eighteenth-century individualism also recedes in his thought as he places greater stress on social solidarity.[1] Saint-Simon's final work, *New Christianity* (1825), even argues for a form of religion that will satisfy man's emotional needs and supply a set of moral principles to unify society.[2] Such modifications of the idea of progress ensured that it would not be rejected as an eighteenth-century curiosity. His own evolution kept pace with the changing temper of the time.

Auguste Comte was responsible for the next phase of its development. Beginning as secretary to Saint-Simon, Comte threw off his patronage in an acrimonious quarrel over their joint publications in 1824.[3] Attacks of insanity, delusions of grandeur and an acutely unhappy home life provided ample fuel for the fire of his vitriolic temper, but Comte continued to retain an extensive network of admirers. His fame rested primarily on the *Positive Philosophy* (1830–42), a reworked course of lectures delivered in Paris. Comte's positive philosophy was the erection of Newtonian method into a speculative system. Positivism taught that all knowledge is based on observation, experiment and the ascertaining of scientific laws. In the past man's consciousness had passed through the theological stage, in which all phenomena are attributed directly to God, and the metaphysical stage, in which there is still a search after primary causes conceived as abstractions. Now man had reached the final, positive stage, in which knowledge of the relation of observed facts is recognized to be all that is possible.[4] Comte claimed that the law of the three stages, which applied to all disciplines, had been confirmed in a fit of madness in 1826 during which his mind regressed through the metaphysical to the theological stage before returning by the same path to positivism and sanity.[5] His own task (his debt to Saint-Simon becoming very apparent here) was to apply the positive method to the study of societies. The resulting sociology would lay bare the laws of how societies are structured ('social

1. Manuel, *The Prophets of Paris*, p. 127.
2. *Ibid.*, pp. 138–48.
3. *Ibid.*, pp. 252–60.
4. D. G. Charlton, *Positivist Thought in France during the Second Empire, 1852–1870* (Oxford, 1959), p. 29.
5. Manuel, *The Prophets of Paris*, p. 281.

statics') and how societies develop over time ('social dynamics').[6] Progress in Comte is therefore both assured in the law of the three stages and to be investigated through social dynamics.

Comte's thought was to be a major influence on Durkheim and through him on the development of sociology as a discipline, but he himself became dissatisfied with the drily detached tone of his earlier writings. In the mid-1840s he fell in love and was convinced of 'la prépondérance nécessaire de la vie affective'.[7] He found an outlet for his feelings in organizing a new religion, the Positivist Church of Humanity. He issued a positivist calendar of 'saints' who had worked for human progress, composed a positivist catechism and declared in 1857 that he would in future sign circulars 'High Priest of Humanity'.[8] Comte admitted that he had passed through two phases in his career, the first as a new Aristotle, the second as a new St Paul.[9] In England John Stuart Mill, who had been deeply influenced by the earlier Comte, turned away from his erstwhile mentor with the lament that 'others may laugh, but we could far rather weep at this melancholy decadence of a great intellect'.[1] Yet some found the new religion satisfying in many parts of the world. In Brazil in particular members of the upper classes who wished to mark their independence of mind by breaking with the Catholic Church were attracted to the religion of humanity. The Brazilian flag bears to this day the positivist motto, 'Order and Progress'.[2] Comte was one of those responsible for the active diffusion of the idea of progress, albeit in unaccustomed trappings, in the mid-nineteenth century.

Other propagators of the ideal of human improvement abounded. In France there was the visionary Charles Fourier who looked to a future when there will be thirty-seven million poets like Homer, thirty-seven million philosophers like Newton and thirty-seven million writers like Molière – and when the oceans will consist of lemonade.[3] In England there was Charles Dickens who preached in many of his novels a doctrine of improvement and who ranged dummy books round his study walls under the general heading *The*

6. Charlton, *Positivist Thought in France during the Second Empire*, p. 30.
7. 'The inevitable primacy of the life of the affections.' *Ibid.*, p. 24.
8. Manuel, *The Prophets of Paris*, p. 267.
9. Charlton, *Secular Religions in France*, p. 47.
1. J. S. Mill, *Auguste Comte and Positivism* (London, 1866), p. 199.
2. Manuel, *The Prophets of Paris*, p. 274.
3. Charlton, *Secular Religions in France*, p. 168.

Wisdom of our Ancestors with individual titles like 'Ignorance', 'Superstition', 'The Block', 'The Stake', 'The Rack', 'Dirt' and 'Disease'.[4] The values of the Enlightenment spread down to lower social groups with the development of the popular press. A desire to improve themselves and so to push forward the advance of civilization became the accepted attitude of the skilled workers of Britain in their friendly societies and mechanics' institutes.[5] The Great Exhibition in the Crystal Palace, with its visible proof that technology and prosperity were advancing together, evoked in 1851 something like a national celebration of the possibilities of progress both material and moral.[6] In the following year in France Eugène Pelletan voiced the widespread mood by proclaiming progress 'la loi générale de l'univers'.[7]

Nor did the vogue for the idea evaporate. It was powerfully reinforced by the current of thought associated with evolution. Charles Darwin himself saw confirmation for contemporary patterns of social thinking in his theory:

> As natural selection works solely by and for the good of each being, all corporeal and mental endowments will tend to progress towards perfection.[8]

Although social Darwinism, especially in America, could hold that life is essentially competitive so that the weak inevitably suffer,[9] evolutionary thought had a strong tendency to optimism. 'Higher life', in the phrase of the time, would emerge. This expectation was popular partly on account of reasons unconnected with Darwin. The Enlightenment's belief in the constancy of human nature had withered in the face of objections from romantic theorists that mankind is marked by variety.[1] An evolutionary view offered an explanation

4. Humphry House, 'The Mood of Doubt', *Ideas and Beliefs of the Victorians: An Historic Revaluation of the Victorian Age* (London, 1949), p. 72.
5. T. R. Tholfsen, *Working Class Radicalism in Mid-Victorian England* (London, 1976), esp. pp. 61–65.
6. E. L. Woodward, '1851 and the Visibility of Progress', *Ideas and Beliefs of the Victorians*, pp. 55–62.
7. 'The general law of the universe.' Charlton, *Secular Religions in France*, p. 199.
8. Charles Darwin, *The Origin of Species* (1859: London, 1897), p. 402.
9. Richard Hofstadter, *Social Darwinism in American Thought, 1860–1915* (Philadelphia, 1944), esp. pp. 43–45.
1. *Cf.* below, pp. 92f.

of the variations as different stages in the same process.[2] Herbert Spencer, who worked out the basis of an evolutionary social theory before Darwin published *The Origin of Species*, could gain a large audience for a bold message:

> Progress . . . is not an accident, but a necessity. . . . What we call evil and immorality must disappear. It is certain that man must become perfect.[3]

An age that could listen complacently to so startling a set of assertions was well described by John Morley as one 'that lives on its faith in progress'.[4]

PROGRESS AND HISTORIANS

The temper of the age could not but affect its historians. It showed itself primarily in what Sir Herbert Butterfield labelled 'the Whig interpretation of history', the tendency of nineteenth-century (and later) historians to interpret the past in the light of the present and so to commend history's winners.[5] Protestants and Whigs rather than Catholics and Tories are treated sympathetically, for they, according to this reading of history, contributed to the achievements of the historian's own day. So general was this attitude that historians opposed to reforms in their own time joined in the approval of the progressives of the past. Thus Henry Hallam, who was fearful of the changes that parliamentary reform might bring in its train, shows no sympathy in his *Constitutional History of England* (1827) for those who had resisted earlier innovations.[6] This approach is nothing other than the feeding of assumptions about progress into historical writing, commonly at an unconscious level. It is clearly derived from two characteristic features of this theory of history. There is the conviction that the past tells a story of improvement.

2. J. W. Burrow, *Evolution and Society: A Study in Victorian Social Theory* (Cambridge, 1966), p. 98.
3. Herbert Spencer, *Social Statics* (London, 1851), pp. 79f.
4. John Morley, *Machiavelli* (Romanes Lecture), (Oxford, 1897), p. 23. The idea of progress did, however, provoke some literary figures of late nineteenth-century England into expressing dissent. *Cf.* J. H. Buckley, *The Triumph of Time: A Study of the Victorian Concepts of Time, History, Progress, and Decadence* (Cambridge, Mass., 1967), pp. 53–93.
5. Sir Herbert Butterfield, *The Whig Interpretation of History* (London, 1931).
6. *Ibid.*, p. 4.

And there is the belief that the values of the present – among Whig historians often the values of civil and religious liberty – are unchanging. This second opinion encourages anachronistic appraisals that Butterfield deplores – of Luther, for instance, as the herald of modern freedoms.[7] The Whig view, as Butterfield puts it, organizes history according to 'an unfolding principle of progress'.[8]

Thomas Babington Macaulay, whose *History of England* (1848–55) was the most celebrated historical work of the nineteenth century in the English language, well exemplifies the Whig interpretation. He did not, in the manner of eighteenth-century historians, deliberately plan his material in order to illustrate the grand pattern of human improvement. But Macaulay believed passionately in progress. Chapter three of his *History* contrasts the social conditions of 1685 with those of 1848, consistently to the advantage of his own time.

> The more carefully we examine the history of the past, the more reason shall we find to dissent from those who imagine that our age has been fruitful of new social evils. The truth is that the evils are, with scarcely an exception, old. That which is new is the intelligence which discerns and the humanity which remedies them.[9]

Macaulay set himself to correct what he saw as a weakness in Hume's *History of Great Britain*, his preparedness to exonerate the Stuarts.[1] He wanted to vindicate those who struggled against seventeenth-century absolutism. His method was to exploit the techniques for conjuring up time and place that vitalized the novels of Sir Walter Scott. If this were done, he had written twenty years before, we should not 'have to look for the wars and votes of the Puritans in Clarendon, and for their phraseology in Old Mortality'.[2] But Macaulay normally preferred to make vivid only those who, like the Puritans, were on the side of liberty. The worldview of the

7. *Ibid.*, p. 78.
8. *Ibid.*, p. 45.
9. T. B. Macaulay, *The History of England from the Accession of James the Second*, ed. C. H. Firth (London, 1913), 1, p. 412.
1. Hume, *The History of Great Britain*, p. 44.
2. T. B. Macaulay, 'History', *The Edinburgh Review*, 48 (May 1828), p. 365. *Old Mortality* is the covenanting novel of Sir Walter Scott, on whose significance *cf.* below, p. 107.

Stuart court is left unilluminated. His imaginative sympathy, as Butterfield says of Whig historians as a class, stops 'at a point that could almost be fixed by formula'.[3]

If the Whig interpretation was the most pervasive way in which the idea of progress affected British historiography, the associated belief that historical development is law-governed as found in Comte or Spencer was taken up with enthusiasm by a number of historians at home and abroad. Henry Buckle, the writer of a *History of Civilization in England* (1857–61), was convinced that history is a science on the Newtonian model:

> Whoever is at all acquainted with what has been done during the last two centuries must be aware that every generation demonstrates some events to be regular and predictable, which the preceding generation had declared to be irregular and unpredictable; so that the marked tendency of advancing civilization is to strengthen our belief in the universality of order, of method and of law.[4]

In France Buckle's equivalent was Hippolyte Taine, a prolific historian and critic, who wrote in 1864 that 'History is a science analogous not to geometry, but to physiology and zoology'[5] – that is, empirical and concerned with living beings. Although Taine later modified his position, he was acclaimed as the leader of a positivist school of historiography concerned to write about the laws of human behaviour in the past. J. B. Bury, the author of the best-known study of the idea of progress, is usually put in the same category as Buckle and Taine on account of his pronouncement about history being a science.[6] It is clear, however, that he rejected the view that historical generalizations are laws that can be used as a basis for prediction together with several other of the inferences from believing in scientific history drawn by his predecessors.[7] Yet Bury remains

3. Butterfield, *The Whig Interpretation of History*, p. 95.
4. H. T. Buckle, *Introduction to the History of Civilization in England* (1857), ed. J. M. Robertson (London, n.d.), p. 3.
5. Quoted by W. O. Chadwick, *The Secularization of the European Mind in the Nineteenth Century* (Cambridge, 1975), p. 205.
6. *Cf.* above, p. 4.
7. D. S. Goldstein, 'J. B. Bury's Philosophy of History: A Reappraisal', *The American Historical Review*, 82 (1977), esp. p. 898.

another instance of a historian drawn towards the ideal of remodelling history in a scientific manner by his sympathy for a belief in progress.

Lord Acton, Bury's predecessor in the Regius Chair at Cambridge, had none of Bury's academic reserve over progress. Bury pointed out that the idea of progress itself suggested that the doctrine would be superseded as civilization advanced.[8] Acton declared roundly: 'Not to believe in Progress is to question the divine government.'[9] Acton was a Roman Catholic, albeit one who had grave doubts about the proceedings of the First Vatican Council of 1869–70, and he was also a classic nineteenth-century liberal. Providence he identified with a progress that operates according to regular law:

> There is as much difference in the old and new notion[s] of God before and since the discovery of the laws of history as before and since the discovery of law in nature. And the science which describes it is the Philosophy of History. But its results, from Bossuet and Vico to Buckle and Ferrari are not comparable, in solidarity and completeness to those of inductive science.[1]

The remedy was to study broad sweeps of the past more thoroughly so that the laws of history could be identified as firmly as those of physics or astronomy. He himself projected a history of liberty, which he believed to be the central theme of world history.[2] Acton was trying to integrate the Christian view of history with the idea of progress. Aspects of the Christian view had to be casualties. 'We expect no miracles, because of our experience. Providence needs none.'[3] Progress gained the upper hand.

ASSESSMENT OF THE IDEA OF PROGRESS

The idea of progress has suffered vicissitudes in the twentieth century. The First World War struck a blow at more facile versions of popular optimism. It took a bold spirit to declare in 1916 that progress is 'a fact as well as an ideal' and that

8. Bury, *The Idea of Progress*, p. 352.
9. Acton Collection, Cambridge University Library, MS Add. 4987, f.55. *Cf.* Lionel Kochan, *Acton on History* (London, 1954), p. 113.
1. Acton Collection, Cambridge University Library, MS Add. 4916, f.7.
2. *Ibid.*, 4991, f.198.
3. *Ibid.*, 5692, f.30.

> The present war seems to many of us the supreme struggle of our better nature to gain the mastery over . . . obstructions . . .[4]

But men like the author of these words, F. S. Marvin, a school inspector influenced by Comte, continued to entertain confidence in the possibilities of human improvement, especially through education. The second war struck a second blow. The President of the American Historical Association in 1946, S. B. Fay, who had retired from a Harvard chair, confessed that it was difficult to believe that the previous half-century had been marked by social progress. He concluded that advances did not come automatically, but were probably the result of man's purposeful effort.[5] These embers, however, were fanned into a stronger flame by the material prosperity that western nations enjoyed in the quarter century following the Second World War.[6] Progress seemed a fruit of the planned economy. Despite the more recent waning of the popular mood of optimism, it would probably be true to say that elements of the idea of progress remain widely diffused – though less widely diffused in the world of scholarship than in the mind of the man in the street.

What of its validity? 'Put a flint knife by a computer . . .',[7] we are told, and the conclusion is inescapable. Material progress would certainly be hard to deny. Knowledge and the ability to apply knowledge to technical problems have advanced. But that says nothing about moral progress. The napalm bomb is as much a triumph of applied science as penicillin. How increased human knowledge has been put to use shows small sign of having improved over the centuries. The late Roman emperor Heliogabalus is said to have had people executed before him because he liked to see red blood on green grass.[8] But the twentieth century can hardly claim a moral superiority when it has witnessed the extermination of millions of Jews purely on the ground of their racial identity. To uphold any theory that human virtue has advanced is a bold position

4. F. S. Marvin, 'The Idea of Progress', *Progress and History*, ed. F. S. Marvin (London, 1916), pp. 21, 16.
5. S. B. Fay, 'The Idea of Progress', *The American Historical Review*, 52 (1947), pp. 245f.
6. Sidney Pollard, *The Idea of Progress: History and Society* (London, 1968), p. 184.
7. J. H. Plumb, 'The Historian's Dilemma', *Crisis in the Humanities*, ed. J. H. Plumb (Harmondsworth, 1964), p. 42.
8. R. M. Hare, *Freedom and Reason* (Oxford, 1963), p. 161.

to adopt in the face of such evidence. Bury wrote that to believe in progress is 'an act of faith'.[9] Perhaps the late twentieth century would want to say on reflection that it is an act of credulity.

Since the faith in progress has no generally accepted source of authority, it has shown marked variations. In particular, there has been a divergence over the future course of history between two forms of the idea. In the stronger form, as held for instance by Condorcet or Comte, the future is held to be certain because in some sense the historical process is predetermined. On this view it is possible to discover from the past the laws of how human society developed and so to predict the future. In the weaker view, which grew stronger from the mid-nineteenth century and is held by most modern advocates, all sense of the inevitability of history is banished. Human freedom on this view prevents any supposition that history must develop in a certain direction. The stronger view inherits the measure of determinism in the Christian doctrine of providence; the weaker, normally held by those who have been further away from the Christian roots of the idea, rejects determinism entirely. Only if the future is in some way guaranteed can human confidence in what lies ahead be sustained. Despite the sanguine attitude of its protagonists, the weaker view of progress current today offers no certain grounds for hope.

A second consequence of the variations in the theory of progress is that there is disagreement over what the idea implies for human behaviour today. Professor Sidney Pollard of the University of Sheffield concludes his study of its evolution by writing that the idea of progress is a necessary substitute for supernatural sanctions in giving us assurance that morality is not relative.[1] If God does not reveal moral standards, then history shows that they are nevertheless unchanging. Professor J. H. Plumb, Master of Christ's College, Cambridge, however, declares that history should never bc used to sanction morality. On the contrary, what history shows is that there has been a welcome increase in the area of liberty in living.[2] The divergence is grounded in a difference between what the two historians discern in the pattern of progress: for Professor Pollard, there has been little if any change in human character over recorded

9. Bury, *The Idea of Progress*, p. 4.
1. Pollard, *The Idea of Progress*, pp. 181, 201.
2. J. H. Plumb, *The Death of the Past* (London, 1969), pp. 140f.

history; but for Professor Plumb, 'mankind has improved, materially alas more than morally, but nevertheless both have improved'.[3] Professor Pollard does not share Professor Plumb's criterion for assessing progress, a belief that liberty is the supreme value. Both writers show the confidence characteristic of those who hold to the idea of progress that their values are right, although one holds that morality is absolute and the other that it must be allowed to change. Variations in criteria lead to variations in conclusions. It therefore becomes highly doubtful whether the idea offers any guidance over what values to accept.

Furthermore there is a serious moral objection to the whole notion of progress. If man is advancing, those who live at an earlier period work and suffer for the sake of those who come later. Commemoration by posterity is their only reward. Individuals at the earlier stages are treated not as ends in themselves, but as means to the end of human improvement. Belief in progress can all too readily lead to a willingness to treat our contemporaries as dispensable in the name of some greater good to be enjoyed by future generations. Much of the bloodshed of the French Revolution received a shallow justification in the supposed demands of progress. The door is opened to sacrificing others for the sake of an imagined utopia as soon as we deny each of them the possibility of personal fulfilment. And individuals desire such fulfilment in their own right. This the theory of progress does not offer. Even when it manages to generate hope, the idea of progress confines the realization of hope to others.

3. Pollard, *The Idea of Progress*, p. viii; Plumb, *The Death of the Past*, p. 142.

5 Historicism

'The spiritual . . . has a historical aspect under which it appears as change, as the contingent, as a passing moment . . . and . . . every event has a spiritual aspect by which it partakes of immortality.'

Jakob Burckhardt, *Reflections on History.*

The word 'historicism' is now the normal name given to the school of historical thought that dominated Germany from the rise of romanticism in the late eighteenth century down to the recent past. The word has been used in other ways. Best known is Sir Karl Popper's onslaught on any form of the belief that the future can be predicted on the basis of the course of the past, an idea that he labels 'historicism'.[1] Popper's conception of historicism is not the subject of this chapter. Our concern is with what has been called 'historicism' in Germany since the 1880s.[2] It is a set of ideas that has proved almost as influential in western thought as the idea of progress. Indeed, in Germany and countries such as Sweden and Hungary that are strongly swayed by German intellectual currents, historicism has been more influential than the idea of progress. Its impact on the Anglo-Saxon climate of opinion has been far less marked, chiefly because of the language barrier. Yet it has filtered through to affect a number of fields, especially theology. Historicism ranks as one of the chief ways of understanding the historical process in the modern world.

The central idea in historicism is that all cultures are moulded by history. The name 'historicism' bears witness to this conviction that the customs and beliefs of any group are the products of the group's historical experience. Nothing can be understood in isolation from its past. Hence, for instance, the doctrines of a school of philosophy must be appreciated not only as attempts to grasp abstract truth but

1. Sir Karl R. Popper, *The Poverty of Historicism* (London, 1960), p. 3.
2. G. G. Iggers, *The German Conception of History: The National Tradition of Historical Thought from Herder to the Present* (Middletown, Conn., 1968), pp. 287–90.

also as expressions of attitudes that have grown up in the society where the philosophers live. Thus the teachings of Socrates could be propagated only in the free atmosphere of Athens. Customs and beliefs are like flowers that will flourish only in a particular soil. Historicists placed stress on the nation as the ground where particular values take root. Luther was therefore seen less as a champion of international reformation in the church than as a German national hero. He embodied the conviction, the hard work and the aptitude for ideas of the German nation. The explanation of why different nations have different flairs lies chiefly in language. The way in which a nation speaks determines its stock of ideas. Hence historicists conceived the nation as the area where a particular language is spoken. Historicism formed the kernel of nineteenth-century nationalism, the ideological driving force behind the unification of Italy and Germany alike. Wherever Italian was spoken should be part of a united Italy; wherever German was spoken should be part of a united Germany. Historicism had major political implications.

A second strand in historicist thought is concerned with how we appreciate groups other than our own. We know the customs and beliefs of the groups to which we belong. But how do we grasp the significance of customs and beliefs elsewhere? People in other societies, on the historicist premise, have values different from our own. People in other periods also had different values. The resulting problem is specially acute for a historian. How can he break out of his own thought-world in order to penetrate the thought-world of other places and times? The historicist answer is that we have a faculty of intuition. A human being enjoys a gift of empathy for other human beings that allows him to grasp the significance of what others do. Luther's distance from us in time does not prevent us from making sense of his actions. The process of intuition historicists often called 'understanding' (*Verstehen*). It is a form of inter-personal perception that transcends the rational. It is not achieved, most historicists held, by reason at all, for reason is fitted for investigating only the non-human world. But the technique of intuition enables us to overcome the barriers that separate us from other parts of the human world. Understanding is the distinctive method of the disciplines that study man, the historical sciences.

The two salient beliefs of historicists both bear the marks of reaction against the Enlightenment. The belief that all cultures are moulded by history is a contradiction of the idea of progress itself.

The historical process, according to so many of the Enlightenment thinkers, is a straight line passing upwards through various improving stages of social organization. Historicists, by contrast, held that there is nothing linear about history. A goal of history – such as human perfection – that so often appears in early statements of the idea of progress is absent from historicism. Although historicists often retained some Christian notion of an end of the world, they did not allow it to influence their view of history to any significant degree. History, in their view, is not teleological. Consequently, it is not true that each stage in human development is transitory, without value in itself, significant merely as a stepping-stone towards the further shore of the ideal society. On the contrary, each age has its own intrinsic worth. This is the context of the well-known dictum of Ranke, by common consent the greatest practitioner of history in the historicist manner: 'Every epoch is immediate to God . . .'[3] Any age, that is to say, is responsible for its own standards. It is not answerable to posterity. The scorn of the *philosophes* for the standards of previous generations as superstitious and barbaric was therefore misplaced, a sign of their lack of a historical sense. In a similar way, the historicist stress on 'understanding' represents a break with the Enlightenment. Reason, according to the *philosophes*, is the measure of all things. No, replied the historicists: reason is not the measure of man. Reason is incapable of grasping the significance of human behaviour. A special faculty alone is capable of that. Reason is not omnicompetent, just as the idea of progress does not sum up the significance of the past. Historicism, then, developed in reaction against the Enlightenment.

PRECURSORS OF HISTORICISM

There had been anticipations of historicism before the Enlightenment. In sixteenth-century France a number of gifted historians, men who were humanists and strongly influenced by legal studies, discarded the normal Christian framework of the time and broke through the constraints of following classical patterns. Jean Bodin, probably the best-known of them, drew a characteristic historicist contrast between the study of human history and the study of the non-human world, what he called 'causes hidden in nature', pointing

3. Leopold von Ranke, *The Theory and Practice of History*, ed. G. G. Iggers (Indianapolis, 1973), p. 53.

out that the disciplines have different methods.[4] Again, La Popelinière, a Huguenot historian, concluded that works of history themselves are moulded by the historical process – a drastic move, in the historicist manner, towards treating anything as the result of its historical evolution.[5] This group of writers seems to have had no well-known successors in France, although their legal approach to history became entrenched in southern Italy and affected seventeenth-century constitutional thought in Britain.[6] Furthermore Bodin in particular undoubtedly influenced the greatest precursor of historicism, an early eighteenth-century Florentine professor of rhetoric, Giambattista Vico.[7]

Vico came to a position similar to that of the German historicists of the romantic period because he was opposing a similar style of mechanistic thinking. The German historicists were to react against the Enlightenment; Vico reacted against Cartesianism, the tradition of thought begun by the early seventeenth-century French philosopher, Descartes. The only opinions worthy of the title 'knowledge', according to Descartes, are reached by deductive reasoning from undoubted premises. Certainty is attainable only in disciplines that can be made to approximate to mathematics. History is nothing like mathematics: so much the worse for history – which, according to Descartes, omits so much in its account of the past that 'what is retained is not portrayed as it really is'.[8] Vico embraced Cartesian views in his early years, but later reacted against its denigration of history. He defended history as a truth-finding discipline in his *New Science* of 1725 (revised 1730 and 1744). He emphasized, just as the historicists were to do, that history has a method different from other disciplines. He began with the common-sense principle that the maker of an object is best placed to understand it. Man can understand something of nature by experimenting on a part of it,

4. Jean Bodin, *Method for the Easy Comprehension of History* (1566), quoted by George Huppert, *The Idea of Perfect History: Historical Erudition and Historical Philosophy in Renaissance France* (Urbana, Illinois, 1970), pp. 93f.
5. La Popelinière, *History of Histories* (1604), quoted by Huppert, *The Idea of Perfect History*, pp. 162ff.
6. J. G. A. Pocock, *The Ancient Constitution and the Feudal Law* (Cambridge, 1957), esp. p. 18.
7. Sir Isaiah Berlin, *Vico and Herder: Two Studies in the History of Ideas* (London, 1976), p. 49n.
8. René Descartes, 'Discourse on Method', *The Philosophical Works*, ed. E. S. Haldane and G. R. T. Ross, 1 (Cambridge, 1911), p. 85.

but only God, as its creator, can understand the whole. Natural science can therefore discover only partial knowledge. The whole of mathematics might certainly be understood by man since he invents the premises, but the resulting knowledge is of an artificial abstraction. Mathematics can therefore reveal knowledge that is merely fictional. History produces knowledge of reality, of 'the world of nations', as Vico put it, 'or civil world'. And history can produce knowledge of the whole of the world, 'which since men had made it, men could come to know'.[9] Historical knowledge is possible by examining our own human minds, which have an affinity with the minds of men in the past. By asserting something very similar to the later German notion of interpersonal intuition, Vico believed that he had vindicated historical knowledge from Descartes' criticisms.

Vico was also intending to restore the traditional Catholic division of history into the sacred and the profane. The Roman Catholic Church had come to insist that the history of the people of God should be written in terms of the operation of providence. There can be little doubt that Vico wrote with a conscious Christian purpose, to refute those who were beginning to treat sacred history as an area of historical inquiry without a providential framework.[1] He therefore insisted that God made special interventions in the history of the Hebrews, but he was prepared to concede to critics of Christian history that providence among other nations operates only through the development of human customs. Indeed, he may have thought himself compelled by his own principles to deny that providence is a direct, transcendent power in the area beyond the pale of sacred history. According to the Christian view, God is the maker of history. But if God is its maker, Vico supposed, man cannot be. A mental affinity for people in the past would become impossible, and so Vico's defence of historical knowledge would crumble. Divine control of history is minimized in order to guarantee that man should be the maker of his own history. Despite his Christian purpose, Vico's teaching shows how the Christian view of the past was disintegrating in his day. In his thought were elements of all the other schools of thought about the past. There is an anticipation of the doctrine of

9. *The New Science of Giambattista Vico*, trans. T. G. Bergin and M. H. Fisch (Ithaca, New York, 1968), p. 96.
1. A. D. Momigliano, 'Vico's *Scienza Nuova*: Roman "Bestioni" and Roman "Eroi",' *Essays in Ancient and Modern Historiography* (Oxford, 1977), pp. 254ff.

progress in his discernment of a development of civilization among all nations from forests through huts, villages and cities to academies;[2] Marx applauded his axiom that man is the maker of history;[3] and Vico gave prominence to the idea that civilization passes through the same cyclical pattern in every nation. But it is as a proto-historicist, delighting in the variety of human customs, languages and cultures moulded by history, that Vico was to have his greatest influence. It is no accident that he was most celebrated in the earlier nineteenth century, especially by Niebuhr in Germany and by Michelet in France,[4] at the high water-mark of historicism.

THE BACKGROUND OF HISTORICISM

Historicism itself developed in late eighteenth-century Germany. The Enlightenment that flourished in France and Britain came late to Germany. Only after mid-century did it begin to have a marked effect on German thought. The philosophers of the German Enlightenment, the *Aufklärer*, were not swept along in the early waves of enthusiasm for 'enlightened' ways. They respected the intellectual achievements of the French *philosophes*, but were sufficiently detached to be critical even of their central ideas. The key to the distinctive quality of the German Enlightenment is its high estimate of tradition. In France, what was traditional was likely to be treated with contempt; in Germany, it was likely to be treated with esteem. The customs of the small German principalities, for instance, were valued by men who frequently owed their incomes to the local rulers. Two aspects of German tradition were specially formative of their idea of history. Religion of a markedly other-worldly type had put down deep roots in German soil, and historical research characteristic of the age of erudition had become normal. Hence the *Aufklärer* were dismayed by the scorn for revealed religion evident in the writings of Voltaire and his contemporaries. And they feared that philosophical history in the French or Scottish manner paid too little attention to the detail of the past. Even while borrowing many of the ideals of the Enlightenment in western Europe, the Germans mod-

2. G. P. Gooch, *History and Historians in the Nineteenth Century* (London, 1952), p. 9.
3. Karl Marx, *Capital*, 1 (1867: Moscow, 1961), p. 372n.
4. Berlin, *Vico and Herder*, p. 137.

ified them.[5] The modifications in the field of historical thought produced historicism.

The religious contribution to the rise of historicism came chiefly from pietism. This movement, under the leadership of Gottfried Arnold, had done much in the late seventeenth and early eighteenth centuries to revitalize the official Lutheranism of Germany. Pietism laid such stress on personal religion that it verged on mysticism. The chief contributions of the movement were two, to lay the foundations of the technique of 'understanding' and to give a sense of purpose to men concerned with history. Arnold had contrasted reason with the spiritual illumination that he called *Sophia*. Reason is capable only of making logical distinctions, but *Sophia* is 'the power of the most Holy Trinity which at once reveals, transfigures and heralds'.[6] Special intuition, especially of the meaning of the Bible, is the method of discovering important truths. The contrast was an assumption that lived on in the minds of the many thinkers of the German Enlightenment who had received a pietist upbringing. They broadened the application of special intuition to documents other than the Bible. The historian, they therefore came to believe, has a direct, non-rational understanding of historical evidence that enables him to know what happened in the past.[7] The second contribution of pietism was to infuse its sense of religious zeal into the German Enlightenment. The *Aufklärer* were predominantly clergymen, and frequently theologians. Their aim was the defence of revealed religion for an educated public. Johann Lorenz von Mosheim, for instance, published in 1754 *An Ecclesiastical History Ancient and Modern* in order to show how and why Christianity had changed over time and so to vindicate its essence. Mosheim's successors were particularly intent on showing the value of biblical history. These men were engaged in Christian apologetic against trends of thought that they feared were making for godlessness.

The tradition of seventeenth-century antiquarianism also contributed to the emergence of historicism. In the German universities the

5. P. H. Reill, *The German Enlightenment and the Rise of Historicism* (Berkeley, Calif., 1975), pp. 1f., 36ff.
6. Arnold, quoted by Erich Seeburg, *Gottfried Arnold* (Darmstadt, 1964), cited by Reill, *The German Enlightenment*, p. 27.
7. Joachim Wach, *Das Verstehen* (1926–33), cited by Reill, *The German Enlightenment*, p. 225.

age of erudition lived on.[8] One of the most distinguished of the *Aufklärer*, Johann Christoph Gatterer, who was to become Professor of History at Göttingen, issued as his first publication in 1738 a detailed genealogy of a Nuremberg family – a typical work of painstaking research.[9] Such men were impressed by the coherent pattern discerned in the past by Voltaire and his like in France. They began to feel dismayed that Germany lagged so far behind France in concentrating on intensive quarrying of the minutiae of the past to the exclusion of broad reflection on the course of history. Yet at the same time they felt the French were becoming too cavalier with the hard detail of what happened in the past and imposing too rigid a framework of interpretation. Classical historians, they noticed, used rhetoric to good effect without the hard-and-fast rational categories of the *philosophes*. Gatterer and a number of his contemporaries began to commend the combining of traditional German erudition, the French method of analysis and the ancient model of persuasive narrative. This synthesis, they believed, would end the German reputation for pedantry, yet at the same time give scope to the German genius for digging out detail. The Germans, Gatterer once remarked, were a people exactly suited to the production of learned footnotes.[1] The synthesis was achieved. As historians subsequently began to write on Gatterer's principles, they integrated the research method of philology with the generalizing method of philosophy – as Vico had done in Italy and as Gibbon was doing in England.[2] The effect was to preserve in German scholarship the eye for detail that had marked the Europe-wide movement of erudition of the late seventeenth century. The encyclopaedic footnotes of many a twentieth-century German treatise bear witness to the vitality of the tradition.

Arising from the continuation of the quest for detail was a stress, particularly at Göttingen, on the need to ensure the accuracy of what was written as history. This was no sudden or qualitative leap in

8. On the age of erudition, *cf.* above, pp. 61ff.
9. P. H. Reill, 'History and Hermeneutics in the *Aufklärung*: The Thought of Johann Christoph Gatterer', *The Journal of Modern History*, 45 (1973), p. 27.
1. Sir Herbert Butterfield, *Man on his Past: The Study of the History of Historical Scholarship* (Cambridge, 1955), p. 38.
2. *The New Science of Giambattista Vico*, p. xxi. A. D. Momigliano, 'Gibbon's Contribution to Historical Method,' *Studies in Historiography* (London, 1966), p. 44.

standards of criticism, as it is sometimes represented. It was a stage in the increasingly widespread desire for historical accuracy that began in the later Middle Ages and which is still, in the late twentieth century, by no means universal, even in the western world. If the process had a single most marked acceleration, it undoubtedly came in the seventeenth, not in the eighteenth, century, when the antiquarian vogue seized Europe. Admittedly, the seventeenth century applied critical standards chiefly to activities auxiliary to history – to philology and genealogy, to the editing of texts. But this remained strikingly true of the *Aufklärer*. Gatterer wrote no major work of history as such. His colleague at Göttingen, August Ludwig Schlözer, produced as the climax of his career not a historical study but an edition of the Russian *Chronicle of Nestor* (1802–09).[3] And their contemporaries concentrated on philological researches, lectures and programmatic essays on how history should be written. Perhaps the chief reason for the later neglect of Gatterer and Schlözer – and the eighteenth-century German Enlightenment generally – is the absence of any monument of historical scholarship equivalent to Gibbon's *Decline and Fall* or Niebuhr's *History of Rome*. This omission was the immediate corollary of advancing critical standards. The Göttingen historians wanted to revise the history of every nation – but only after reconsidering the validity of all the evidence. The earliest historicists therefore concentrated on the sources, publishing their conclusions in learned journals. The number of predominantly historical periodicals in Germany rose from three in 1700 to 131 in 1790.[4] The nineteenth century was to enjoy the fruit of their labours on the documents.

IDEALISM AND ROMANTICISM

As historicism took shape around the turn of the nineteenth century other bodies of thought were emerging in Germany – idealism and romanticism. Historicism was closely allied with both. Philosophical idealism, whose great protagonist was Immanuel Kant, was like historicism in being a reaction against the Enlightenment. Kant rejected the view that knowledge is passively assimilated by the human mind. This was to turn against the sensationalism that was

3. Butterfield, *Man on his Past*, pp. 55f.
4. *Ibid*, p. 37.

held, for example, by David Hume.[5] The mind, according to Kant, imposes 'categories' on sense impressions received from the outside world. Only by means of the categories – such concepts as plurality, causality and necessity – can we organize our experience. The mind is therefore active in the acquisition of knowledge. Because this is an argument that *ideas* are essential for understanding the world, it can be classified as a form of idealism. It represents a break with the empiricism of the Enlightenment, the belief that experience alone is needed for understanding the world. Idealism rapidly became the strongest current in German philosophy after the publication of Kant's mature views in the 1780s.[6] Its stress on the role of ideas was widely diffused and became axiomatic in historicist thought. History, it was generally held, is essentially concerned with ideas. It is not about pure ideas, but about a reality whose development is subject to ideas. This view of the nature of history was propounded, for instance, by Wilhelm von Humboldt, the architect of the Prussian education system, in a lecture 'On the Historian's Task' delivered before the Prussian Academy of Sciences in 1821. The trend of ideas, he explained, constitutes historical truth.[7] The history of ideas, *Geistesgeschichte*, became deeply entrenched in German historical tradition. Philosophical idealism had a marked impact on the theory and practice of history.

If idealism was a characteristic intellectual expression of the turn of the nineteenth century, romanticism was the characteristic cultural expression of the period. Romanticism was similarly a reaction against the norms of the eighteenth century. Nature had been conceived as an intricate structure of cause and effect passively awaiting dissection by the human reason. Now nature was seen as an organic whole that actively influences human beings. It is worthy of respect, even of something akin to worship. For Wordsworth nature was 'the nurse, the guide, the guardian of my heart, and soul of all my moral being'.[8] Nature fulfilled the role of God. There was a tone of diffuse religiosity about the romantic movement in European

5. *Cf.* above, pp. 77ff.
6. On Kantian idealism, *cf.* below, p. 118.
7. Wilhelm von Humboldt, 'On the Historian's Task', Ranke, *Theory and Practice*, pp. 9f.
8. William Wordsworth, 'Lines written a few miles above Tintern Abbey', *Lyrical Ballads* (1798), lines 110ff., ed. R. L. Brett and A. R. Jones (London, 1963), p. 116.

thought. Romanticism, it has been said, was 'spilt religion'.[9] The divine was thought to be everything – or, to be more precise, in everything. Romantics like Wordsworth and Coleridge in England discerned the divine in the natural world of crags and seascapes, flowers and storms. Their poetry was meant to distil the mystical, spiritual experience of those who lived in awareness of the 'Wisdom and Spirit of the Universe.'[1] Romanticism was charged with a sense of the divine abroad in the world.

Historicism was of a piece with the romantic tide that swept Germany. Goethe, the greatest of German romantics, was not a theorist or practitioner of history. Yet Goethe is quite reasonably treated in the best-known German study of the subject as the climax of the rise of historicism.[2] He stood for the same values as the historicists. In particular they shared the feeling that the world is impregnated with the divine. The human world does not differ from the natural world in that respect. God is at work in history. Ranke illustrates this well in an essay that he wrote 'On the Character of Historical Science':

> It is not necessary for us to prove at length that the eternal dwells in the individual. This is the religious foundation on which our efforts rest. We believe that there is nothing without God, and nothing lives except through God.[3]

There was a strong sense of the divine underpinning of the historical process. Each group, historicists held, is shaped by history. But history is in turn working out the purposes of the God who is present in it. The variety of customs that have emerged over time do not suggest that God is at work in the history of some peoples, but not in the history of others. On the contrary, the variety of customs gives evidence of the manifold wisdom of God. The religiosity of the times strongly coloured the historicist worldview.

The Christian purpose of the *Aufklärer* in the second half of the

9. T. E. Hulme, 'Romanticism and Classicism', *Speculations*, ed. Herbert Read (London, 1936), p. 118, quoted by M. H. Abrams, *Natural Supernaturalism: Tradition and Revolution in Romantic Literature* (London, 1971), p. 68.
1. William Wordsworth, *The Prelude*, Book 1, line 401, ed. Ernest de Selincourt, 2nd edn, revised by Helen Darbishire (Oxford, 1959), p. 26.
2. Friedrich Meinecke, *Historism: The Rise of a New Historical Outlook* (1932), trans. J. E. Anderson (London, 1973), pp. 373–495.
3. Ranke, *Theory and Practice*, p. 38.

eighteenth century lay behind much of the diffuse religious feeling in German thought at the turn of the nineteenth century. The apologetic aim of some of the early *Aufklärer* led to no watering down of historic Christianity.[4] Increasingly, however, theologians felt it wise to modify orthodoxy in order to make it more readily defensible in the intellectual climate of their day. Contemporary aesthetic theory, for example, was applied to the Bible. Johann David Michaelis, a Göttingen scholar, treated the biblical documents as 'sacred poetry', rich in myth but weak in logic, whose meaning must be distilled by critical analysis.[5] Nineteenth-century British theologians were to call such efforts 'neologizing'. The tendency was to reinterpret Christianity as a form of the religious sentiment common to all men. The process entailed discarding aspects of biblical teaching that did not appeal to the spirit of the age. The idea of providence was an early casualty. Human beings, according to Michaelis, cannot discern particular instances of divine providence:

> Our views are too confined, and we know too little of the whole chain of causes and effects, to determine what the wisdom of the Deity should ordain . . .[6]

A historian who uses the notion of providence is guilty of presumption. The religious tone of German thought did not mean that there was a return to a Christian view of history. On the contrary, historicism represents a move away from a traditional Christian providentialism.

THE FORMATION OF A NATIONAL TRADITION

The *Aufklärer* were also responsible for developing another feature of romantic thought, a stress on organic development. Like Vico, they were eager to reject a mechanistic worldview. Their particular foe was the influence of Johann Christian von Wolff, the dominant intellectual force in mid-eighteenth-century Germany. Wolff had attempted to apply deductive logic, in the Cartesian manner, to all fields of thought. Every item of knowledge, according to Wolff, is

4. This is true, for instance, of J. M. Chladenius, on whom *cf.* below, pp. 162–65.
5. Reill, *The German Enlightenment*, pp. 82, 193ff., 241.
6. J. D. Michaelis, *Introduction to the New Testament* (4th edn, 1788), trans. Herbert Marsh (Cambridge, 1793–1802), 3, p. 108, quoted by Reill, *The German Enlightenment*, p. 128.

atomistic, separate from every other item. According to the *Aufklärer*, on the contrary, every item is related to another. Schlözer wrote an essay on 'the interconnectedness of events'.[7] History began to be seen not as a series of isolated occurrences, but as an organic development. Growth, on the analogy of the natural world, became a key concept. Groups, communities and nations grow to maturity and wither away, but during the whole process each keeps its own individuality. The most influential exponent of such ideas was Johann Gottfried von Herder.

Herder, who rose through various ecclesiastical appointments to hold the highest church office in Saxe-Weimar, is known chiefly for his *Reflections on the Philosophy of the History of Mankind* (1784–91), a rambling work but one that fully expresses the spirit of early German romanticism. Herder's central importance lies in his statement of what Sir Isaiah Berlin has recently described as 'pluralism' – that is, the contention that each culture has values that cannot justly be compared with the values of other cultures.[8] This cultural relativism is at the opposite pole from the preparedness of thinkers of the progress school to compare the past unfavourably with the present. Herder did not disdain the 'unenlightened' Middle Ages, but on the contrary delighted in the rich variety of mediaeval life. To him, more than to any other writer of the time, belongs the credit for introducing a favourable attitude towards the Middle Ages. He did not entirely reject the notion of progress, but held that it can take place only within a given nation and cannot be measured on any single scale. Each nation, he wrote, contains the 'ideal of its own perfection, wholly independent of all comparison with those of others.'[9] Language is the characteristic that divides one nation most clearly from another. The language gives each nation a corporate identity, a personality. Herder was therefore distressed when Germans aped the language of the French. 'Germans,' he urged, 'speak German! Spew out the Seine's ugly slime!'[1] Herder was an exponent of a historical philosophy that was based on pride in the German language. The continuing bond of historicism with the language was

7. Butterfield, *Man on his Past*, p. 8.
8. Berlin, *Vico and Herder*, p. 153.
9. Herder, *Yet Another Philosophy of History* (1774), quoted by Berlin, *Vico and Herder*, p. 206.
1. Herder, *Works*, 27, p. 129, quoted by Berlin, *Vico and Herder*, p. 182.

at once to encourage its popularity in German-speaking lands and to restrict its appeal elsewhere.

It would be wrong to see in Herder a political form of nationalism. Herder was a cultural nationalist, but at the same time he was a cosmopolitan. He did not sympathize with the aggressive policies of Frederick II of Prussia.[2] There was no political edge to historicism until the Napoleonic Wars. Then, however, with the patriotic tide of resentment against French aggrandisement and the French philosophy that had loosed revolutionary anarchy on Europe, Germans began to identify their national prestige with convictions such as those of Herder. Napoleon had given all Europe a code of laws based on universal 'rational' principles; Savigny and Eichhorn at Berlin, developing Herder's ideas, argued that laws should be peculiar to one people and develop organically with the life of that people. Similarly, historians began to argue, or rather to assume, that each state embodies distinctive national traditions. The behaviour of states can be assessed not by universal principles, but only by the standard of how far the state is expressing its proper spirit. Ranke came close to believing that states are above morality.[3] A further consequence was that German historians paid inordinate attention to foreign policy for as long as the historicist tradition held sway. In Ranke's writing this concentration led to a relative neglect of political conflict within states in order to concentrate on external relations.[4] The idea of the corporate personality of the state became an axiom integral to the German historicist tradition.

HISTORICISM IN HISTORIOGRAPHY

It was also during the Napoleonic Wars that men turned from preparing the materials of history to historiography proper. Georg Friedrich Creuzer was a pioneer of history written within a romantic framework with his study of the origins of Greek poetry (1810–12).[5] Far more influential was another book first published in this period,

2. Johann Gottfried von Herder, *Reflections on the Philosophy of the History of Mankind* (Chicago, 1968), p. xxi.
3. Ranke, *Theory and Practice*, p. li.
4. *Ibid.*, p. lxvii.
5. A. D. Momigliano, 'Friedrich Creuzer and Greek Historiography', *Studies in Historiography*, p. 82.

the *History of Rome* (1811) by Barthold Georg Niebuhr, who lectured at the newly established University of Berlin. Niebuhr blended the fragmentary sources for early Roman history – lawcodes, inscriptions, poetry, ballad-literature (to which category he consigned much of Livy) – into a coherent story of a perennial struggle for power between patricians and plebeians, an interpretation that was to enjoy a remarkable longevity and that has not yet been exorcized from the text books. It was, for its day, a *tour de force*, replacing the traditional accounts of brief phases of republican history based on the ancient historians with a unitary and vivid narrative. Niebuhr could not have achieved his feat without making the typically historicist assumption that poetry and myth express the inner spirit of a nation, and so treating as sound evidence what would now be approached with great caution. He also assumed (following Vico) that all nations go through similar cycles of development, so that the historical experience of Germany could be used to throw light on the story of Rome.[6] Such techniques may not appear to be the methods of a critical historian, but they were the stock-in-trade of a historicist and brought Niebuhr wide acclaim.

Through Niebuhr the ideas of historicism spread beyond Germany. In England a group of scholars with an Oxford background, the so-called 'Liberal Anglicans', read Niebuhr avidly. Of this group the best known is Thomas Arnold, Headmaster of Rugby and subsequently Regius Professor of Modern History at Oxford. Arnold learned German in 1825 in order to read Niebuhr, a work, as he put it at the time, of 'extraordinary ability and learning'.[7] It moulded all his thought. His inaugural lecture at Oxford is a manifesto of historicist views. Modern history, he argued, is the study of 'national personality', which is the product of race, language, institutions and religion, and persists down the ages.[8] He turned into a passionate Germanophile. He appointed the first German master at an English public school within a year of becoming headmaster at Rugby.[9] And

6. A. D. Momigliano, 'Perizonius, Niebuhr and the Character of Early Roman Tradition', *Essays in Ancient and Modern Historiography*, pp. 234f.
7. A. P. Stanley, *The Life and Correspondence of Thomas Arnold, DD* (London, 1844), 1, p. 44.
8. Thomas Arnold, *Introductory Lectures on Modern History* ... (London, 1845), p. 25.
9. J. S. G. Simmons, 'Slavonic Studies at Oxford: The Proposed Slavonic Chair at the Taylor Institution in 1844', *Oxford Slavonic Papers*, 3 (1952), p. 129.

he took over from two of the other Liberal Anglicans the superintendence of the translation of Niebuhr into English.[1] Through interest in Niebuhr, Arnold came to an awareness of Vico's views. He did not, as a clergyman, concur in Vico's belief that nations advance to civilization without divine interposition, but was fascinated by his notion of cyclical recurrence.[2] Historicism, however, was to sway the fancy of British historians rather than to convince their mind. The aspect of historicism that entered the British historical tradition was its delight in the colour and variety of past ages. The chief influence making for a romantic view of history in Britain was not a historian but a novelist, Sir Walter Scott. The appreciation of mediaeval culture that Germany owed to Herder, Britain owed to Scott.[3] It was Sir Walter Scott who fired the imagination of Macaulay and of many subsequent British historians like Sir Ernest Barker.[4] The romantic in British historiography was to be found in its literary expression rather than in its intellectual assumptions.

In Germany, however, the historicist tradition dominated intellectual life. Its greatest exponent in the practice of history was a man born in 1795 and influenced by Niebuhr while at university, Leopold von Ranke, whose long life did not end until 1886. Ranke was the author of a long series of histories of European powers including the papacy. He is usually represented in Anglo-Saxon historical literature as the exemplar of value-free objectivity. His dictum that the historian must concern himself only with 'what actually happened' has become the most common of commonplaces on historical thought. But this is a distorted image of the man, founded on a mistranslation. Ranke's phrase, *wie es eigentlich gewesen*, contains an adverb, *eigentlich*, which certainly means 'actually' in twentieth-century German usage. In Ranke's own nineteenth-century usage, however, it usually meant 'essentially'. His phrase, then, should properly be rendered 'what essentially

1. Stanley, *Thomas Arnold*, 1, p. 45.
2. Duncan Forbes, *The Liberal Anglican Idea of History* (Cambridge, 1952), p. 71. P. W. Day, *Matthew Arnold and the Philosophy of Vico* (Auckland, New Zealand, 1964), pp. 5f.
3. H. R. Trevor-Roper, *The Romantic Movement and the Study of History* (London, 1969), pp. 4–9.
4. On Macaulay, *cf.* above, p. 86. Sir Ernest Barker, *Age and Youth* (London, 1953), pp. 251ff.

happened.'[5] Ranke was not saying that the past must be accurately recorded by a historian whose mind need not colour the process. On the contrary, he was saying that the historian's mind must penetrate to the inwardness of events. He was expressing the normal historicist belief that intuition enables the historian to divine the essence of the past.

Nor was Ranke a champion of the collecting of facts in the manner of Buckle or Acton.[6] He did believe in intensive archival research. But in this he was not digging out a mass of facts as an alternative to being guided by his own ideas about the past. For one thing, research was itself enjoined by the historicist mentality as a whole. When Ranke did systematic work on the reports of Venetian ambassadors to supply a detailed account of court intrigues in early modern Europe, he was not breaking free from the prejudices of his age. He was following the principles of the *Aufklärer*. Again, his ideas about the past entered fully into his historical work. His belief in the corporate personality of states led him to seek its expression in the relations of the European powers. If the state reveals its character in international dealings, these should receive a historian's prime attention. That might entail neglect, for instance, of popular movements – which, as Acton once noted, Ranke did neglect.[7] Another of his historicist views, that nations develop organically, explains his policy when in the editorial chair of the *Historisch-Politische Zeitschrift* on behalf of the Prussian government (1831–36). He steered a middle course between reaction and liberalism, arguing that interruptions in national growth are to be deplored.[8] His historical assumptions led directly to a political stance. Ranke is certainly an exemplar of thorough research, but in no sense was his work value-free.

One of the reasons for the misrepresentation of Ranke as a mere collector of facts is that his successors in public favour in Germany, members of 'the Prussian School', chose so to depict and to criticize him. After 1848, when attendance at Ranke's lectures was dwindling, J. C. Droysen, the founder of the Prussian school, was arguing that he had not sufficiently glorified German national aspirations in his

5. Ranke, *Theory and Practice*, p. xix.
6. *Cf.* above, pp. 87f.
7. Butterfield, *Man on his Past*, p. 88.
8. Ranke, *Theory and Practice*, p. xxix.

history. Droysen, like his contemporary Heinrich von Sybel, came to be more appreciative of positivist history as exemplified by Buckle, yet reaffirmed the central historicist claim that the methods of the natural sciences cannot be applied to history.[9] At the turn of the twentieth century Max Weber, though drawn further towards positivism, was nevertheless preoccupied with the issue of the proper distinctive method of the sciences of man.[1] Even if the tradition of historicism was being diluted, it flowed on into the twentieth century. Its influence on German scholarship remained. The flight of academics from Hitler's tyranny in the 1930s introduced a leavening of their ideas into Anglo-Saxon scholarship, but no more than a leavening.[2] In the 1960s many German historians were still defending a method that concentrated on justifying their country's past role in the international arena against the contention of Fritz Fischer that Germany must bear the responsibility for the outbreak of the First World War.[3] The academic debate on this issue bears testimony to the continuing, if declining, influence of the statist element in German historicism.

HISTORICIST THEORY

In the later historicist tradition the most important theorist of history was Wilhelm Dilthey, a professor at Berlin who died in 1911 but whose thought exerted a strong posthumous influence. His achievement was to elaborate (albeit inconsistently) the historicist notion of intuition. History, the whole tradition held, is concerned with the understanding of human action by methods different from those of the natural sciences. The laws of science cannot grasp the particular features of any instance of human behaviour, charged as it is with intention. Human intention can only be intuited. The process of 'understanding', according to Dilthey, is not so much an irrational jump of feeling as an intelligible method, guided by principles that can be laid down – principles that Dilthey called 'hermeneutics'. Dilthey found in the early nineteenth-century theologian Schleier-

9. Iggers, *German Conception*, pp. 104–09.
1. *Cf.* below, pp. 158f.
2. A. D. Momigliano, 'Historicism in Contemporary Thought', *Studies in Historiography*, p. 227.
3. J. A. Moses, *The Politics of Illusion: The Fischer Controversy in German Historiography* (London, 1975).

macher principles for interpreting the Bible (the traditional meaning of the word 'hermeneutics'), and recognized that they can be applied to any documents.[4] Further, according to Dilthey, human beings can be studied as though they were documents. Parts and wholes, whether of documents or of human situations, can be understood only by seeing them in relation to one another. Just as Schleiermacher had held that biblical verses must be understood in their context, so human action can be grasped only in its context. Here was Dilthey's doctrine of the 'hermeneutic circle': a part must be understood through its setting in the whole; the whole must be understood through recognizing the significance of its parts. Interpretation is therefore a process of allowing part and whole to interact in the mind.[5] Dilthey succeeded in giving an account of what historians do that many others were to find persuasive.

A similar, although less carefully worked out, historical epistemology was developed in England by R. G. Collingwood, Waynflete Professor of Metaphysical Philosophy at Oxford, who died in 1943. Collingwood's papers on the subject, comprising a survey of theorists of history over the centuries and an exposition of his own views, were collated and published posthumously as *The Idea of History*. This book stands squarely in the historicist tradition. Its central contention Collingwood had already given to the world in *An Autobiography*, a simple statement of his views to which *The Idea* adds little of definite doctrine. Historical knowledge, he claims in the *Autobiography*, 'is the re-enactment in the historian's mind of the thought whose history he is studying'.[6] The historian must penetrate beyond the outside of an event to the 'inside', to the thought of the person in the past, and totally identify his mind with, say, that of Nelson. 'I plunge beneath the surface of my mind', he writes, 'and there live a life in which I not merely think about Nelson but am Nelson'.[7] Historical events are unique in having an inside that can be mentally re-enacted, the task of the historian alone. The events of nature have nothing but an outside, so that the scientist is excluded from exploring the mental world of man.[8] The contrast

4. R. E. Palmer, *Hermeneutics: Interpretation Theory in Schleiermacher, Dilthey, Heidegger, and Gadamer* (Evanston, Illinois, 1969), pp. 94ff.
5. H. P. Rickman, ed., *W. Dilthey: Selected Writings* (Cambridge, 1976), pp. 9ff.
6. R. G. Collingwood, *An Autobiography* (London, 1939), p. 112.
7. *Ibid.*, p. 113.
8. R. G. Collingwood, *The Idea of History* (London, 1946), p. 214.

establishes for Collingwood that history has its own distinct methodology, a claim on which he repeatedly insists. His doctrine that a historian must become mentally identified with a historical agent may seem startling, but its purpose is to support the familiar historicist belief that history differs entirely from natural science.

Collingwood had come to this apparently idiosyncratic position, according to his own account in the *Autobiography*, as a result of his historical research on Roman Britain.[9] It seems likely, however, that his own research did no more than confirm ideas that he had drawn from Vico, the only theorist whose account of historical epistemology escapes criticism in *The Idea*.[1] In 1913 he published a translation of a pamphlet by the Italian philosopher Benedetto Croce entitled *The Philosophy of Giambattista Vico*. Collingwood was therefore strongly attracted to Vico from a very early stage in his career. Those who knew Collingwood agree that in conversation he would acknowledge that Vico, 'a kind of abandoned quarry of marvellous ideas', had influenced him more than anyone else.[2] Collingwood, it has been suggested, differs from Vico in holding that the task of mental identification with a person in the past is an easy one, whereas Vico admitted its difficulty.[3] Collingwood, however, does not write of the process as easy. He is not concerned with its ease or difficulty, but only with its nature. His remarks on the arduousness of historical research might suggest that he believed it to be difficult. It seems clear that Collingwood seized on Vico's central principle, that man can understand the past because he is its maker, and made it his own. He did develop it somewhat, but only to the extent of expounding the meaning of Vico's statement that the principles of 'the world of civil society', the human past, are 'to be found within the modifications of our own human mind.'[4] Collingwood's theory of historical knowledge is essentially that of Vico.

Historicist theory has had repercussions on areas far broader than the discussion of what the historian does. In France, for instance, it

9. Collingwood, *An Autobiography*, p. 117.
1. Collingwood does, however, criticize Vico's pattern of historical cycles in *The Idea of History*, p. 264.
2. Sir Isaiah Berlin, 'Giambattista Vico', *The Listener*, 28 September 1972, p. 391. T. M. Knox in Collingwood, *The Idea of History*, p. viii.
3. Sir Isaiah Berlin, 'The Philosophical Ideas of Giambattista Vico', *Art and Ideas in Eighteenth-Century Italy* (Rome, 1960), p. 227.
4. *The New Science of Giambattista Vico*, p. 96.

affected social theorists from the time of Saint-Simon onwards.[5] In Britain its belief that time and place shape people's behaviour transformed economic theory in the late nineteenth century.[6] In Italy, together with Hegelianism, Vico's thought in particular formed the background for perhaps the greatest twentieth-century Italian intellectual achievement, the aesthetic and historical philosophy of Benedetto Croce.[7] In Germany the historicist stress on the corporate personality of the nation formed the foundation of Hitler's *völkisch* philosophy of life.[8] The nation in National Socialist thought was defined less in terms of language than of race, yet its central role in history and its superiority to normal moral conventions bear the marks of historicist styles of thinking. In Germany the deeply embedded idea of intuitive understanding also did much to shape philosophical trends. Dilthey's method was taken up by Martin Heidegger, whose *Being and Time* (1927) was intended as a preliminary hermeneutic study but became the early classic of existentialism. In a chaotic world, according to Heidegger, man must recognize the certainty of death and so steel himself to follow a life of decisive activity. Such ideas were to become popular in the wake of the Second World War, especially through the writings of Jean-Paul Sartre.[9] Existentialism can perhaps be regarded as the *reductio ad absurdum* of historicism. Human life, in the opinion of the existentialists, is not simply shaped by history, but is reduced to meaninglessness by being part of the flux of events. All that remains for man is to accept that the world is a place of absurdity and futility.

ASSESSMENT OF HISTORICISM

Historicism is a tradition of thought all too little known in the Anglo-Saxon world. It represents a sustained attempt over nearly two centuries to grapple with the question of the significance of the historical process. It has deeply affected the way history has been

5. *Cf.* above, pp. 81f.
6. A. W. Coats, 'The Historist Reaction in English Political Economy, 1870–90', *Economica*, new series, 21 (1954).
7. A. D. Momigliano, 'Reconsidering B. Croce (1866–1952)', *Essays in Ancient and Modern Historiography*, pp. 347ff.
8. Michael Oakeshott, *The Social and Political Doctrines of Contemporary Europe* (Cambridge, 1939), p. 201.
9. M. D. Biddiss, *The Age of the Masses: Ideas and Society in Europe Since 1870* (Hassocks, Sussex, 1977), pp. 249f, 322f.

written from the time of Niebuhr onwards. And it has affected almost every field of human thought. Yet it has been little considered as a body of thought by speakers of English. There has sometimes been a preparedness to assimilate its insights in small doses, in economics or theology for instance, but its overall thrust has been sadly neglected. Collingwood's approach to historical issues is normally treated as eccentric precisely because the body of thought that he represents is not appreciated. German emigrés apart, there have been few thinkers who have delved in depth into historicism. Thomas Arnold and his circle were exceptional. No historicist *tradition* has emerged in the English-speaking world. The explanation lies chiefly in ignorance of German. Translation has usually been confined to works that are likely to draw public attention, and so to items that impinge on existing Anglo-Saxon debates. Expositions of the premises of the German debates have begun to appear only in recent years. Historicism needs to be estimated not as an intellectual vagary but as a mainstream way of understanding the historical process.

Yet it is open to serious criticism. The main historicist idea is that human groups are moulded by history. To a great extent this is undeniable. It is a premise of the argument of this book that the ways people think are affected by social and intellectual conditions. But historicism takes a further step. It holds that the flux of history eliminates any constancy in man. There is no such thing as human nature. Man, wrote Schlözer, 'is nothing by nature'.[1] This was to reject the view of man held down the centuries in western thought and accepted by the *philosophes* of the Enlightenment. Man had normally been supposed to be in all societies and in all ages the same. There is surely an element of truth in this view too. Human beings, as Hume saw, had similar characteristics whether they lived in ancient Greece or Rome or in modern France or England.[2] People have the same type of motive, the same order of feelings, the same type of thinking. There is something that human beings have in common. Historicism over-reacted against the Enlightenment. The *philosophes*, it is true, had defined too precisely the qualities that mark off man as human. Their notion that man is defined by his

1. A. L. Schlözer, *Vorstellung seiner Universalhistorie* (Göttingen, 1772), 1, p. 26, quoted by G. G. Iggers, *New Directions in European Historiography* (Middletown, Conn., 1975), p. 15.
2. *Cf.* above, pp. 77f.

power of reason was inadequate. But that does not mean that all human characteristics are determined by circumstances. Historicism underestimates the extent to which human nature is constant.

The historicist idea of how we obtain knowledge of the past is also questionable. The historian, it is said, can intuit the mental world of people long dead. This process of formulating ideas by inference from the evidence was characterized by Von Humboldt as being like the work of a creative artist.[3] There lies its weakness. How is the artist to know whether he has created a faithful likeness of the people of the past? His very creativity may lead him astray. There is no objective criterion for determining how accurately the historian reflects the past. According to the historicists of the romantic era this problem does not arise. Intuition, because it is personal knowledge, is inherently superior to the imposition of rational categories on the human world. Dilthey, however, recognized that the lack of a criterion of accuracy was a reproach to the whole idea of 'understanding'. His hermeneutic circle was an attempt to draw up a methodology for historicism. Yet it is very doubtful whether there would be agreement between any two historians on how to apply Dilthey's technique. To this subject we must return in chapter seven.[4] Here it must be noted that historicist methodology is extremely difficult to formulate in other than the vaguest terms.

Historicism seems to be fertile soil for dangerous doctrines. It contends, following Herder, that nations are the chief actors on the historical stage. Most of the tradition has gone beyond him in urging that particular nations are singled out by their prowess for greatness. The Prussian school of historians in the late nineteenth century made a major contribution to German militarism. The historical writing of Droysen was one of the factors that made Bismarck's work possible. And the Nazis were able to exploit the image of a glorious German past that the historians had created. The problem here is not simply that historicism concentrated attention on the nation or that it had a right-wing tendency to accept whatever was traditional. The historicists claimed more. They often argued that it was their duty to promote with a single eye the greatness of Germany. The historian's cognition, according to Droysen, must be

3. Von Humboldt, 'On the Historian's Task', Ranke, *Theory and Practice*, p. 14.
4. *Cf.* below, pp. 147f.

conditioned by belonging to the German state, nation and religion. He despised an 'emasculated objectivity'.[5] This was to transform the unavoidable commitment of the historian into an unchangeable ideological straitjacket that restricted his critical powers. Moreover, criticisms by historians of other nationalities were ruled out of court because they could not express the spirit of Germany. The deeds of the German state were beyond debate. A dubious claim about the centrality of nationhood in the historical process led on to nationalist excesses by historians – and by statesmen too.

The overriding problem of historicism is its lack of foundations. The determinant of men's beliefs, it holds, is history itself. The historical process is therefore a patchwork quilt of different attitudes and customs. Is there any ground for saying that some are right and others wrong? In the wake of the First World War even men deeply immersed in the German tradition of historical thought began to have doubts on this score. Ernst Troeltsch, a historical theologian at Berlin, diagnosed in 1922 a 'crisis of historicism'.[6] Historical study, he argued, had undermined 'all firm norms and ideals of human existence'.[7] The flux of history alone seemed responsible for the prevailing values in different human societies. In earlier historicism romantic religiosity had upheld the belief that God is the source of what is right in all societies over time. Troeltsch himself continued to claim that without the idea of God 'or something analogous' the formulation of objective values is impossible.[8] Historicism depended on religion for its intellectual plausibility. Religious belief, however, was ceasing to be the fashion amongst the educated. Neither Troeltsch nor his twentieth-century successors in the historicist tradition proved able to discover an alternative to divine guarantees for judgments of value. Historicism collapsed into historical relativism. There was no ground for preferring one custom to another, one moral code to another or even, most crucially,

5. J. G. Droysen, *Historik: Vorlesungen über Enzyklopädie und Methodologie der Geschichte*, ed. Rudolf Hübner (Munich, 1937), quoted by Iggers, *German Conception*, p. 112.
6. Ernst Troeltsch, 'Die Krisis des Historismus', *Die Neue Rundschau*, 33 (1922), cited by Iggers, *German Conception*, p. 189n.
7. Ernst Troeltsch, 'Das neunzehnte Jahrhundert', *Gesammelte Schriften*, 4, p. 628, quoted by Iggers, *German Conception*, p. 189.
8. Ernst Troeltsch, *Historicism and its Problems* (Tübingen, 1922), p. 184, quoted by Robert Morgan, 'Troeltsch and the Dialectical Theology', *Ernst Troeltsch and the Future of Theology*, ed. J. P. Clayton (Cambridge, 1976), p. 46.

historicism to another worldview. The whole historicist perspective stood revealed as an arbitrary preference. The 'crisis' that Troeltsch analysed goes a long way towards explaining why historicism has declined in the twentieth century. Confidence in it as a worldview has ebbed, even if elements of its teaching survive in western thought. Far from revealing the true significance of the historical process, historicism eventually undermined its own premises.

6 Marxist history

'The *entire so-called history of the world* is nothing but the creation of man through human labour . . .'.

Karl Marx, 'Economic and Philosophic Manuscripts of 1844'.

Marxism is not so much a political programme or an economic analysis as a historical worldview. History is at its heart. The preferred name of its proponents for the whole Marxist perspective is 'historical materialism', a phrase coined by Engels in 1892 as an equivalent for what he had also called 'the materialist conception of history'.[1] Neither term was used by Marx himself, but both fairly represent his central belief that material conditions mould human history. This was to reject what Marx dismissed as the 'idealistic view of history', any belief that ideas are responsible for shaping human destinies.[2] How men produce their means of subsistence, according to Marxism, is the key to historical change.

Beyond such basic assertions about the Marxist view of history it is difficult to go without careful explanation. The problem is that Marxism has been distorted both by its friends and by its foes. The exponents of Marxism have often adapted it to make it more readily understood by the masses or else modified it to suit the exigencies of changed political circumstances. In their eagerness to discredit so subversive a body of ideas the opponents of Marxism have frequently misidentified the target of their criticisms. On the one hand, in official Communism, the views of Marx, Engels and Lenin have been blended and codified as orthodox 'Marxist-Leninism'. On the other, among hostile commentators, there has been an equal preparedness to attribute the theories of Marx's successors to Marx himself. Both camps have long dwelt in ignorance of Marx's own

1. The phrase 'the materialist conception of history' was first used by Engels in 1859. Z. A. Jordan, *The Evolution of Dialectical Materialism: A Philosophical and Sociological Analysis* (London, 1967), p. 37n.
2. Karl Marx and Frederick Engels, *The German Ideology* (1845–46), ed. Roy Pascal (London, 1938), p. 28.

position, for their knowledge of him was confined to the relatively few works in print. At least three-quarters of his writings remained unpublished at his death.[3] One work pivotal for interpreting the body of his thought was not published in Russian until 1939 and in English until 1973.[4] Hence the opinions of few men have been so thoroughly misrepresented. It is essential to sift out the views of Karl Marx from the beliefs commonly attributed to him.

Further, the significance of his views can be grasped only by analysing how they emerged. His frame of mind was constructed in mid-nineteenth-century Germany and so deeply affected by historicism. Yet he also early encountered the tradition of thought associated with the idea of progress. Marxism was engendered by the interaction of the two schools in a particularly acute mind. It is not simply that Marx drew diverse elements from historicism and the idea of progress. Rather, he took over an earlier fusion of the two traditions and reworked it. The earlier fusion was the system of George William Frederick Hegel, whose all-encompassing philosophy was the marvel of Germany in the decade after his death in 1831. As a law student at Berlin in 1837 Marx reported to his father that he 'had got to know Hegel from beginning to end'.[5] Although Hegel was perhaps most celebrated for his *Lectures on the Philosophy of World History*, Marx's views on history developed in engagement with the whole Hegelian worldview. Accordingly it is to Hegel that we must turn.

THE HEGELIAN BACKGROUND OF MARX

Hegel's philosophy can best be understood as a response to that of Kant.[6] In the theory of knowledge Kant's belief that the mind actively constructs the world of experience led him to conclude that the world of experience differs from the world as it really is, beyond experience. He contrasted the knowable world of *phenomena* ('things as they appear') with the unknowable world of *noumena* ('things as they are in themselves'). This distinction Hegel boldly denied. The world

3. Perry Anderson, *Considerations on Western Marxism* (London, 1976), p. 3.
4. Karl Marx, *The Grundrisse: Foundations of the Critique of Political Economy (Rough Draft)* (Harmondsworth, 1973), p. 7n.
5. Karl Marx, 'Letter to his Father', *Karl Marx: Early Texts*, ed. David McLellan (Oxford, 1972), p. 8.
6. *Cf.* above, pp. 100f.

that is known is the world of *noumena* in Kant's sense. Hegel grounded this claim on the belief that the mind is responsible for creating the external world. There can be, according to Hegel, no reality beyond experience. Hegel summed up his views in the dictum, 'The real is the rational and the rational is the real.'[7] He meant that the real world is knowable to the mind; and that the mind is all there is ultimately in the real world. Hegel was laying great stress on mind because he believed that the particular human mind is a manifestation of the eternal Mind (*Geist*), which is the equivalent of God in his thought. The human mind creates the world in knowing it because it is part of the great creative Mind (or God). Hegel is therefore classified as an absolute idealist. The ideas of the mind are wholly responsible for the external world.

The pattern to be discovered in the world, it follows, is the same pattern that operates in the mind. Both patterns are called the dialectic, which is perhaps the best known feature of the Hegelian system. It is usually described as a triad of thesis, antithesis and synthesis, but these terms are not used by Hegel. He calls the dialectic 'the grasping of opposites in their unity'.[8] In the historical process, as in logic, a moment is succeeded by its opposite, which in turn is succeeded by the unity of the opposites. The unity then becomes the first moment of a new phase. For instance, according to Hegel, the family as the central social unit in the Middle Ages was superseded by the rise of 'civil society', which, in its commercial individualism, tended to break up the family. Subsequently the two opposites were superseded by the state, which supplied ideal conditions for ethical life by uniting the solidarity of the family with the commercial individualism of civil society.[9] The triadic pattern is regularly discerned in various sections of world history. It bears the hallmarks of the idea of progress. The thread of linearity runs through it, there is confidence in a goal being achieved and it embraces a firm scale of values. Each feature was modified by Hegel's environment in historicist Germany. The shifts between moments make the line jagged rather than straight, the goal is often Hegel's own day rather than the future and the supreme value being

7. Quoted by G. R. G. Mure, *The Philosophy of Hegel* (London, 1965), p. 23. A less memorable translation is given in *Hegel's Philosophy of Right* (1821), trans. T. M. Knox (Oxford, 1952), p. 10.
8. *Hegel's Science of Logic*, trans. A. V. Miller (London, 1969), p. 56.
9. *Hegel's Philosophy of Right*, pp. 105–223.

generated is freedom understood in a thoroughly romantic way as self-realization. Yet the idea of progress contributed the underlying structure of Hegel's understanding of history.

While still a student, Marx was drawn into the circle of the 'Young Hegelians', a group committed to the trenchant criticism of Christianity. Hegel had defended the consistency of his philosophy with Lutheran orthodoxy, and many of his followers did the same. The Young Hegelians, on the contrary, used Hegelian categories to assert the truth of atheism. By 1841 Marx was contemplating the launching of a journal to be entitled *Atheistic Archives*.[1] The Young Hegelians, however, came to pay more attention to politics. The Prussian authorities censored their atheistic propaganda, and resentment of government policy rapidly developed into opposition to the government itself. Marx was swept along with them. In 1841 his friends were already seeing in him an extreme revolutionary.[2] Discussion of Hegelianism led Marx to a radical stance in religion and politics alike.

In 1843 Marx determined to settle accounts with Hegel by composing a 'Critique of Hegel's Philosophy of Right'. Marx had already pointed out in a newspaper article that a majority of the poor in Prussian lands were technically without any rights because they were not members of groups recognized by the state. These people were treated by Hegel merely as a threat to the stability of the state, yet according to Hegelian premises the state should guarantee the enjoyment of a self-fulfilling freedom for all.[3] There was a contradiction in the heart of the institution that Hegel made the culmination of history. Marx argues in the 'Critique' that the Hegelian state, far from acting in the interests of man in general, acts according to the direction of vested interests. It is a mask for the economic individualism of what Hegel had called 'civil society'. The state is not at the apex of history. Instead of extolling the state, according to Marx, we should aim for 'democracy', in which all will share power.[4] Here is the germ of the later Marxian idea that history is leading up towards communism, where no state survives to neglect

1. *Karl Marx: Early Texts*, p. xiv.
2. *Ibid.*
3. Heinz Lubasz, 'Marx's Initial Problematic: The Problem of Poverty', *Political Studies*, 24 (1976), pp. 27–34.
4. Karl Marx, 'Critique of Hegel's "Philosophy of Right",' *Karl Marx: Early Texts*, p. 65.

or oppress the mass of the people. Even though he was to continue to think and express himself in a Hegelian manner, Marx had made his declaration of intellectual independence from Hegel.

MARX'S THEORY OF HISTORY

In Marx's expositions of his views on the historical process the starting-point is that man is the maker of his own history. This proposition emerged partly from Marx's encounter with the thought of Ludwig Feuerbach, whose *Essence of Christianity* (1841) had attempted to show that theology is a mystified form of anthropology. Feuerbach held that man is not, as Hegel had taught, essentially part of Mind. Yet he equally rejected the traditional materialist view going back to the eighteenth century that man is merely a cog in a mechanistic universe. Feuerbach's philosophy set man in the middle of the stage.[5] Marx was attracted by this anthropocentrism, but at the same time felt that Feuerbach had omitted the salient quality of man as an active being. Feuerbach had not progressed beyond a Lockean view that man is the passive recipient of sense experience. As Marx puts it in his third thesis on Feuerbach:

> The materialist doctrine that men are products of circumstances and upbringing, and that, therefore, changed men are products of other circumstances and changed upbringing, forgets that it is men who change circumstances and that the educator must himself be educated.[6]

Marx argued that Hegel had done greater justice to man as an active being, even if in Hegel human activity is purely mental. The true view, according to Marx, is that (following Feuerbach) man is part of the material world and that (following Hegel) he participates in creating the world. This was how the foundation of historical materialism was laid.

Marx's starting-point was by no means an abstract one. He was claiming that it is natural for man to engage in productive labour. He based the contention on common sense:

> . . . we must begin by stating the first premise of all human

5. Jordan, *Dialectical Materialism*, p. 19.
6. Karl Marx, 'Theses on Feuerbach', Karl Marx and Frederick Engels, *Collected Works*, 5 (London, 1976), p. 7. This version was edited by Engels, but seems to reflect Marx's meaning well.

> existence and, therefore, of all history, the premise, namely, that men must be in a position to live in order to be able to 'make history'. But life involves before everything else eating and drinking, housing, clothing and various other things. The first historical act is thus the production of the means to satisfy these needs, the production of material life itself.[7]

The essential form of human activity is therefore production. Marx dismissed recent German thought for failing to recognize this 'fundamental fact'. 'It is well known', he writes, 'that the Germans have never done this, and they have never, therefore, had an *earthly* basis for history and consequently never a historian.'[8] To observe that need spurs man to labour is the beginning of historical wisdom.

The second major element in Marx's historical theory grows out of the first. The way in which men supply their needs, the mode of production, shapes all aspects of their life together. Working to create the means of subsistence is a definite way of life.

> As individuals express their life, so they are. What they are, therefore, coincides with their production, both with *what* they produce and with *how* they produce. Hence what individuals are depends on the material conditions of their production.[9]

Marx is not saying merely that economic activity in some sense *causes* the pattern of social life. Rather he is arguing that social life essentially *consists in* working to satisfy needs. A particular mode of production embraces man's relation with other men as well as man's relation with the natural world.[1] The legal, political, religious, aesthetic and philosophical aspects of life, what Marx sums up as ideology, are all conditioned by the core of human life, the mode of production. 'It is not the consciousness of men that determines their being, but, on the contrary, their social being that determines their consciousness.'[2] There is in this epigram an underlying polemic against Hegel and his doctrine that the mind creates the world. The

7. Marx and Engels, 'The German Ideology', Marx and Engels, *Collected Works*, 5, pp. 41f.
8. *Ibid.* p. 42.
9. *Ibid.* pp. 31f.
1. Derek Sayer, 'Method and Dogma in Historical Materialism', *The Sociological Review*, 23 (1975), p. 780.
2. Karl Marx, 'Preface to *A Contribution to the Critique of Political Economy*' (1859), Karl Marx and Frederick Engels, *Selected Works* (Moscow, 1951) 1, p. 329.

saying also reveals the debt of Marx to historicism. Marx believed as strongly as Herder or Ranke that customs and ideas are generated by social conditions in a particular group. He went beyond Herder or Ranke in holding that how men gain their living is the decisive aspect of social conditions. Yet in his conviction that production shapes ideology Marx shows the continuity of his ideas with the underlying historicist assumptions of the Germany of his day.

The third major feature of Marx's understanding of history is his scheme of historical periods. Like Hegel, Marx identifies stages in the formation of society. Like Hegel also, Marx analyses with particular care the stage that both men termed 'civil society' – or, as the phrase in Marx is usually translated, 'bourgeois society'. Marx may well have been influenced in this area of his thought by theorists of the idea of progress such as Saint-Simon.[3] Earlier views were, however, transformed to coincide with the priority given by Marx to production. At certain points in history, according to Marx, the development of the mode of production outpaces changes in the politico-legal structure of society. 'Then begins an epoch of social revolution. With the change of the economic foundation the entire immense superstructure is more or less rapidly transformed.'[4] Such social revolutions separate the stages of history. In each stage the division of labour gives rise to conflicts between social groups having different modes of production, the 'classes' of Marxist thought. The ruling class is the one that controls the dominant mode of production. 'The handmill gives you society with the feudal lord; the steam mill, society with the industrial capitalist'.[5] Asiatic, ancient, feudal and bourgeois phases have already emerged. The bourgeois stage is the last in which there is class conflict, for it will be superseded by a revolution with the proletariat in the vanguard. The proletariat, as the great majority of the population, has no particular interests and so will not antagonize other groups in the socialist society that is to come. The linearity and confidence in the future characteristic of the idea of progress are very much in evidence.

The question arises of whether this is a fatalist view of history.

3. Jordan, *Dialectical Materialism*, pp. 119, 122ff.
4. Marx, 'Preface to *A Contribution to the Critique of Political Economy*', Marx and Engels, *Selected Works*, 1, p. 329.
5. Karl Marx, *The Poverty of Philosophy* (London, 1941), p. 92. For a detailed study of social development according to Marx, *cf.* W. H. Shaw, *Marx's Theory of History* (London, 1978).

It is the opinion of Sir Isaiah Berlin that in Marx's thought the pattern of history is determined independently of human agency. Forces that are 'impersonal and irresistible' truly govern the world.[6] Many others, Marxist and non-Marxist, have agreed that Marx believed in historical inevitability. They can quote Marx's dictum that 'the natural laws of capitalist production' are 'working with iron necessity towards inevitable results'.[7] When Marx wrote this passage in the preface to the first German edition of *Capital*, however, he was using a popular style to persuade his German readers that analysis of the British economy was relevant to their own country. The passage is not one marked by expository precision. The word 'iron', for instance, is an epithet taken from Goethe, not a technical term. Marx himself was at pains to protest against treating parts of *Capital* as an account of universal patterns that were destined to shape world history. The book, he pointed out, contains a 'historical sketch of the genesis of capitalism in Western Europe', not 'an historic – philosophic theory of the general path every people is fated to tread.'[8] Nor did he claim that economic forces dictate the course of events on a smaller scale. For Marx, economic forces do not exist as entities separate from man. Human activity, as we have seen, is in his view essentially concerned with production and so economic. Consequently economic developments depend upon human decisions. The processes of history, according to Marx, are determined by no agency other than man.

What, then, is to be made of Marx's use of the word 'laws'? He cannot mean that laws inexorably govern the affairs of men. It is also clear that he did not make use of historical laws for prediction in the manner of the classic theorists of the idea of progress like Condorcet or Saint-Simon.[9] Laws for Marx can be equated with 'tendencies' – as they are, for example, in the passage from the preface to the first German edition of *Capital* that is quoted above. They are generalizations about social trends. No man is at liberty to act as he pleases, for he is immersed in a social stream that limits

6. Sir Isaiah Berlin, *Historical Inevitability* (London, 1954), p. 22.
7. Karl Marx, 'Preface to the First German Edition of the First Volume of *Capital*' (1867), Marx and Engels, *Selected Works*, 1, p. 407.
8. Karl Marx to the editorial board of the *Otechestvenniye Zapiski*, November 1877, Karl Marx and Frederick Engels, *Selected Correspondence* (Moscow, 1956), p. 379.
9. Paul Thomas, 'Marx and Science', *Political Studies*, 24 (1976), p. 10.

his options. As Marx puts it in a historical essay that he composed about the French revolution of 1848:

> Men make their own history, but they do not make it just as they please; they do not make it under circumstances chosen by themselves, but under circumstances directly encountered, given and transmitted from the past.[1]

What men have freely done in a previous generation has turned the historical process in a certain direction. A Marxian law is no more than a description of the way in which human possibilities happen to have worked out.[2] Marx did not deviate from his initial premise that man, not fate or law, is the maker of history.

ENGELS' THEORY OF HISTORY

The name of Frederick Engels is usually coupled with that of Karl Marx. It is frequently assumed that the views of the two men coincided. They did, after all, collaborate in a number of works, including not only the famous *Communist Manifesto* of 1848 but also *The German Ideology* of 1845–46 in which the basic Marxian premises about history were laid down over against Hegel and Feuerbach. Engels also constructed, in 'Ludwig Feuerbach and the End of Classical German Philosophy' (1886), an analysis of the broad sweep of European history that seems consistent with the main axioms of Marx's historical theory.[3] Yet the whole cast of mind of the two men differed. Marx was a philosopher by temperament and by training and was content to spend day after day at seat 07 in the reading room of the British Museum. Engels left school in 1837 before taking his matriculation examination, and entered on a career in the family business that was interrupted only by a year of voluntary military service.[4] His convictions about class conflict were formed not by philosophical reflection but by experience of

1. Karl Marx, 'The Eighteenth Brumaire of Louis Bonaparte' (1852), Marx and Engels, *Selected Works*, 1, p. 225.
2. Helmut Fleischer, *Marxism and History* (London, 1973), p. 79.
3. Frederick Engels, 'Ludwig Feuerbach and the End of Classical German Philosophy', Marx and Engels, *Selected Works*, 2, pp. 354–62.
4. Frederick Engels, *The Condition of the Working Class in England*, ed. W. O. Henderson and W. H. Chaloner (Oxford, 1958), pp. xxviif.

Manchester.[5] He enjoyed intellectual pursuits, especially keeping up with developments in natural science, but in a piecemeal rather than a systematic way. Although he admired Hegel and was briefly a member of a Young Hegelian club,[6] he did not obtain a firm grasp of Hegelianism in the manner of Marx. It was typical that when the two men expressed their conviction that the state would come to an end following the proletarian revolution, whereas Marx always used a Hegelian technical term in saying the state would be 'sublated' (*aufgehoben*), Engels used a biological metaphor in declaring that it would wither away.[7] Engels had the interests and attitudes of a nineteenth-century general reader, albeit an extremely assiduous one.

Engels' scientific concerns modified the structure of Marxian thought. He believed that history could be investigated by the same methods that were achieving great results in the field of natural science. Marx was the first to do so. 'Just as Darwin discovered the law of development of organic nature, so Marx discovered the law of development of human history. . .'[8] Nature and history are closely related in Engels' thought. Both are in a state of flux. Both operate according to what he calls in Hegelian fashion dialectical laws. In the *Anti-Dühring* (1878) Engels attempts to show that the dialectical laws of the two processes even follow the same pattern. Engels claimed after Marx's death that the *Anti-Dühring* contained 'the views held by Marx and myself'.[9] Marx, however, did not commit himself to the opinions of his colleague.[1] He nowhere offers surmises about the functioning of the laws of nature or hints that the dialectic is a way of seeing history.[2] Marx in *Capital* does express his esteem for Darwin and refers to laws that apply to the human as well as the natural world.[3] But Engels went far further. It seems clear that

5. Frederick Engels, 'On the History of the Communist League', Marx and Engels, *Selected Works*, 2, p. 311.
6. *Karl Marx: Early Texts*, p. xii.
7. Shlomo Avineri, *The Social and Political Thought of Karl Marx* (Cambridge, 1968), p. 202.
8. Frederick Engels, 'Speech at the Graveside of Karl Marx' (1883), Marx and Engels, *Selected Works*, 2, p. 153.
9. Frederick Engels, 'Special Introduction to the English Edition of 1892 of *Socialism: Utopian and Scientific*', Marx and Engels, *Selected Works*, 2, p. 87.
1. Jordan, *Dialectical Materialism*, pp. 9ff.
2. Terrell Carver, 'Marx and Hegel's *Logic*', *Political Studies*, 24 (1976), p. 66.
3. Karl Marx, *Capital*, 1 (1867: Moscow, 1961), pp. 341n, 305f.

he ventured speculations on the nature of the universe that Marx never contemplated. In so doing he enveloped the Marxist theory of history in an all-embracing cosmology.

Engels also reinforced the features in Marx's thought that leaned towards positivism. Philosophy might understand a static universe, he argues, but only dialectical thinking is adequate for grasping a reality that is in flux. When the presuppositions of philosophy give way to the insight of dialectics, research in any discipline can gain 'real positive knowledge of the world'.[4] The phrase sounds like an echo of Comte.[5] Historians, for instance, are capable of establishing incontrovertible truth about the past. Like Buckle or Taine, Engels believed that historical research would lay bare a pattern of progress, 'the history of the development of society'.[6] There could be a science of man. Engels recognized that there is a problem in discerning the 'scientific' laws that apply in human affairs. Men do not appear to act solely according to laws, for they pursue consciously determined goals. Yet he was sure this problem could be surmounted.[7] History is entirely analagous to nature as an object of study, according to Engels, for the two are integrally related. Engels went beyond Marx in approximating his views to those of contemporary theorists of positivism.

Yet Engels shifted the emphasis in Marxism less far towards positivism than some younger Marxist writing in the last years of his life around 1890. Their 'most amazing rubbish', as Engels called it, asserted that the economic side of life alone determined all other aspects of human existence.[8] In the mode of production they saw cause, in everything else effect. Engels was protected from thinking so simplistically in terms of cause and effect because of his version of Hegelianism. He discerned a dynamic interaction between forces in history, not a mechanical abstraction. 'What these gentlemen all lack', he wrote, 'is dialectics.'[9] They were applying by rote a central

4. Engels, 'Feuerbach and the End of Classical German Philosophy', Marx and Engels, *Selected Works*, 2, p. 331.
5. *Cf.* above, p. 82.
6. Engels, 'Feuerbach and the End of Classical German Philosophy', Marx and Engels, *Selected Works*, 2, p. 353.
7. *Cf.* below, pp. 154f.
8. Engels to J. Bloch, 21–22 September 1890, Marx and Engels, *Selected Works*, 2, p. 444.
9. Engels to C. Schmidt, 27 October 1890, *Selected Works*, 2, p. 450.

principle common to Marx and Engels, the priority of material conditions in shaping the life of society, and did not recognize with both men that any epoch is formed by all the factors at work in it.

> Without making oneself ridiculous (wrote Engels), it would be a difficult thing to explain in terms of economics the existence of every small state in Germany, past and present, or the origin of the High German consonant permutations. . .[1]

Engels would accept no single-cause determinism. He applied a dictum of Marx to 'Marxists' who did do so: 'All I know is that I am not a Marxist.'[2]

Engels elaborated his own view of how factors interacted in history in a series of letters written in the 1890s. He rejected economic reductionism.

> According to the materialist conception of history, the *ultimately* determining element in history is the production and reproduction of real life. More than this neither Marx nor I have ever asserted. Hence if somebody twists this into saying that the economic element is the *only* determining one, he transforms that proposition into a meaningless, abstract, senseless phrase.[3]

Marx and he had been bound in their political writings to lay chief stress on the derivation of political, legal, philosophical and religious ideas and practices from the economic basis, but they had not supposed that their form was derived directly. Non-economic spheres develop their own internal dynamic. The further a particular sphere lies from the sphere of production, the greater relative independence it exhibits. Thus whereas trade patterns follow production patterns closely, philosophy and religion are far less immediately dependent on the changes in the mode of production.[4] Moreover politics, law, philosophy and religion in turn affect economic developments.[5] Engels therefore tried to combat the tendencies that were becoming increasingly apparent in his last years to apply the materialist conception of history as a rigid formula. His criticisms were directed

1. Engels to J. Bloch, 21–22 September 1890, *Selected Works*, 2, p. 443.
2. Engels to C. Schmidt, 5 August 1890, *Selected Works*, 2, p. 441.
3. Engels to J. Bloch, 21–22 September 1890, *Selected Works*, 2, p. 443.
4. Engels to C. Schmidt, 27 October 1890, *Selected Works*, 2, pp. 445–50.
5. Engels to F. Mehring, 14 July 1893, *Selected Works*, 2, p. 452.

against those 'whom it serves as an excuse for *not* studying history'.[6] He himself was responsible for making Marxism more of a dogmatic worldview with positivist leanings, but he resisted those who were taking the process further.

THE TRADITION OF MARXIST THEORISTS

The next generation of theorists conceived their task in a way similar to Engels. They would systematize and disseminate the theories of Marx. For all of them this entailed restating and defending historical materialism in particular, since both they and their opponents recognized Marx's theory of history as the kernel of his thought. Thus the Germans Franz Mehring and Karl Kautsky wrote respectively *On Historical Materialism* (1893) and *The Materialist Conception of History* (1927) and the Italian Antonio Labriola composed a series of *Essays on the Materialistic Conception of History* (1896). Most influential at a theoretical level, however, was the Russian Georgy Plekhanov, whose writings played a decisive role in the conversion of Lenin to Marxism.[7] His chief work, *The Development of the Monist View of History* (1895), is a rebuttal of the criticism that Marxism is a form of economic determinism. He shows that Marxists allow for the influence of politics and mass psychology on economic development.[8] Like Engels, Plekhanov rejects other misrepresentations of the Marxist case. He demonstrates with considerable erudition that although Marxists see human behaviour as susceptible to description in terms of law, they do not fail to recognize the creative role of individuals in history.[9] He argues that Marxism does not arbitrarily isolate 'factors' that influence the historical process, but points to the 'one history, the history of their own social relations' determined by the productive forces.[1] And Plekhanov ventures to correct other Marxists, as when he claims that Labriola

6. Engels to C. Schmidt, 5 August 1890, *Selected Works*, 2, p. 441.
7. Jordan, *Dialectical Materialism*, p. 183.
8. Georgy Plekhanov, *The Development of the Monist View of History* (1895: Moscow, 1956), pp. 200–12.
9. Georgy Plekhanov, *The Role of the Individual in History* (1898: London, 1940).
1. Georgy Plekhanov, *The Materialist Conception of History* (1897: London, 1940), p. 60.

attributes too much significance to race in the creation of ideology.[2] In these controversies Plekhanov frequently uses illustrations drawn from history and reveals a familiarity with contemporary developments in historical method across the whole of Europe. He was very much a historian protesting against any suggestion that Marxism impoverishes historiography.

Yet at the same time Plekhanov was contributing to the process of defining Marxist orthodoxy. Even if in later years he himself became suspect, in his own day he helped to delimit what he was the first to describe as 'dialectical materialism'.[3] His interests did not lie in the field of natural science, but he stressed more than Engels the bond between the theory of history and the theory of the natural world. He pinned more precisely on the notion of 'contradiction' as an explanation of the process of flux discerned by Engels in both nature and history. Contradiction is to be found, according to Plekhanov, supremely in the struggle for existence. Darwin had discovered the struggle for existence in the environment of nature; Marx had discovered a similar struggle, the class struggle, in the environment of history. 'That is why one can say that Marxism is Darwinism in its application to social science . . .'[4] History became a branch of evolution. This cosmology was a far cry from the simplicity of Marx's own view of human history as response to felt needs, even though Plekhanov had capably defended the practical application of this view from misunderstandings. Plekhanov resisted over-rigid interpretations of Marxist history itself, but at the same time propagated a more dogmatic conception of the place of history in a Marxist worldview.

In the generation of theorists that succeeded Plekhanov and his contemporaries, attention shifted away from history to economic and political analysis. The years before and after the Russian revolution of 1917 demanded the making of history rather than concern with its nature. Nikolai Bukharin, one of Lenin's lieutenants who published a *Theory of Historical Materialism* in 1921, was an exception, but Lenin himself was more typical in studying Russian and international capitalism and writing short works on the political demands of the hour. Lenin commented that times had changed since Marx

2. *Ibid.*, p. 25.
3. Jordan, *Dialectical Materialism*, p. 184.
4. Plekhanov, *Monist View*, p. 274 n.

and Engels had laid stress on *historical* materialism rather than historical *materialism*.[5] Now he had to insist on the importance of materialism rather than a particular understanding of history. Consequently he went further along the road travelled by Engels and Plekhanov in grounding Marxist theory of history in a broader philosophy of the world. Materialism for Lenin meant essentially epistemological realism, the belief that what is perceived is real.[6] Materialism in history, on Lenin's view, is deducible from that more fundamental realism - although in what way is not entirely clear. Marxist history is presented in Lenin's mature works as part of a self-consistent and incontrovertible system that all loyal party members must embrace. The party line on the nature of history was defined even more closely by Lenin's successor as ruler of Russia, Joseph Stalin. His own *Dialectical and Historical Materialism* (1938) was less a theoretical exploration than a handbook of orthodoxy in this area. Through the agency of the Third International it was guaranteed that similar views would be expressed by representatives of Communist parties outside Russia. The most capable statement of the mainstream Marxist view in English was *Historical Materialism* (1953) by Maurice Cornforth. It well reflected the way in which Marxist theory had developed since Engels by treating the subject in the second volume of a trilogy on *Dialectical Materialism*.

Contemporary with the emergence of a Marxism that toed the ideological line there developed a tradition of thought far less constrained by pressures to conform. This phenomenon has been styled 'Western Marxism' both to differentiate it from the Stalinism that emanated from Russia and to draw attention to the roots of most of its theorists in western Europe. In face of the failure of Communist revolutions outside Russia following the First World War, Western Marxists characteristically withdrew from a political activity that seemed futile and devoted themselves primarily to philosophy. In Italy Antonio Gramsci, eliminated from politics by imprisonment, generated a theory that was to become widely influential half a century later explaining the non-revolutionary attitude of the proletariat as a result of 'cultural hegemony' exercised by the

5. V. I. Lenin, 'Materialism and Empirio-Criticism' (1909), K. Marx, F. Engels and V. I. Lenin, *On Historical Materialism: A Collection* (Moscow, 1972), p. 437.
6. *Ibid.*, p. 445.

ruling class.[7] In Germany the Frankfurt school similarly turned to the elaboration of theory. Founded at the University of Frankfurt in 1923 to promote Marxist studies, an Institute of Social Research functioned there until forced to move to the United States following the Nazi coup of 1933, but returned to Frankfurt in 1950.[8] Although its first director had been a historian, it was guided from 1930 by Max Horkheimer into a concern with social theory. The school early followed its Hungarian associate, the literary critic Georg Lukács, in recognizing the cruciality of the Hegelian influence on Marx.[9] It also perceived the importance in Marx's thought of the human condition. Members of the school advocated Marxism with a human face long before the Prague spring of 1968, but its realization was felt to be unlikely. Consequently the Frankfurt school tended to pessimism about the course of history. This tendency was reinforced by the school's favourable estimate of writers from the heyday of German historicism. Horkheimer and his colleague Theodor Adorno drew especially on Schelling to develop the view that man's growing ascendancy over nature is not a matter of progress but has led to greater oppression. These writers generated a correspondingly unfavourable estimate of the Enlightenment.[1] Walter Benjamin, another colleague, imagines the course of events as a massive catastrophe that strews wreckage at the feet of the angel of history, who is blown by a storm:

> This storm irresistibly propels him into the future to which his back is turned, while the pile of debris before him grows skyward. This storm is what we call progress.[2]

So vivid an image was born of frustration at the apparent impossibility of attaining the goals of Karl Marx. Progress was commonly dismissed as a hallucination.

No such reservations about the future have troubled recent Marxist theorists in Russia. V. Kelle and M. Kovalson, in a handbook on

7. Antonio Gramsci, *Letters from Prison*, ed. Lynne Lawner (London, 1975), pp. 42f.
8. Martin Jay, *The Dialectical Imagination: A History of the Frankfurt School and the Institute for Social Research, 1923–1950* (London, 1973), pp. 10, 29, 286.
9. Georg Lukács, *History and Class Consciousness* (1923: London, 1971), pp. xliii-xlvi.
1. Anderson, *Western Marxism*, pp. 81f.
2. Walter Benjamin, *Illuminations* (London, 1970), p. 260.

Historical Materialism published in 1973 for western consumption, trumpet their confidence in progress. The pattern in history is defined as 'a forward movement, a movement along an upgrade leading from a lower state to a higher one'.[3] This view, which contrasts with seeing development as 'cyclical movement along a circle' or as Providence steadily working to achieve some goal for history, was first proclaimed, say the authors, 'by the enlighteners of the 18th century'.[4] Each social formation develops according to laws, although these laws should not be imposed on history (as was done 'by bourgeois sociologists like Herbert Spencer') but discovered in the historical process itself.[5] Distinctive Marxist elements are introduced. The criterion of social progress is the stage reached by the development of the productive forces; the motive power of progress is 'antagonism' (or contradiction); and 'in our epoch the general progressive tendency for social conditions to change is determined as advance towards socialism and communism'.[6] Yet the overall framework is the idea of progress. Marxism-Leninism is presented as a scientific analysis of social development. Denials of the idea by western non-Marxists are explained as a consequence of 'the obvious signs of decline of the capitalist formation (world wars, insoluble contradictions, *etc.*)'.[7] Even the Moscow English-language publishing house calls itself 'Progress Publishers'. In contemporary Soviet literature the process that began with Engels of closing the gap between Marxism and the idea of progress has reached a fresh high point. Recent Western Marxism sees little hope in the future; recent Soviet Marxism sees a great deal.

MARXIST HISTORIOGRAPHY

There was a dearth of applications of Marxist theory to the writing of history until the twentieth century. Engels in the 1890s still used to draw attention to Marx's short study of the French revolution of 1848, *The Eighteenth Brumaire of Louis Bonaparte* (1852), as a

3. V. Kelle and M. Kovalson, *Historical Materialism: An Outline of Marxist Theory of Society* (Moscow, 1973), p. 303.
4. *Ibid.*, pp. 303, 311.
5. *Ibid.*, p. 310.
6. *Ibid.*, pp. 307, 312.
7. *Ibid.*, p. 306.

model of historiography.[8] At the turn of the century there were pioneer works by German Marxists: Eduard Bernstein wrote on the English revolution of the seventeenth century, Franz Mehring on aspects of German history and Karl Kautsky on such themes as the radical Reformation.[9] Surprising omissions nevertheless remained. In the wake of the Russian Revolution it was realized that there was no satisfactory brief sketch of Russian history from the Marxist standpoint. M. N. Pokrovsky, who had already written a number of longer works including the four-volume *Russian History from the Earliest Times* (1910–14), composed a *Short History of Russia* (1920) to fill the gap.[1] Pokrovsky dominated Russian historiography and academic life generally from the revolution until his death in 1932. The training of Russia's first cohort of Marxist historians was in his hands. 'History is the politics of the past,' ran his creed, 'without which one is unable to practise politics of the present.'[2] Heroized in his lifetime, Pokrovsky was sharply criticized after his death. With some justice he was charged with 'legal Marxism', a mechanistically applied economic determinism that neglected what Engels had insisted on – the reciprocal interaction of ideology with material relations.[3] Fault was found with his periodization, for it suggested that Russia had experienced a more advanced capitalist economy than the party line admitted.[4] And he was tarred with the brush of 'cosmopolitanism' for failing to stress the achievements of the Russian people.[5] The last charge was a corollary of the whipping up of national feeling by Stalin from the mid-1930s. The fate of Pokrovsky's reputation is a sign of the domination of history, as of all disciplines, by Stalinism. Despite the relative relaxation of control over historiography in Russia since Stalin's death, there has been no

8. *E.g.* Engels to J. Bloch, 21–22 September 1890, Marx and Engels, *Selected Works*, 2, p. 444.
9. Eduard Bernstein, *Cromwell and Communism* (1895: London, 1930). Franz Mehring, *Absolutism and Revolution in Germany, 1525–1848* (1892–1910: London, 1975). Karl Kautsky, *Communism in Central Europe at the Time of the Reformation* (1894: London, 1897).
1. A. G. Mazour, *The Writing of History in the Soviet Union* (Stanford, Calif., 1971), pp. 8ff.
2. M. N. Pokrovsky, *Istoricheskaia nauka i borba klassov* (Moscow, 1933), p. 360, quoted by *ibid.*, p. 11.
3. Mazour, *The Writing of History in the Soviet Union*, pp. 14, 361.
4. *Ibid.*, pp. xiv, 15, 20.
5. *Ibid.*, pp. 15ff.

sign of the emergence of a historian of a stature comparable to that of Pokrovsky.

Outside Russia and her Communist satellites, probably the greatest impact of Marxist history has been in France. The Marxist interpretation of the French Revolution as a bourgeois uprising against a feudal nobility in particular has attained the status of historical orthodoxy. Jean Jaurès, the leading French Social Democrat, began the tradition with his *Histoire socialiste de la révolution française* (1901–04) in which he complains that the revolution had been isolated as a political event from its economic background.[6] Perhaps the greatest contribution to the Marxist interpretation was made by Georges Lefebvre in a series of books beginning with his *Paysans du Nord* of 1924. Lefebvre's pupil Albert Soboul, whose most distinguished book was *Les sans-culottes parisiens en l'an II* (1958), is the chief contemporary protagonist of the Marxist view.[7] It is instructive to note the ground occupied by Soboul's critics. François Furet and Denis Richet in *La Révolution* (1965–66) argue that the interpretation of the revolution as a 'feudal against bourgeois' class struggle misrepresents the remarkable unity of late eighteenth-century French educated society, in which nobles and bourgeois intermingled freely. They take issue with the Marxist contention that the classes were distinct and antagonistic. Richet nevertheless agrees with Soboul that capitalism originated in France before 1789, but holds that the bourgeois class did not come to power until the late nineteenth century. One of the chief opponents of the Marxist interpretation, that is to say, entirely accepts the validity of Marxist categories like capitalism and the bourgeois class. Furet, the other opponent, has taken a step even nearer to the Marxists. He takes Soboul to task for vulgarizing Marxism by replacing the mode of production with the class struggle as its central feature. The right application of Marxism has become a matter of concern to its critics.[8] To a quite remarkable extent the debate about the French Revolution takes place on Marxist premises.

In Britain Marxism has been rather less prepared to mould

6. G. G. Iggers, *New Directions in European Historiography* (Middletown, Conn., 1975), p. 146.
7. Geoffrey Ellis, 'The "Marxist Interpretation" of the French Revolution', *The English Historical Review*, 93 (1978), p. 353.
8. *Ibid.*, pp. 363–66.

historical debate and rather more content to contribute to it. The explanation is probably that British historians have usually treated Marxism, in the phrase of Christopher Hill, as a technique of analysis, not a dogma.[9] Marx would no doubt have approved. The effect has been to encourage tendencies already at work in British historiography, especially those promoted by R. H. Tawney, a Christian socialist for whom Marxism was an irrelevance.[1] Recognition of the importance of economic history, as in Tawney's *The Agrarian Problem in the Sixteenth Century* (1912), and of the social influences on human thinking, as in his *Religion and the Rise of Capitalism* (1926), would have taken place had Marxism never existed. Yet there have been historians more or less committed to Marxism, among whom the most distinguished has perhaps been E. P. Thompson, the author of *The Making of the English Working Class* (1963), who left the Communist Party in 1956 over the suppression of the Hungarian uprising. A younger generation of Marxist scholars has displayed its colours most openly. Foremost among them is Perry Anderson, whose *Passages from Antiquity to Feudalism* (1974) and *Lineages of the Absolutist State* (1974) analyse the broad sweep of European history from Pericles to Louis XIV with great virtuosity. In the writings of Anderson and his contemporaries British Marxist historiography, still strongly empirical but more obviously immersed in theoretical categories, has attained a new maturity.

The method of a historian shaped by Marxism has seldom been analysed more trenchantly than when in 1975 the American scholar J. H. Hexter subjected the works of Christopher Hill to scrutiny in *The Times Literary Supplement*. Hill, perhaps the most prestigious of British seventeenth-century historians, was taken to task for his techniques of 'source-mining' (extracting quotations on a narrowly defined subject) and 'compulsive lumping' (fitting the evidence into a grand thesis). In the 1940s Hill had been the up-and-coming Marxist historian in Britain. By 1975, however, he had long since ceased to be a mainstream Communist, and Hexter dismissed the idea that his method could be a hangover from his earlier Marxist

9. Christopher Hill, 'Marxism and History', *The Modern Quarterly*, new series, 3 (1948), p. 52.
1. *Cf.* D. W. Bebbington, 'R. H. Tawney as a Historian', *Christian Graduate*, 25 (1972).

commitment.[2] Yet in the exchange that followed battle was joined over whether or not it can be assumed that ideology reflects changes in the mode of production, a central Marxist axiom. Hill declared that, 'Capitalism is in fact with us today, as it was not in the Middle Ages; and Ideas have changed accordingly'.[3] Hexter took exception to the word 'accordingly', criticizing it as a clear instance of lumping.[4] E. J. Hobsbawm, an eminent Marxist economic historian, contributed a letter defending the assumption that ideas change in accordance with economic developments.[5] The validity of the Marxist view of history was at issue. But in the low-key ideological debates peculiar to the Anglo-Saxon academic world the nub of the controversy was not made explicit. The approach of Marxist historians in Britain has hitherto been refined and gentlemanly, even self-effacing.

ASSESSMENT OF THE MARXIST VIEW

The question dividing Hill and Hexter demands attention in any assessment of historical materialism. Does the way people gain their living mould their ideas? The view of Marx, it has already been established, was not that the mode of production follows some predetermined path, with ideology reflecting its inexorable course. The Marxist view cannot justly be branded as fatalist. Nor, as Engels was at pains to point out, should Marxists hold that economic factors determine ideological developments to the exclusion of any influence of ideas over economics. The relationship between the two is reciprocal, or, as Engels put it, 'dialectical'. Yet there remains the Marxist belief that change in the mode of production is the prime motor of all that happens in the fields of law, politics, philosophy and religion. That man's devices for satisfying his material needs have affected all these fields can hardly be doubted. Law has often been enacted to protect private interests in agriculture and industry; and imagery of the market-place was much over-used as a vehicle

2. J. H. Hexter, 'The Burden of Proof', *The Times Literary Supplement*, 24 October 1975, pp. 1251f.
3. Christopher Hill to the editor, *The Times Literary Supplement*, 7 November 1975, p. 1333.
4. J. H. Hexter to the editor, *The Times Literary Supplement*, 28 November 1975, p. 1419.
5. E. J. Hobsbawm to the editor, *The Times Literary Supplement*, 12 December 1975, p. 1489.

for doctrinal exposition by nineteenth-century preachers. The crux of the matter, however, lies in whether or not the many-sided cultural achievement of man can be explained in terms of production alone as 'the ultimately determining element in history'.[6]

It is difficult, first of all, to believe that great works of art simply reflect – however remotely – the way men labour for food, clothing and shelter. Marxism offers little explanation of the timeless appeal of Shakespeare to people in societies with entirely different modes of production. Nor, more importantly for our purposes, does it explain why artistic achievements took place when they did. There have been attempts to identify the structure of patronage as the explanatory factor. This does suggest why Shakespeare included so many scenes of low comedy (to appeal to the 'groundlings' among his potential audiences), but it does not go so far as to show why a man should have the genius to compose *King Lear* at the turn of the seventeenth century. Historicism, for all its weaknesses, can at least offer an explanation in terms of the reflection of artistic ideals. It is difficult, though, to see how the economic development of society can be seen as the ultimately determining factor behind artistic achievement.[7] Secondly, many bodies of ideas like nationalism cannot be explained satisfactorily on Marxist premises. Marx himself supposed that capitalism would foster a spirit of international solidarity, but national feeling won triumphs in his own day (in Germany and Japan, for instance) and has continued to play a major part in world affairs in the twentieth century.[8] Nationalism has been glossed as something like an imposition on the people to divert them from revolutionary struggle, but such an interpretation does scant justice to the popular roots of patriotic ardour. It is demonstrably wrong in cases such as Poland, where Communist rule has not mitigated nationalism. Thirdly, there is the problem for Marxists that ideas can stir people to action even when their economic interests point another way. Thus it has been convincingly shown that the abolition of the slave trade in 1807 was not the result of the declining profitability of West Indian plantations (as the Marxist interpretation of Eric Williams had alleged) but a consequence of Enlight-

6. Engels to J. Bloch, 21–22 September 1890, *Selected Works*, 2, p. 443.
7. *Cf.* Gorden Leff, *The Tyranny of Concepts: A Critique of Marxism* (London, 1969), pp. 167–74.
8. Anderson, *Western Marxism*, pp. 114f.

enment and evangelical humanitarianism.[9] It seems evident, therefore, that the priority given by Marx to production as an all-embracing explanatory factor was mistaken. His view was, after all, an intuition arising from a desire to rebut Hegel. Historical materialism was not the result of mature reflection on world history, but the fruit of reaction against a particular idealist philosophy.

Because the structure of authentic Marxism was a response to its Hegelian background, it drew largely on Hegel's own sources for its view of history. Its yoking together of elements from the idea of progress and from historicism opens it to the criticisms already made of both. Although like the idea of progress it claims to offer hope for the future, the hope is always deferred. The highest fulfilment for man is only striving for posterity. Furthermore, individuals in the present may have to sacrifice themselves for the sake of those to come. In the hands of the powerful such a doctrine can sanction the elimination of any who do not concur in the chosen path to the future. The Marxist worldview was sterile in the face of Stalinist tyranny. Marxism drew from historicism on the other hand its relativism of standards. Men are so moulded by their time and place as to be incapable of attaining values that are unequivocally right. Although Marx criticized capitalism from a moral standpoint, he held that morality in bourgeois society functions as an instrument of class oppression. Moral judgments therefore lack an objective foundation, at least until the coming of socialism. Similarly Engels delighted in his rejection of absolute truth.[1] Marxism has been left with no moral standard by which to assess historical events. The gauge of progress has to be non-moral, such as the degree of production achieved, according to contemporary Soviet theory; or else, if there is no standard by which to assess progress, the whole notion of progress dissolves, as among the theorists of Western Marxism. In either case, the assurance of a future where morality is upheld fades. The Marxist view of history invites man to an uncertain hope.

9. Roger Anstey, *The Atlantic Slave Trade and British Abolition, 1760–1810* (London, 1975), esp. pp. 53, 91–235.
1. Engels, 'Feuerbach and the End of Classical German Philosophy', Marx and Engels, *Selected Works*, 2, p. 331.

7 The philosophy of historiography

'[There is a] justification of history as a search for concrete causes . . .'

M. M. Postan, *Fact and Relevance: Essays on Historical Method.*

'An historical interpretation grows the more barren the more it imposes causal relations on its protean subject matter. The more profound our historical insight, the less use we have for so-called causal explanations.'

Oswald Spengler, *The Decline of the West*, as translated by J. H. Huizingar, *Dutch Civilisation in the Seventeenth Century and Other Essays.*

In the twentieth century, Marxists have been remarkable for urging that an understanding of the historical process should shape the way in which history is written. It has been far more common to say that philosophies of history should not influence historiography – often on the ground that they have no claim on our attention at all. Philosophy of history done in the manner of Hegel or Marx, the depiction of grand patterns in the past, has been dismissed as arbitrary and unwarranted theorizing. It is categorized, following the terminology of the philosopher C. D. Broad, as 'speculative philosophy of history'.[1] Such speculation, it is often assumed, can be treated as a curiosity left over from more metaphysically inclined ages and is not a matter worthy of serious attention in the present. Yet there has been growing interest in what is called the 'critical philosophy of history', the scrutiny of how historians write. It is 'critical' because it criticizes the process of composing history. The activity is normally undertaken by philosophers rather than by historians, and is often accorded a place in the curriculum of philosophical studies in British universities. Its name is perhaps unnecessarily opaque. Philosophical reflection on what historians do

1. W. H. Walsh, *An Introduction to Philosophy of History* (London, 1967), p. 16.

explains itself better when it is called 'the philosophy of historiography'.

Writers in this field usually appear to be making dispassionate analyses, uninfluenced by other theorists. Yet their statements are largely formed by two contrasting ways of looking at the subject – two ways which themselves have a history. Their ideas can be recognized as growing to a surprising extent out of the two traditions that were discussed in chapters four and five. The two schools of thought about historiography are rooted in the alternative worldviews which emerged in the eighteenth and early nineteenth centuries, one being associated with the Enlightenment and the other being thrown up in the romantic era. Contemporary philosophy of historiography shows traces either of the positivism that was so clearly related to the idea of progress or of the idealism in whose atmosphere historicism was born and sustained. More often than not such writers show no awareness of being aligned with alternative traditions of thought. But when they philosophize about historical method without an appreciation of the background of their views, it does not mean that they are relatively free from influences deeply embedded in the past. On the contrary, it is likely to mean that they have not heard of previous criticisms levelled against ideas similar to their own and so that they offer faithful copies of the doctrines of their predecessors. Whether they realize it or not, contemporary philosophers of historiography display traits inherited from earlier schools of thought.

This debt to the past reveals that opinions about historiography are grounded in convictions about the historical process. Philosophers of historiography may not consciously entertain ideas about the significance of world history. Such ideas, however, are implicit in the bond between today's schools of thought about how history is written and past schools of thought about how history is made. It follows that C. D. Broad's division of the philosophy of history into 'speculative' on the one hand and 'critical' on the other is not as sharp as it may at first sight appear. The critical is an offshoot of the speculative. Philosophy cannot safely ignore questions about the significance of the historical process while concentrating on such technicalities as the method of historical explanation. It is of course true that philosophers may choose to pay greatest attention to these technical topics, but they need to be aware that such matters cannot be divorced from broader enquiries about the patterns in history.

The philosophy of historiography is a branch of traditional interest in the meaning of history.

POSITIVISTS AND IDEALISTS

The philosophy of historiography deals with a range of difficult questions. What is the role of causation in historical explanation? How detached should the historian be from his subject-matter? What part does intuition play in the historian's grasp of the past? The variety and complexity of such questions dictate that there are differences, often quite marked, between writers who hold similar positions. Yet answers to the controversial questions in the field divide writers broadly into two camps. There is a strong tendency for a given writer to belong to one or other of the two schools of thought that inherit the traditions of the Enlightenment or of romanticism. Different labels have been proposed for the two camps: realists against idealists, positivists against anti-positivists or the logical-empiricist approach against the hermeneutic-dialectical approach.[2] It will be convenient here to call them positivists and idealists.

The positivist school draws most of its support from the Anglo-Saxon world. It holds that there are regularities that can be established in human behaviour. The technique of the historian is consequently a matter of empirical investigation to establish general laws. There is no method peculiar to history. Positivists in modern historiographical debate would not wish to endorse the classic positivism held by Comte in the nineteenth century.[3] Few contemporary positivists would wish to go so far as to agree with Buckle or Taine about historical method.[4] Yet their conviction of the power of empirical method – of fact-finding and generalizing – justifies their being called positivists. This remains true even though some, like Sir Karl Popper, would repudiate the label 'positivist' on the ground that they reject opinions that they regard as basic to positiv-

2. Harriet Gilliam, 'The Dialectics of Realism and Idealism in Modern Historiographic Theory', *History and Theory*, 15 (1976), pp. 232f. P. L. Gardiner, 'The Concept of Man as Presupposed by the Historical Studies', *The Proper Study* (Royal Institute of Philosophy Lectures, 4, 1969–1970) (London, 1971), pp. 15–18. Gerard Radnitzky, *Contemporary Schools of Metascience* (Göteborg, 1971), pp. xv–xix.
3. *Cf.* above, pp. 82f.
4. *Cf.* above, p. 87.

ism.[5] A belief that history uses essentially the same methods as other social sciences is the common bond of the positivist school.

Idealists, whose stronghold is in Germany, believe on the contrary that historical method is unique. Whereas a scientist aims to formulate general laws, the historian concentrates on illuminating particular individuals and events. Many advocates of an idealist position would go so far as to claim that human beings cannot be studied by the methods of science at all. Human actions are charged with intention, which cannot be explained in terms of scientific categories. Idealism in this sense cannot be equated with the idealism of Kant or of any other philosopher.[6] Some writers about historiography who stand in the camp here called idealist, like R. G. Collingwood, have repudiated the term as a description of their own philosophical stance.[7] Yet they are idealist in the basic sense that they stress that men have ideas. That is what makes human beings distinctive; and that in turn makes the history of human affairs distinctive. A belief in the autonomy of history is the hallmark of the idealist school.

The controversy between positivists and idealists has impinged on the historical community in recent years in the form of the debate over the relation of history to sociology. A few historians have taken up their pens to contribute. Best known are probably the views of E. H. Carr, whose Trevelyan lectures at Cambridge in 1961 were published as *What is History?*, and its rebuttal by G. R. Elton in *The Practice of History* (1967). Carr argues, among other points, that 'the more sociological history becomes, and the more historical sociology becomes, the better for both'.[8] Elton replies that the two disciplines are intrinsically different:

> History may fairly concern itself with past social relationships, and the historian may often be well advised to count heads; but it should always be recognized that, since history must analyse and relate the story of past change and must concern itself with particular people as well as categories, historical studies derived

5. Ralf Dahrendorf, 'Remarks on the Discussion of the Papers by Karl R. Popper and Theodor W. Adorno', T. W. Adorno *et al.*, *The Positivist Dispute in German Sociology* (London, 1976), pp. 125f.
6. *Cf.* above, pp. 100f.
7. R. G. Collingwood, *An Autobiography* (London, 1939), p. 56.
8. E. H. Carr, *What is History?* (Harmondsworth, 1964), p. 66.

> from sociological influence can never be more than a small part of the whole enterprise.[9]

The divergence of opinion was given a sharp edge both because the introduction of sociology as a new discipline was still a lively issue in the academic politics of Cambridge in the 1960s and because Elton took exception to the left-wing political implications that he discerned in Carr's view. But the issue was one of substance. Carr was adopting on this particular question the positivist stance that history has no distinctive method to separate it from sociology, a form of science. Elton, in stressing the concern of history with 'particular people', was expounding an aspect of the idealist case for the autonomy of history. The battle was fought over ground familiar to philosophers of historiography.

The same topic has occupied other historians in recent years. Alan Bullock, who was to achieve fame in the following year as the biographer of Hitler, was asked to write on 'The Historian's Purpose' shortly after the launching of the journal *History Today* in 1951. His central theme in the article is that the essential concern of the historian is not with the general propositions of the sociologist, but wtih individual events. 'His whole training teaches him to break down rather than build up generalizations, to bring the general always to the touchstone of particular, concrete instances.'[1] History therefore differs from sociology. The historian's attention to the particular, similar to that of the novelist or dramatist, can be more fruitful than the generalizations of the sociologist. Like Dostoyevsky or Shakespeare, the historian reveals a great deal about human nature that is beyond the reach of a technique that puts people in categories. Bullock was expounding a version of idealism. A quarter of a century later, the same writer, by now Lord Bullock and ex-Vice-Chanceller of Oxford, repeated his warning that history should not be treated as a social science. Individual decisions like that of Hitler to attack Russia in 1941 have enormous historical impact. Generalization, therefore, must not divert the historian from the traditional cultivation of an eye for the event, the person, the

9. G. R. Elton, *The Practice of History* (Sydney, 1967), p. 28.
1. Alan Bullock, 'The Historian's Purpose: History and Metahistory', *History Today* (February 1951), pp. 9f.

particular.[2] His message remained the same: history is not sociology. Perhaps unconsciously, Bullock was once more making out a case for idealism. The debate on the relation between history and sociology has done more in Britain than any other aspect of the subject to bring to the surface divergent views over the nature of historiography.

CONTRASTS BETWEEN POSITIVISTS AND IDEALISTS

Many other debates in the philosophy of historiography have been generated by the disagreement between positivists and idealists. It is therefore possible to analyse the central issues in this area in terms of their opposing viewpoints. The starting-place must be their contrasting attitudes to their subject-manner. Human beings, according to the positivist school, can be treated as subjects for inquiry in exactly the same way as the natural world. There is no reason in principle why methods developed for the investigation of soil, flowers or birds should not be applied to man. The task may prove harder, since man is a more complex phenomenon, but it is not essentially different. History is therefore to be regarded as one of the social sciences that imitate the techniques of the natural sciences. The idealists argue on the contrary that man must be treated in a different way from the natural world. Human beings differ not in degree but in kind from soil, flowers or birds, for they enjoy (or enjoyed) consciousness. Research must adapt itself to its subject-matter, and so human beings should be treated differently from the non-human world.[3] A distinctive historical method must be adopted for the study of man. Thus a positivist like the American C. G. Hempel can urge that the assimilation of historical method to the techniques of the natural sciences illustrates 'the methodological unity of empirical science'.[4] An idealist rejects this belief that there exists only a single method, in history as in all disciplines. For him history is unique.

The two schools are equally divergent on the issue of historical explanation. How does the historian explain events? The positivist answers that it is a matter of identifying causes. The factors leading

2. Lord Bullock, *Is History becoming a Social Science?* (Cambridge, 1977), pp. 13, 19f.
3. *E.g.* Jürgen Habermas, 'The Analytical Theory of Science and Dialectics', Adorno *et al.*, *The Positivist Dispute*, p. 134.
4. C. G. Hempel, 'The Function of General Laws in History', *Theories of History*, ed. Patrick Gardiner (Glencoe, Illinois, 1959), p. 356.

up to an event must be scrutinized in order to discover whether and to what extent they were responsible for it. Thus it can be established that economic rivalry was a cause of the First World War. There is scope for debate about the importance relative to other factors of economic rivalry, but that it was in a common-sense way a cause of the war few would doubt. The idealist, however, questions the whole concept of causation when applied to the human world. A lighted match can be the cause of a forest fire in the natural world, but human beings have ideas about what they want to do. Their actual intentions, not abstractions external to the human mind like economic rivalry, explain why events occur. History is about mental life. 'All history', wrote Collingwood, 'is the history of thought.'[5] Since historical agents think, their reasons for acting are qualitatively different from what can be captured in the language of causation. The positivist can reply that agents may misconceive their reasons for acting. Freud, he can claim, has shown as much. Hence human intentions constitute slippery ground for historical explanation. The positivist sees the identification of a range of causes, which may include an agent's motives, as a far surer path to historical truth. But the idealist remains unconvinced that human activity can in any intelligible sense be 'caused'.

A third area of disagreement is over the use of laws. The historian, according to the positivist school, can employ general laws in a way analagous to their use by a natural scientist. The laws in the historian's case are generalizations of a psychological or sociological kind that are not normally stated. Once preceding circumstances have been established, reference (often subconscious) to the generalization shows what event ensued. Thus a historian might say that drought and sandstorms in the 'dust-bowl' conditions of the American mid-west of the 1930s were the reasons why farmers migrated to California. He is assuming the general hypothesis that people tend to move to regions offering better conditions for agriculture.[6] The idealist school contends that this is a false account of historical procedure. The historian does not believe in laws stating that when certain necessary and sufficient conditions are fulfilled, events follow.

5. Collingwood, *An Autobiography*, p. 110.
6. This is the example supplied in the classic statement of this view by C. G. Hempel, 'The Function of General Laws in History', *Theories of History*, ed. Gardiner, pp. 349f.

His concern is not with regularities but with the unique. Human activity is too spontaneous to be subject to artificial generalizations. In a famous presentation of this case in 1894 Wilhelm Windelband, Rector of the University of Strasburg, distinguished the historical sciences from the natural sciences precisely because they do not aim to discover laws but to depict 'human lives in the full richness of their unique development, preserved in their living individuality'.[7] No laws govern how personalities express themselves. Positivists may concede that the elucidation of laws is not the historian's objective, and yet contrive to argue that law-like generalizations play a crucial role behind the scenes in history writing. The issue of the place of laws in historiography is another question that is unresolved.

Fourthly, there is the question of method. The positivist stands for empiricism. He means that the historian collects items of evidence which support a broader conclusion. The conclusion is accepted as true if its supporting evidence is relevant and non-trivial. It can be subjected to further investigation that will either continue to validate it or else reveal instances that show it to be false. The great advantage of this approach is that it permits 'inter-subjective testability'.[8] One scholar can investigate the conclusions of another on an agreed procedural basis. No such advantage is entailed by the idealist account of method. The historian's task, according to an idealist, is to recapture the mental world of past human beings. The task is achieved by a technique that can only be used in obtaining knowledge about the world of persons: 'understanding' *(Verstehen)*. It is the technique we use for knowing other persons in ordinary life, a form of imaginative appreciation. As such, it is both irreducible to a set of rules and private to each practising historian. The idealist can claim that his account is nearer to a description of what a historian actually does. Whereas he does not normally adopt any consistent form of empirical method, he does try to cultivate imaginative appreciation. Yet the technique of 'understanding' is all too open to the positivist charge that as a characterization of method it is far

7. Wilhelm Windelband, *Präludien, Aufsätze und Reden zur Philosophie und ihrer Geschichte* (7th and 8th edns, Tübingen, 1921), 2, p. 152, quoted by G. G. Iggers, *The German Conception of History: The National Tradition of Historical Thought from Herder to the Present* (Middletown, Conn., 1968), p. 149.
8. Sir Karl R. Popper, *The Logic of Scientific Discovery* (London, 1959), p. 47.

from rigorous. The claim to 'understand' seems close to the mystical. Once again, the two schools are divided over method.

A fifth area of divergence is over the theory of truth used in history. This is not a matter that much troubles positivists. They accept the common-sense view of what constitutes truth, usually called the correspondence theory. Aristotle formulated this view neatly: 'To say of what is that it is not, or of what is not that it is, is false, while to say of what is that it is, or of what is not that it is not, is true.'[9] Statements, that is to say, must correspond with reality. In history, a statement about the past must represent accurately what happened in the past. But such a view, according to idealists, is simplistic. We cannot know for certain, they claim, what is the reality of the human world in the present, let alone in the past. Our understanding of other people cannot be total, so that there is no reality within our grasp with which statements about people can correspond. Coherence must replace correspondence as the criterion of truth. A statement is true if it coheres with other statements that we can make. Napoleon, we say, was ambitious. The statement is true because we can also say that he rose to become Emperor, that he wished to conquer Europe and that he returned undaunted from Elba. To claim that Napoleon was ambitious fits in with our other beliefs about him. Idealists argue that parts of reality can be understood only in relation to the whole. The validity of an account depends on how well it makes sense of the totality of experience. This 'making sense' is the task of the human sciences, including history – a task analysed most notably by the German philosopher Hans-Georg Gadamer in his *Truth and Method* (1961). Idealist concern with the systematic application of the principle of coherence is commonly dismissed by positivists as an unnecessary enterprise, but it is the foundation of much contemporary theory about disciplines like history that take man for their object.

The question of how far the historian should write from a detached standpoint also divides positivists from idealists. Objectivity in the sense of dispassionate treatment of evidence can readily be defended on positivist grounds. History, according to the positivists, uses a method essentially no different from that of other disciplines. Hence the attitude of the historian should not differ from that of the natural

9. Aristotle, *Metaphysics*, 1011 b 26f., trans. W. D. Ross, *The Works of Aristotle Translated into English*, ed. J. A. Smith and W. D. Ross, 8 (Oxford, 1908).

scientist. History 'demands the same kind of dedication, the same ruthlessness, the same passion for exactness, as physics'.[1] There should be no sense of involvement with the subject-matter. This, however, the idealists deny outright. The historian must have empathy for his subject-matter. Since he writes about people, he must bring his experience of living among people to his work. He will try to identify himself with the human beings of the past just as he tries to identify himself with the human beings of his own day. 'Understanding', wrote Dilthey, 'is a rediscovery of the I in the Thou.'[2] Historical knowledge is a matter of personal engagement. Positivists criticize this position for its apparent preparedness to sacrifice the rigour of an academic discipline. Our grasp of the personalities we encounter in ordinary life is notoriously slight: how can we hope to use this frail tool to prise out historical truth? It is far better to try to analyse from a distance. Many idealists would reply that objectivity is properly not a matter of distancing oneself at all, but of treating the object of research in its own terms. Historical research cannot but deal with human beings as personalities, men and women of ideas, feelings and emotions. Detachment seems to the positivist to be the historian's goal; to the idealists it seems to be a misleading will-o'-the-wisp.

Underlying the division between the two camps is a fundamental philosophical issue, the debate between determinism and freewill. Are human beings free to act as they choose? The positivist case appears to lead to the conclusion that they are not. Some commentators would claim that the positivist use of the notion of cause implies a deterministic assessment of human behaviour. If an action is caused, it is not free. Even if positivists argue that this is to misconstrue the way in which the word 'cause' is used, it remains true that positivists are committed to the existence of laws. Only by means of laws can individual instances of behaviour be explained. If there are laws, then human action must conform to them. Accordingly a measure of prediction is possible. The future will follow the same laws as the past. All this implies determinism. Idealists therefore urge that they are the champions of human freedom. Theirs, they claim, is the method of examining a man's unconditioned actions

1. John Passmore, 'The Objectivity of History' (1958), *The Philosophy of History*, ed. Patrick Gardiner (London, 1974), p. 160.
2. H. P. Rickman, ed., *W. Dilthey: Selected Writings* (Cambridge, 1976), p. 208.

that are the outcome of his own intentions alone. Their rejection of laws is an assertion that each human being is free. The historian 'discovers the freedom of man as an historical agent'.[3] There are distinguished thinkers on both sides who do not concur in the conclusions of their colleagues. Popper, who stands broadly with the positivist school, is no friend of determinism; and Oakeshott, a leading idealist, considers historical events necessary.[4] Yet there is a general divergence between the positivists who entertain determinism and the idealists who uphold freewill.

THE BACKGROUND OF THE TWO SCHOOLS

The differences between the two schools have generated most of the controversies in the philosophy of historiography in the twentieth century. In each of the seven areas - subject-matter, explanation, the possibility of laws, method, the theory of truth, detachment and determinism - the issue has polarized theorists into positivists and idealists. The differences hang together. It is consistent for the positivist who holds that history's subject-matter does not render the discipline different in kind from that of the natural scientist to say that the historian can use the scientist's empirical method, the scientist's correspondence theory of truth and the scientist's detached technique. Similarly it is consistent for the idealist who holds that history's human subject-matter differs in kind from that of the natural scientist to defend a distinctive historical method of 'understanding', with its corollaries of the coherence theory of truth and a strong empathy for human beings. There is a stark dichotomy of standpoints on the whole range of issues. The question then arises of why in the philosophy of historiography so many of the battles should be fought out between only two camps. We might have expected to discover instead a large range of separate conflicts between thinkers of a wide variety of standpoints. The existence of the two schools of thought demands explanation. It can be explained in terms of their background.

Both schools are not simply the product of twentieth-century theorizing about history, but possess intellectual lineages going back

3. R. G. Collingwood, *The Idea of History* (London, 1946), p. 318.
4. Sir Karl R. Popper, *The Open Society and its Enemies* (London, 1962), 2, p. 85. Michael Oakeshott, *Experience and its Modes* (Cambridge, 1933), pp. 129f.

to the eighteenth century. Positivism descends from the idea of progress; idealism has its roots in historicism. The inheritance of the two schools is evident in their differing views of method. The empirical approach of the positivists reflects the philosophical climate of the eighteenth century that fostered the idea of progress. To investigate human behaviour by means similar to those of Newtonian science is still the pattern advocated by the positivists. There must be painstaking scrutiny of the evidence to establish whether or not individual instances permit a generalization. The task of contemporary scholars, according to the positivist philosophers, is exactly what was envisaged by the disciples of Newton and Locke two centuries ago, the creation of a science of man. Popper, perhaps the most sophisticated representative of a broadly positivist point of view, recognizes the antecedents of his viewpoint. 'I am an old representative of the Enlightenment', he declares, 'and a liberal – and even a pre-Hegelian one.'[5] The idealists, on the other hand, reveal their debt to historicism in their claim that 'understanding' is the essence of method. To understand human beings is to appreciate their qualities in the manner of Herder. It entails the use of imagination to conjure up the nature of the past, as Niebuhr did for ancient Rome. The idealist school looks for its inspiration not to the Enlightenment of Britain and France but to the romantic movement in Germany.

The continuity of positivism with the school of progress is not confined to the area of method. The same continuity is evident at the other points where positivism and idealism diverge. The positivist belief that history need not differ in approach from the natural sciences even though it takes human beings for its subject-matter is identical with an eighteenth-century premise. The Enlightenment likewise held that knowledge of the human world is in principle as attainable as knowledge of the natural world. The consequent positivist view that events involving people are as much *caused* as any happening in nature has been the normal assumption of those inheriting the Enlightenment worldview. It was upheld, for instance, by Comte, the high priest of positivism, as much as it is by contemporary positivists. Although the hope of Hume or Buckle that history might discover the laws governing human behaviour has now

5. Quoted by Dahrendorf, 'Remarks on the Discussion of the Papers by Karl R. Popper and Theodor W. Adorno', Adorno *et al.*, *The Positivist Dispute*, p. 129.

been transferred to psychology and sociology, it remains true that the positivist school believes that historiography is about laws. The eighteenth-century assumption of a correspondence theory of truth has been sustained down to contemporary positivists. Today's ideal of detachment in the historian can also be paralleled from the past. Acton wrote: 'The object is: objectiveness – get at things, without any disturbing, refraction-medium.'[6] And positivist leanings towards determinism recall the insistence of so many theorists of progress in the eighteenth and nineteenth centuries, with Condorcet at their head, that progress is inevitable. The characteristic features of the positivist school have been the standard implications of the idea of progress.

In a similar way idealist contentions about writing history coincide with traditional historicist views. Dilthey's case for the independence of history as the discipline that investigates man is a classic statement to which contemporary idealists still appeal. The idealist stress on human action being charged with ideas was already fully formulated by Wilhelm von Humboldt, the founder of the University of Berlin, in a lecture 'On the Historian's Task' delivered before the Prussian Academy of Sciences in 1821.[7] The rejection of laws of human development on the ground that actions are unique in their cultural settings was formulated even earlier, by Herder. Von Humboldt was voicing the idealist belief in coherence as the criterion of true history when he declared of the historian, 'Differently from the poet, but in a way similar to him, he must work the collected fragments into a whole.'[8] The doctrine of empathy was the stock-in-trade of historicists in the nineteenth century as much as it is of idealists in the twentieth. And the belief that human history shows man to be free goes back to historicist origins in Vico. Just as contemporary positivism has emerged from theories of progress, so contemporary idealism has emerged from historicism. It is not merely that in the two cases there happens to be an overlap of opinion. Rather, contemporary theorists of historiography are divided between two long-standing traditions of thought.

Although theorists frequently seem to be unconscious of standing

6. Acton Collection, Cambridge University Library, MS Add. 5692, f.30.
7. Wilhelm von Humboldt, 'On the Historian's Task', Leopold von Ranke, *The Theory and Practice of History*, ed. G. G. Iggers (Indianapolis, 1973), pp. 9f.
8. *Ibid.*, p. 6.

in a tradition, some do appeal to their predecessors. This is particularly true of participants in German controversies over the nature of the historical sciences. Gadamer, for instance, presents the case for the use of 'understanding' and all the other apparatus of the idealist school in a treatise that locates his own approach in a tradition consisting especially of Schleiermacher, Dilthey and Heidegger.[9] Debate in Germany can be conducted as a series of claims and counter-claims to be the true heirs of Kant.[1] Recognition of the historical background of the controversy is less common in the English-speaking world. Yet in Britain and America there are cases where discussion has been developed in terms of thinkers from the past. M. M. Postan, for instance, treats Adam Smith as the inspiration of economic history as a social science and Kant as the deplorable progenitor of idealist methodologies.[2] The distinguished American historian of ideas P. O. Kristeller, in protesting against the classification of history as a social science, both appeals to Dilthey and tempers Dilthey's views with those of his contemporary, the neo-Kantian philosopher Heinrich Rickert.[3] There are writers fully aware that the present-day division of opinion over the practice of history stretches back for two centuries.

MARXIST THEORY OF HISTORIOGRAPHY

A third group of analysts of historiography, not so far discussed in this chapter, is the most self-conscious about standing in a tradition – the tradition of Marx and Engels.[4] This school is emphatic on one of the issues separating positivists from idealists. Detachment, claim the Marxists, is impossible. The historian's social class forms his ideology and hence his approach to writing history. Detachment is even undesirable. A present-day historian ought to be committed to the cause of the proletariat. Beyond this issue, however, Marxists have been neither distinctive nor united in their views. One explan-

9. Hans-Georg Gadamer, *Truth and Method* (1961: London, 1975).
1. *E.g.* by K. O. Apel and K. R. Popper. Adorno *et al.*, *The Positivist Dispute*, pp. xxxiiif., 90.
2. M. M. Postan, *Fact and Relevance: Essays on Historical Method* (Cambridge, 1971), pp. 23, 11.
3. P. O. Kristeller, 'Some Problems of Historical Knowledge', *The Journal of Philosophy*, 58 (1961), pp. 98f.
4. There is an interesting Marxist analysis in G. S. Jones, 'The Pathology of English History,' *New Left Review*, 46 (1967).

ation of their lack of a consistent attitude is that they have paid greater attention to the historical process than to historiography. They have understandably been more concerned to vindicate the Marxist analysis of the past than to reflect on the nature of that analysis. Another explanation lies in the indebtedness of Marxism to the other two traditions of thought about history. Marx, as was seen in chapter six, derived much of his thinking from Hegel, who had blended elements drawn from theorists of progress with elements of historicism. The Marxist tradition from Marx down to the present day has inhabited an intellectual world where the other two traditions have continued in differing degrees to flourish. Marxist commentary on historiography has therefore been attracted towards either one or the other of the twin poles of positivism and idealism.

Marx himself seems to have accepted the positivist premise that man is as much a subject for science as is nature. He prophesied: 'Natural science will later comprise the science of man just as much as the science of man will embrace natural science; they will be one single science.'[5] There was therefore no inherent reason not to use empirical method in human studies like history, and many of his followers have felt free to do so. Yet on the other hand when Marx applies the word 'laws' to the historical process it is clear that his usage is not that of the positivists. Marxian laws refer not to universal generalizations about human behaviour but to trends in a particular social setting.[6] Present-day philosophers of historiography in the idealist camp, at least in Germany, describe laws in an identical way.[7] Marx drew on both positivist and idealist elements in the thought-world of his day. Since he left no treatise on the details of how to write history, the way in which the diverse elements should be combined has remained open for debate. Although Marx achieved something of a synthesis of the other two schools, the synthesis was unstable.

Engels pushed the centre of gravity in Marxism towards positivism. In his esteem for the achievements of natural science, he had no doubt that its generalizing method was applicable to man. He was, however, aware of the central idealist objection that history

5. *Karl Marx: Early Texts*, ed. David McLellan (Oxford, 1972), p. 154.
6. *Cf.* above, pp. 124f.
7. *E.g.* Jürgen Habermas, 'The Analytical Theory of Science and Dialectics', Adorno *et al.*, *The Positivist Dispute*, pp. 138f.

differs from nature because its subject-matter consists of thinking agents. The historian writes of 'men acting with deliberation or passion, working towards definite goals; nothing happens without a conscious purpose, without an intended aim.' [8] Hence, according to idealists, human activity must be described in its uniqueness. Engels rebutted the objection by arguing that when wills conflict in the flux of history, one intention nullifies another. Hence human intentions can be ignored and generalization about social affairs is legitimate. In history, as in nature, there are 'hidden laws and it is only a matter of discovering these laws'.[9] Engels reached an entirely positivist conclusion. The historian Plekhanov was more loyal to Marx than was Engels, for he discerned 'an antinomy, the first part of which was general laws, and the second part was the activities of individuals'.[1] Plekhanov, that is to say, argued that both general laws (as urged by positivists) and individuals (as urged by idealists) are makers of history. Indeed he added an intermediate category, the particular historical situation, as a third factor that was responsible for events in the historical process.[2] Plekhanov held a balance between the positivist and idealist positions. But it was Engels, not Plekhanov, who was to remain authoritative for the mainstream Marxist tradition.

The approximation of Marxist method in historical studies to positivism has won the day in contemporary Russia. There historiography has the task of establishing laws.[3] The dependence of a positivist philosophy of historiography on the idea of progress, usually tacit in English-language discussions, is made explicit in Russian historical theory. It is the laws of progress that historians are expected to analyse. In the Western Marxism that has broken free of Soviet domination, however, there has been a fusion with national philosophical traditions. In Germany this has given rise to the blend of Marxism and historicism characteristic of the Frankfurt school.[4] In that quarter have emerged some of the staunchest cham-

8. Frederick Engels, 'Ludwig Feuerbach and the End of Classical German Philosophy' (1886), Karl Marx and Frederick Engels, *Selected Works* (Moscow, 1951), 2, p. 354.
9. *Ibid.*
1. Georgy Plekhanov, *The Role of the Individual in History* (London, 1940), p. 56.
2. *Ibid.*, p. 59.
3. *Cf.* above, pp. 132f.
4. *Cf.* above, pp. 131f.

pions of what has been called in this chapter the idealist philosophy of historiography. It is perhaps odd that men in a Marxist tradition should defend an aspect of the idealism that Marx criticized in Hegel. Adorno of the Frankfurt school has admitted that he has been forced back from the standpoint of Marx to the position of the Young Hegelians.[5] Marxism has therefore been modified in opposite directions in Russia and Germany. Russian Marxist theory of historiography has veered towards positivism while German Marxist theory has gone so far towards idealism as to cease to be Marxist. Marxism has shown itself to be an impermanent means of bridging the gulf between the other two schools in the philosophy of historiography.

RESOLVING THE DEBATE

There remains a striking contrast between two ways of conceiving what the historian does. Apart from the deep roots of both positivism and idealism in the past, other factors help to reinforce the division. One factor is that different specialisms encourage historians to sympathize with one camp or the other. Economic historians are often attracted by a positivist stance. They take for granted that impersonal forces such as supply and demand exert a major influence over human destinies. Consequently they are sure that they can formulate law-like generalizations about behaviour and use them as tools of historical explanation. It is no accident that one of the most eminent exponents of the positivist viewpoint in Britain, Professor Postan, is an economic historian. The increasing use of quantitative methods in economic history, and their extension to fresh fields of social history, mean that more historians are inclined to treat human beings *en masse*, their actions as caused by external stimuli and their investigation as a matter of the application of the methods of social science. Such historians naturally incline to positivism. Others, however, tend in the opposite direction. Historians of art and of ideas usually see their subject-matter as the work of creative individuals whose achievement resists all classification in terms of laws. The historian of art feels bound to make an aesthetic response that seems close to what idealists call 'understanding'. The historian of ideas

5. Dahrendorf, 'Remarks on the Discussion of the Papers by Karl R. Popper and Theodor W. Adorno', Adorno *et al.*, *The Positivist Dispute*, p. 128. On the Young Hegelians, *cf.* above, p. 120.

interprets written texts in a way which he is likely to feel is similar to Dilthey's description of the process. Both are prone to reach a conclusion like that of P. O. Kristeller:

> The true meaning of history does not consist in any sociological laws . . ., nor in any expectation of any future progress or doom . . ., but in the intrinsic significance of the products of the human spirit that we are able to discover and to understand. [6]

Historians are shaped, more than many will admit, by their sub-disciplines. The effect is to strengthen the division of opinion over the nature of historiography.

A second factor having a similar effect is the interaction of views of historiography with political allegiance in its broadest sense. The idea of progress emerged in a reformist milieu, but historicism originated in the German reaction against that current of reform. The bonds between positivism and the left on the one hand and idealism and the right on the other have persisted to this day in the English-speaking world. Thus Professor Postan stands with the moderate left in England, but Professor Oakeshott is the philosopher of Conservatism. To favour close relations between history and sociology is still normally the view of the less traditionalist in British universities; to resist close relations is often the hallmark of the traditionalist. In Germany, however, the relationship between views on historical method and political opinions has been reversed. This is largely a consequence of the greater impact of Marxism in Germany. The fusion of Marxism with historicism has outflanked positivism. The fusion has generated 'critical theory', which is not only an anti-positivist philosophy of the human sciences but also offers a tool for the criticism of ideology. By unmasking whatever hinders the understanding (in the technical sense) of human affairs, critical theory is taken to have a practical role. To adopt critical theory is therefore a radical stance; to reject it in favour of a version of positivism is to stand with the German establishment. Thus an advocate of positivism censures Jürgen Habermas, a leading representative of the critical theory developed by the Frankfurt school, for expounding a form of left-wing irrationalism.[7] Political com-

6. Kristeller, 'Some Problems of Historical Knowledge', *The Journal of Philosophy*, 58 (1961), pp. 109f.
7. Hans Albert, 'The Myth of Total Reason', Adorno *et al.*, *The Positivist Dispute*, p. 189.

mitments are interwoven with views on historical theory, albeit in contrasting ways in different countries. There is less concern with resolving the central issues in the philosophy of historiography than with drowning the slogans of the other side.

There have nevertheless been attempts to penetrate beyond the impasse presented by the conflict of positivism and idealism. Hegel made one of the most thorough. Just as his philosophy of history drew on both the idea of progress and historicism, so his philosophy of historiography tried to combine the positivist and idealist standpoints. The positivist view that man must be described as part of a mechanistic world that operates according to laws is true at a certain level on Hegel's account. But the idealist view that man must be described as a free agent consciously seeking goals is also true at another and higher level. The idealist view therefore subsumes the positivist view, both denying and affirming it in typical Hegelian fashion.[8] Hegel regards the idealist standpoint as superior, as might be expected of the idealist philosopher *par excellence.* His analysis of historiography is affected by the idiosyncracies of his system, and so does not do justice to positivism. Yet it is evident that already in the early nineteenth century Hegel recognized the divergence in western thought between the two ways of approaching man's place in history and was attempting to reconcile them.

Another scheme for combining idealism with positivism was proposed by Max Weber, the German sociologist at the turn of the twentieth century whose thought towers over the subsequent development of social science. He argued that models of explanation based on understanding (in the idealist manner) and on causality (in the positivist manner) must both be applied to human affairs. Understanding, according to Weber, creates a range of possible constructs of any human phenomenon, but all are charged with the subjectivity of the person who conceives them. Causality must then be imported in order to discover which of the constructs corresponds with reality. He employs this technique in his famous work on the Protestant spirit and capitalism. He first depicts the Protestant and capitalist mentalities as he understands them (as 'ideal types' in his terminology) and then tries to establish from the evidence a causal link between the two. Weber supposed that the use of causality made his

8. B. T. Wilkins, *Hegel's Philosophy of History* (Ithaca, New York, 1974), pp. 85–92. On Hegelian method, *cf.* above, p. 119.

conclusions objective, but the central weakness in his approach is that the validity of the causal relations depends on the validity of the original constructs. The truth of his thesis, for instance, depends on whether or not he rightly characterized Protestantism and capitalism – an issue on which his judgment has been repeatedly challenged.[9] Weber's piecemeal recipe of using the idealist method and then the positivist method seems inadequate.

Since Weber's time developments have made conditions for the resolution of the conflict a little more favourable. The traditions have interacted more than in the past. Translations of important works have tended to reduce the dominance in the English-speaking world of the positivist school and in the German-speaking world of the idealist school. Representatives of the idealist tradition have been prepared to admit that empirical research has a place, though only a subsidiary one, in the study of man for practical purposes.[1] On the other hand, the bastion of empirical method has been stormed. The historian of science Thomas Kuhn has argued that the traditional view of what a scientist does – in terms of hypothesis, experiment and erection of a law – is erroneous. What happens, according to Kuhn, is this. Individual practitioners of science accept the normal theories of the scientific community until exceptions appear in the course of research. A period of crisis ensues until a new theory gains acceptance by the community. Scientists themselves do not simply use a correspondence theory of truth, but adopt a theory that coheres well with their other views.[2] Kuhn's work suggests that the model of a dispassionate natural scientist presented by positivists to the historian for imitation is misconceived. Historians may well be encouraged to believe that the positivist case has no monopoly of truth.

What then is the path towards identifying the real nature of historiography? The very existence of the two rival interpretations perhaps suggests the best way of advancing the argument. Positivism derives from the idea of progress and idealism from historicism. But

9. Raymond Aron, *Introduction to the Philosophy of History* (1938: London, 1961), pp. 266–70.
1. *E.g.* Jürgen Habermas, 'The Analytical Theory of Science and Dialectics', Adorno *et al.*, *The Positivist Dispute*, p. 141.
2. T. S. Kuhn, *The Structure of Scientific Revolutions* (Chicago, 1962). *Cf.* D. A. Hollinger 'T. S. Kuhn's Theory of Science and its Implications for History', *The American Historical Review*, 78 (1973), esp. pp. 381f.

the idea of progress and historicism themselves came from the same source. Both originated, as chapters four and five showed, in the worldview of Christendom. The idea of progress is a secularized version of Christian linear history. The chief feature discarded was divine control. Likewise, as Nietzsche put it, 'The Protestant pastor is the grandfather of German philosophy.'[3] What historicism had laid aside was mainly the Protestant pastor's belief in a goal of history. Behind the idea of progress and historicism there lies a single inheritance, the Christian understanding of history. It had been modified by interaction with the classical legacy, especially at the Renaissance, but its essentials were the characteristic features of the Christian panorama of the historical process. Implicit in the Christian view of history was a Christian philosophy of historiography. If an attempt is to be made to transcend the opposition between positivism and idealism the brightest prospects lie in going back for guidance to their common ground. Accordingly it is to a Christian view of historiography that we must turn.

A CHRISTIAN PHILOSOPHY OF HISTORIOGRAPHY

The starting-point of any analysis of historiography is its estimate of human beings, the subject-matter of history. Positivism treats man as part of nature, reducing him to 'thinghood'. Idealism treats him as separate from nature, elevating him to a unique status . It is upon the incompatibility of these estimates that the stark contrast between the two schools rests. Raymond Aron, the eminent French scholar, in his *Introduction to the Philosophy of History* (1938) comes to exactly this conclusion. His book, he explains, is intended 'to compare understanding and cause'.[4] He explores first the method of understanding, especially as expounded by Dilthey. He examines the social science methodology based on the concept of cause. Then he tries to synthesize the viewpoints, but finds that they resist combination. 'The complexity of the world of history', he concludes, 'corresponds to a pluralist anthropology.'[5] The divergence between the two ways of looking at historiography, that is to say, is a consequence of a disagreement over the nature of man. Aron pursues

3. Friedrich Nietzsche, *The Anti-Christ* (1895), para. 10 (Harmondsworth, 1968), p. 121.
4. Aron, *Introduction to the Philosophy of History*, p. 266.
5. *Ibid.*, p. 276.

the quest no further. A Christian view of human nature, however, supplies what is lacking: a way of integrating the alternative anthropologies of the positivists and the idealists.

Human beings, on the Christian view, are strangely ambivalent. On the one hand man is an insignificant part of the created world:

> *When I look at thy heavens, the work of thy fingers,*
> *the moon and the stars which thou hast established;*
> *what is man that thou art mindful of him,*
> *and the son of man that thou dost care for him?*[6]

On the other hand, as the psalmist hastens to say in the next verses, man is singled out for greatness:

> *Yet thou hast made him little less than God,*
> *and dost crown him with glory and honour.*
> *Thou has given him dominion over the works of thy hands;*
> *thou hast put all things under his feet.*[7]

Human beings are both made of dust and created in the image of God.[8] There is continuity with nature and yet discontinuity as well. The fissure within man is even sharper because, despite his similarity to a holy God, he is inextricably bound up in sin. He is part and parcel of a world gone wrong as well as enjoying an affinity with a God who embodies the right. The historian takes as his subject-matter human beings that are simultaneously moulded by their debased social and natural surroundings and free to take spontaneous God-like initiatives. Consequently, their behaviour can be described in terms of generalizations about groups, as positivists claim; but it can also be understood as unique activity, as idealists urge. Both cases are valid, but neither offers an exhaustive way of treating the complex phenomenon of man. A Christian anthropology suggests that the techniques commended by positivists and idealists are complementary.

Christian statements of the nature of historiography were seldom spelled out in any detail during the dominance in European thought of the Christian understanding of history. There was no need, for the issues that now divide positivists from idealists had hardly been

6. Psalm 8: 3f.
7. Psalm 8: 5f.
8. Genesis 2: 7; 1: 26.

raised. Only by the mid-eighteenth century were the issues looming on the horizon. The bifurcation of attitudes to history into the Enlightment and romantic schools was then just beginning. Yet it remained the general assumption, especially in Germany, that scholarship was a Christian enterprise. Seventeen years older than J. C. Gatterer, the first distinguished *Aufklärer,* was another theorist of history, Johann Martin Chladenius. Although he is normally considered simply as a precursor of historicism, Chladenius has far greater importance as a thinker who analysed historiography from a standpoint that was neither idealist nor positivist, but more obviously Christian. Born into a family that had been expelled from Hungary for the tenacity of its Lutheranism, Chladenius (or Chladni) became Professor of Theology at Erlangen shortly after its foundation as the only Protestant university in Bavaria in 1743. Chladenius saw his task as the defence of Lutheran orthodoxy, and especially of the historical reliability of the Bible in the face of rationalist criticisms. His method was not to repudiate the rationalist temper of his age outright, but rather to argue that it was inadequate for understanding the Bible. The influential belief of Wolff that all reasoning must be deductive if it is to discover truth suggested that the large historical content of the Bible is of little value. Chladenius argued in his first major work, an *Introduction to the Right Exegesis of Rational Speeches and Writings* (1742), that historical understanding is different from deductive reasoning, yet equally valid.[9] Strict demonstration is not the only avenue to truth. He was defending the usefulness of historical knowledge within a Christian frame of mind.

Chladenius elaborated his viewpoint in his second major work, the *General Science of History* (1752). He analysed the method of the historian, again by contrast with deduction. This was not to adopt the later idealist position that there are two ways of obtaining knowledge, one appropriate for the natural world, the other for the human world. Chladenius believed that the historical sciences should investigate man in his environment and so should embrace natural history as well as history proper. His contrast was not between historical technique and the empirical method of natural science but between historical technique and the deductive method of abstract

9. P. H. Reill, *The German Enlightenment and the Rise of Historicism* (Berkeley, Calif., 1975), pp. 43, 105f.

reasoning.[1] The historian, according to Chladenius, uses a method of argumentation far broader than either the empirical or the deductive. He uses a form of rhetoric. Chladenius was influenced by Christian Thomasius, a late seventeenth-century German scholar who had stressed that rhetoric is a means of engaging with the practical problems of life. Similarly for Chladenius history deals with everyday affairs and so must use the techniques of rhetoric.[2] History is not confined to the empirical method associated with the names of Newton and Locke by Chladenius' contemporaries in Britain and France. His analysis of historiography was not in the tradition that lies behind the positivism of today. He was able to draw on a wider tradition of thought.

At times Chladenius can sound very much like an idealist. He declares, for instance, that 'historical understanding consists of a series of true intuitive judgments that are transmitted from soul to soul through reports, narratives, documents, testimonies, and repetition'. [3] Such a sentence could almost have been written by Dilthey. Yet Chladenius held that the historian is concerned with the identification of causes and formulation of laws much in the way that the positivist account of historiography suggests. Causes and laws, however, do not always form sufficient explanations of human action in themselves. He takes the instance of the resignation by Charles V of the crowns of Germany and Spain in 1556 for the sake of entering a monastery. He retired, it might be said, because of the depressing outcome of several undertakings. It is a valid generalization about human conduct that adversity is discouraging, but such a 'law' is inadequate to explain why he gave up the crowns. The further factor of Charles' failing physical powers can also be treated as a 'cause' of his retirement, but that does not wholly explain his action either. 'The remaining reasons', Chladenius concludes, 'must stem from the individual mentality (*Gedenckenart*) of this monarch.'[4] People act from motives peculiar to themselves. The conclusion in this field may lean slightly towards the idealist position. Chladenius would nevertheless wish to agree with the positivist school that law-like generalizations do guide the historian, and yet to stress the uniqueness of

1. *Ibid.*, p. 106.
2. *Ibid.*, p. 108.
3. J. M. Chladenius, *General Science of History* (Leipzig, 1752), p. 276, quoted by *ibid.*, p. 107.
4. J. M. Chladenius, *General Science of History*, p. 223, quoted by *ibid.*, p. 107.

free human action in the manner of the idealist school. He comes close to doing justice to the categories of causality and understanding alike.

Chladenius performed a further service to a Christian philosophy of historiography by his approach to the question of detachment. The historian, according to the positivists, must stand back from the human beings about whom he writes in order to be dispassionate; but according to the idealists he should cultivate a sense of involvement with them in order to understand. Chladenius delved behind this opposition. He was the first to develop the theory that the historian must write from a point of view. Influenced by Leibniz, he contended that all historical thinking is conditioned by its time. Every work of history is therefore written from a particular vantage point. 'A narration wholly abstracted from its own point of view is impossible', he declares, and 'hence an impartial narration cannot be called one that narrates without any point of view at all, for such simply is not possible.'[5] The historian brings his own convictions to his work. Chladenius stood for the case argued in chapter one, that the point of view of a historian necessarily enters his history.[6] Such a perspective theory of historiography should not be confused with the idealist one. On the idealist view, the historian's subjective grasp of the past is wholly responsible for what he writes. Idealists deny that the past, or even the evidence reflecting the past, exists independently of the historian's mind. According to the perspective theory, however, a finished history is the result of interaction between the historian's judgment and the evidence that represents the factual quality of the past. Evidence exists independently to discipline the historian's work. It is important to notice that a historian's perspective may therefore be altered by historical evidence (or indeed by other means). Presuppositions are open to debate. To claim that historians write from different perspectives is not to hold that their works are immune to criticism from other points of view.[7] Yet recognizing that

5. Chladenius, *General Science of History*, p. 151, quoted by Rudolf Unger, 'The Problem of Historical Objectivity: A Sketch of its Development to the Time of Hegel' (1923), *History and Theory*, Beiheft 11 (1971), p. 71.
6. *Cf.* above, pp. 5–8.
7. This point eliminates the objection mentioned in the otherwise sympathetic treatment of the perspective theory in Walsh, *An Introduction to Philosophy of History*, pp. 110–13. On the way in which evidence may affect historians despite their different perspectives, *cf.* above, pp. 6f.

historians have standpoints prevents capitulation to the positivist argument that historiography should be determined by so-called 'facts'. The perspective theory first formulated by Chladenius takes into account both the subjectivity of the historian (the exclusive emphasis of the idealists) and the objectivity of the past (the exclusive emphasis of the positivists).

It is also possible to bridge the gap between the two schools of thought on another issue dividing them, the question of the theory of truth used in history. The answer lies in a combination of the correspondence and coherence approaches. The validity of a historical statement, it was argued in chapter one, cannot depend on whether or not it corresponds with the past because the past is not available for us to examine. Between us and the past lies the evidence.[8] Yet on the other hand, since the evidence limits the range of possible historical statements, the sole test of veracity is not the degree of coherence of one statement with the others we can make. On this topic Professor W. H. Walsh, who has written one of the most enlightening surveys of the philosophy of historiography, is surely right:

> Whilst denying the proposition that historians know any absolutely certain facts about the past and arguing with the Coherence party that all historical statements are relative, we nevertheless agree with supporters of the Correspondence view in asserting that there is an attempt in history . . . to characterize an independent reality.[9]

In practice historians do use both understandings of truth. They use the correspondence approach when trying to write statements that match the evidence; and they use the coherence approach when trying to ensure that their historical argument is internally self-consistent. Once more it proves valuable to combine the standpoints of the positivist and idealist parties.

It might be objected that the Christian analysis of historiography outlined here is less a fusion of two opposing standpoints than an affirmation of them both that leaves the two unreconciled. It may well be that ways of fusing them more closely could be established, but a tension within the Christian view would remain. This, however,

8. *Cf.* above, pp. 3f.
9. Walsh, *An Introduction to Philosophy of History*, p. 89.

it not a serious objection. A view which tolerates a tension is similar to the Christian position on another aspect of historical theory, the debate between determinism and freewill. This is a question on which Christians have notoriously been divided. The divergence in Protestantism between Calvinists and Arminians has mirrored the contrast in secular thought between determinists and free-willers. The problem arose in Christian theology because there was a desire on the one side to insist that God controls history and on the other to defend human responsibility. Divine sovereignty, especially in human salvation, was what John Calvin stood for; the duty and consequently the freedom to accept salvation were what John Wesley championed. Yet Calvin believed in human responsibility and Wesley in divine sovereignty. Although the contrast between the two positions is real and has important consequences, Calvinism and Arminianism share a worldview in which both God and man are agents of history. In some sense a deed is man's (if only permissively) and God's (if only secondarily). A Christian outlook on history recognizes a fundamental tension - an antinomy - between divine sovereignty and human responsibility. This is no retreat into irrationalism, for secular thought cannot avoid the same tension. Kant's philosophical investigation of the issue led to the identical conclusion that the mind wishes to affirm both that man is determined and that he is free. Christianity adopts a reasonable position in discerning an antinomy between determinism and freewill.

The philosophy of historiography that has been sketched here is analogous. Human behaviour, on a Christian view, is both determined by God and chosen by man. Similarly, human behaviour is both moulded by circumstances and freely undertaken by individuals. Regularity and spontaneity coexist in history. The historian recognizes external influences on human action but also treats human beings as freely responsible for what they do. He wants to use a method that is capable of making generalizations and yet allows for the unique. He is not restricted to empirical method: if he were, it might exclude the recognition that human behaviour is free. Nor is he forced to use the method of understanding: if he were, it might exclude the recognition that man is determined. He uses a method similar to that analysed by Chladenius, at once broader than empiricism and more precise than understanding. Such a philosophy of historiography can treat its subject far more adequately than the views offered by either the positivist or the idealist school.

The controversy between the two schools of thought arises from their isolating one or the other aspect of Christian thought about man. For positivists he is a creature of circumstance; for idealists he is capable of heroic creativity. From that divergence springs the whole debate. It is therefore when the philosophy of historiography rediscovers its Christian roots that it becomes possible to approach a resolution of the questions at issue. Human beings can then be seen whole, as shaped by their context and as shapers of it. Positivists and idealists alike can be appreciated for being right in what they affirm but wrong in what they deny. This is not to contend that people of Christian conviction alone are able to reach such conclusions. It is, however, to point out that when the alternative analyses are combined within a Christian worldview, justice seems to be done to the nature of historiography. The ambiguities of man are seen to explain the ambiguities in the technique of the historian.

8 The meaning of history

'The death and resurrection of Jesus show the meaning God puts on life, and manifest the pattern of history as God himself understands it.'

C. K. Barrett, *History and Faith: The Story of the Passion.*[1]

Philosophies of historiography are part and parcel of philosophies of history. Positivism and idealism, as the last chapter has shown, derive from the idea of progress and historicism respectively. Similarly any Christian view of historiography is bound up with the Christian conception of the historical process. Man in his ambiguous state, 'his fallen greatness' as the eighteenth-century evangelical historian Joseph Milner put it, is the subject of both.[2] History on the Christian view is about human beings who are like God yet habitual wrongdoers, who have immense creative potential yet are enmeshed in a web of circumstance and who are the shapers and yet also the victims of history. Through the tensions of human life, however, God works out the purposes that he will bring to a triumphant conclusion. Such an understanding was the common stock from which the idea of progress and historicism were abstracted. We have established that the one-sidedness of the rival philosophies of historiography can be remedied by integrating them on a Christian foundation. May not the same be true of philosophies of history? It may be possible to do with the idea of progress and historicism what was done with the positivism and idealism that sprang from them. We can seek to unite their affirmations on the basis of their common derivation from the Christian view of history.

We are surely driven to some such task by the inadequacies of the schools of thought about the historical process that have dominated western thought over the last two centuries. In examining theories of progress and the historicist outlook we encountered serious objec-

1. C. K. Barrett, *History and Faith: The Story of the Passion* (London, 1967), p. 36.
2. Joseph Milner, 'Observations on the Use of History', *The Works of the Late Joseph Milner . . .*, 8 (London, 1810), p. 452.

tions. The idea of progress has the merit of offering hope for the future. Yet it seems to fly in the face of the evidence. There is little to suggest that there has been moral improvement in humanity. Episodes in the recent past, such as the concentration camps of the Second World War, suggest that there has been none. Historicism, on the other hand, contends that human beings can find fulfilment in their own time. Yet its own proponents began to point out its fundamental weakness in the inter-war period. Belief in eternal values was evaporating. The variety of values in different societies no longer seemed to reflect anything real. The premises of historicism were revealed as arbitrary. The Marxist fusion of elements from the other two views does not achieve immunity from the criticisms that can be made of them, but on the contrary opens Marxism to those criticisms as well as to fresh ones. Furthermore Marxism has proved to be an unstable synthesis. It has gradually resolved itself into a version of one or the other of the two views of which it was an amalgam. Attempts to inject features of the cyclical theory into western ideas of history have been faulted on grounds of evidence as well as for other reasons. Such considerations draw our attention back to the Christian understanding of history. Is providence a key to the meaning of history?

A Christian understanding supplies something that historicism lacks: confidence in the future. Its keynote of hope is grounded in the twin beliefs that God is guiding history forward in a straight line and that it will in due time reach his goal. Millenarianism may well be an unwarranted interpretation of biblical imagery. Yet belief in the divine superintendence of history and expectations of the end of time provide ample grounds for the Christian hope. There will ultimately be victory for Jesus Christ at the goal of history. Indeed, the decisive engagement has already been fought. The battle against evil was won by Jesus on the cross. At that point God 'disarmed the principalities and powers and made a public example of them, triumphing over them in him'.[3] The outcome of world history is therefore already assured. God will continue to direct the course of events up to their end when the outcome will be made plain. There will be no faltering of his purpose on the way, so that believers are secure even before the end. Thus Christian eschatology, together

3. Colossians 2: 15.

with belief in divine control of the historical process, guarantee the future.

The Christian faith, like the idea of progress, holds out the promise of a bright tomorrow. It contends, however, that it possesses stronger grounds for its promise than the idea of progress. The future is guaranteed not by man, but by God. This contrast explains the weakening over time of theories of progress. In the first flush of enthusiasm for the idea of progress it was commonly held – by Turgot and Priestley, for instance – that God is the author of human improvement. In the second phase exemplified by Comte and Spencer, belief in divine control of the process was discarded, but the conviction that it is bound to continue remained. In the third phase, represented by twentieth-century advocates like S. B. Fay or Sidney Pollard, belief in the inevitability of progress is condemned as a delusion that may inhibit the human effort upon which all progress depends. Theories of progress have become more hesitant as they have travelled further from their Christian background. At the same time as offering firmer grounds for confidence through its belief in God, the Christian view of history is not vulnerable to the central objection to the notion of progress. Although the Christian faith may justly claim to have improved the lot of mankind through humanitarian campaigns such as those to suppress slavery and to encourage literacy, it does not suggest that human nature has changed for the better over the ages. Throughout history, in Joseph Milner's terminology, man has been great, but equally he has always been fallen. Idealistic schemes of the twentieth century like the League of Nations have proved no more effective than smaller-scale projects of the Middle Ages such as the Truce of God. A Christian view of history cannot be criticized on the ground that it ignores the evidence of the continuing weakness and malignity of human beings. It is realistic.

Nor is the Christian view affected by the chief argument brought against the historicist view. Traditional historicism in Germany has waned because of a crisis in confidence. Its nineteenth-century theorists such as Von Humboldt and its practitioners like Ranke could assume a religious sanction for their ideas. Their belief in God allowed them to entertain a cultural pluralism. Each nation's distinctive qualities, they held, are God-given and so cannot be criticized by comparison with the characteristics of other nations. With the decline of theism, at least in intellectual circles, there was no longer any reason to suppose that cultural differences have a justification. Criteria for judgments of value, from the moral to the aesthetic, seemed to lack foundation. It appears that historicism was dependent on Christianity for its vitality. The reverse however is not true. Christian opinion on history is independent of historicism, for Christianity offers a standard of evaluation outside history. God himself is the source and revealer of values. He does not, on the Christian view, encourage a *congeries* of contradictory values to grow up in the soil of history. On the contrary, his standard of right and wrong is eternal. His judgment both within history and at its end vindicates his standard; his mercy allows for human failure to attain it. There is no question of a Christian view of history discovering that its moral foundations have been mined away. Yet at the same time a Christian view shares the historicist conviction that human beings have value in themselves. No human beings are dispensable for the sake of posterity. Human fulfilment is possible in the present. Each generation does stand immediate to God. Christianity generates a view of history that gives historicist insights their due while remaining immune to the main charge against historicism.

A CHRISTIAN PHILOSOPHY OF HISTORY

One of the chief components of the Christian view was discarded by the theorists of progress or else remoulded by the historicists: a belief that God intervenes in the course of history. Eighteenth-century theologians who prepared the way for the idea of progress acknowledged divine control of history overall but refused to admit that God plays a part at specific points. Men of the romantic era saw God in people and institutions much as they saw him in the natural world – in a diffused and general way – rather than in particular events. They were trying to rationalize away an element in the Christian understanding of history that raises one of the problems touched on in chapter three. Why should a God who controls the whole historical process need to interfere at various points? And how are fallible human beings to recognize the divine hand? These questions pose an obstacle to the analysis offered here. Even if a Christian approach resists criticisms of the idea of progress and historicism and combines attractive features of the two schools of thought, it opens itself to criticism on these other scores. Is the notion of particular providences tenable?

Two considerations suggest that belief in divine interventions is integral to a Christian perspective on the world. God's concern, on the Christian view, is not only with the general tendency of the historical process, but also with tiny happenings like the flight of a small bird. Jesus himself drew an inference:

> Are not two sparrows sold for a penny? And not one of them will fall to the ground without your Father's will. But even the hairs of your head are all numbered. Fear not, therefore; you are of more value than many sparrows.[4]

God will pay attention to the minute details of human life. Secondly, that God intervened in history by becoming man and dying for us men and for our salvation is the kernel of Christian faith. The coming of Jesus demonstrates that God is prepared to take a more direct part in human affairs. It has been objected against a belief in divine interventions that it tends to obscure God's superintendence of the historical process.[5] There is no reason, however, why God should not be seen in the whole of history as well as in certain events. The incarnation of Jesus does not contradict a belief in general providence: no more do particular providences. Again, recognition of God's hand in history need not distract attention from the coming of Jesus.[6] Even if some writers such as Bossuet have been so concerned with divine interventions that Jesus has receded into the background, this was not so, for instance, in Milner's church history. Other interventions actually provide a context for the coming of Jesus. It is possible to abuse the idea of particular providences by treating them as a series of vindications of one's own nation in the manner of Mr Podsnap. But the possibility of abusing an idea should not exclude its use. Divine interventions seem to be a necessary element in a Christian view of history.

The working of God in historical events is not, however, obvious. No historian is compelled to acknowledge that particular providences are a reality. God seems to hide himself in history as well as to reveal himself in it. The Christian faith itself offers explanations of why this should be so. First, the purposes of God are veiled even from the believer until the end of time. Again, if God's ways could

4. Matthew 10: 29ff.
5. M. C. Smit, 'The Divine Mystery in History', *Free University Quarterly* (Amsterdam), 6 (1958–59), p. 124.
6. As suggested by *ibid.*, pp. 124f.

be traced exhaustively he would be limited, and so not what Christian faith holds him to be.[7] And if history provided absolutely convincing signs that God is behind it, the unbeliever would stand condemned not for lack of faith, but for ignorance. Hence we should expect there to be no more than suggestions that God intervenes in the world. 'What meets our eyes', declares Pascal, 'denotes neither total absence or manifest presence of the divine, but the presence of a hidden God.'[8] That is true for the believer and the unbeliever alike. The Christian, however, is aware of divine activity not only in the world but also in his own life. Personal experience of the intervention of God inclines him to discern it in the world as well. But he remains a fallible human being who can speak only with diffidence beyond his own experience. He will be cautious about identifying the divine interventions that he believes to take place in the historical process. He does not so much see them as glimpse them. The perception of particular providences, however real they may be, is no straightforward matter.

Yet the task is not beyond us, as a seventeenth-century example may illustrate. The Puritan divine Richard Baxter lived through the Restoration of 1660. He was amazed at the conduct of the army of the Commonwealth. It had conquered three kingdoms, killed the king and dissolved parliaments, but it quietly disbanded 'without one bloody nose' at the Restoration of Charles II. Baxter comments in his autobiography:

> Let any man that hath the use of his understanding judge whether this were not enough to prove that there is a God that governeth the world and disposeth of the Powers of the world according to His Will.[9]

Baxter was not applauding the Restoration as such, for it had led to his ejection from the church and much personal harassment. It was its peaceful mode to which he drew attention. The Almighty, according to Baxter, had overruled. Surely in this instance Baxter had good grounds for discerning God at work. There had been no renewal of civil war. Bloodshed had surprisingly been avoided. God,

7. K. S. Latourette, 'The Christian Understanding of History', *The American Historical Review*, 54 (1949), p. 270.
8. *Pascal's Pensées with an English Translation, Brief Notes and Introduction*, ed. H. F. Stewart (London, 1950), p. 9.
9. Richard Baxter, *Autobiography*, ed. J. M. L. Thompson (London, 1931), p. 92.

he concluded, had displayed his mercy. Baxter may have overestimated the persuasiveness of his case in suggesting that it was sufficient to 'prove' the existence of providence. Perhaps proof of anything is beyond the power of historical evidence. Yet the evidence does suggest that the expected course of events had been diverted in a way which accords with the character of God as the author of peace. Baxter was expressing a faith that was reasonable. More than faith could hardly be expected – 'for we walk by faith, not by sight'.[1] But a reasonable faith can become aware of divine interventions. A claim to discern the hand of God in history need not be extravagant.

Beyond the question of particular providences there looms a larger issue. Any Christian view of history must ultimately take into account the problem of suffering. God's government of the world tolerates suffering. His acts of judgment even use suffering as a means of punishment. How can the spread of the Black Death or the dropping of the atomic bomb on Hiroshima be fitted into a providential scheme? It is impossible to say either that suffering in some sense does not exist, for human beings really experience its agonies; or that God lacks the love and power to remedy it, for love and power are part of God's nature. The problem is at its most acute when we see, with the author of Psalm 73, that the wicked prosper while the innocent suffer. In that case it can be noted that the prosperity of the wicked may not last for ever, and that the innocent are only relatively free from guilt. If it is true that humanity as a whole is infected with sin, perhaps the right perspective on human history is surprise that God's holiness permits him to endure the continued existence of any human beings. Such a perspective would illuminate the breadth of his mercy. And there is a remedy in the future. God is capable of abolishing suffering, perhaps even retrospectively. According to John's eschatological vision of the redeemed, 'God will wipe away every tear from their eyes'.[2] Yet, when all this is said, we still feel that pain is an ugly feature of a world under God's control.

The only ultimate answer lies in the cross of Jesus. If human beings have to bear suffering, God has borne more. Jesus Christ, God manifest in the flesh, underwent mental anguish, human desertion, physical torture and a painful death. More, the sin that

1. 2 Corinthians 5: 7.
2. Revelation 7: 17.

was swallowed up in his death created a schism in God, for the Son was alienated from the Father. That suffering is beyond our comprehension. 'No reason of man can justify God for His treatment of His Son; but whatever does justify it justifies God's whole providence with the universe, and solves its problem.'[3] If the death of Jesus was necessary for putting right what was wrong with the world, it becomes evident that lesser measures could not have sufficed. Perhaps God has not abolished suffering by simpler methods because the death of Jesus guarantees something greater than the immediate abolition of suffering: present liberation from the power of sin and future liberation from the power of death. Further, victory over sin and death was achieved by suffering. This means that suffering can itself be triumphant. To suffer and yet to trust, to suffer and yet to hope – these things are vindicated by God. The cross alone makes the suffering that disfigures human history understandable within God's providence.

The cross of Jesus does more than shape the Christian response to the problem of suffering. The major claims of Christianity about history are summed up by the cross. There Jesus, in fulfilling the prophecies of the Old Testament and creating the theme of the church's preaching, confirmed the vision of history as an ongoing line. The work of Jesus, by opening the kingdom of heaven to all believers, established the Christian hope that God will bring history to a triumphant conclusion. And God's judgment and mercy were demonstrated when he acted in the death of Jesus: the world was judged for rejecting God's Son, and yet mercy was made available for those who believe in him. The crucifixion was the time of achievement, but it is made intelligible by the life of Jesus that preceded it and his resurrection from the dead that followed it. We may therefore wish to agree with the statement by Professor C. K. Barrett which forms the epigraph for this chapter: 'The death and resurrection of Jesus show the meaning God puts on life, and manifest the pattern of history as God himself understands it'.[4]

MODERN STATEMENTS OF A CHRISTIAN VIEW

What has been said about a Christian philosophy of history corresponds quite closely with a number of recent expositions of a

3. P. T. Forsyth, *The Justification of God* (London, 1916), p. 125.
4. Barrett, *History and Faith*, p. 36.

providential understanding of history. Since the Second World War, and more especially in the decade after its close, there have been several notable attempts to wrestle with the problems of faith and history. The primary explanation of the phenomenon undoubtedly lies in the war itself. The struggle against Fascism drove the allied nations to consider what they were defending. The answer was frequently democracy, but very commonly it was Christianity as well. This mood engendered in Britain the Education Act of 1944 providing that religious education should be compulsory. It also fostered consideration of the role of God in world history. The sense of crisis was prolonged as hot war changed into Cold War. Once more the enemy had an ideology, this time Communism, and so again it seemed imperative to explain the opposing Christian standpoint in relation to world events.[5] A further stimulus was the publication in 1946 of R. G. Collingwood's *The Idea of History* with its insistence on historicist lines that the assumptions of Anglo-Saxon historical scholarship deriving from the Enlightenment were erroneous. The challenge to work out a Christian response affected theologians as well as historians. And among theologians, especially those influenced by the decaying historicist tradition in Germany, there was much attention to the question of how far Christian belief rests on historical events.[6] One of the chief monuments to the post-war concern with issues of faith and history, however, is a book little influenced by theological debate but steeped in historical practice. It is *Christianity and History* (1949) by Professor Sir Herbert Butterfield, a Methodist layman and Professor of Modern History at Cambridge.

A major aim of *Christianity and History* is to draw attention to the operation of a general providence:

> that kind of history-making which goes on so to speak over our heads, now deflecting the results of our actions, now taking our purposes out of our hands, and now turning our endeavours to ends not realised.[7]

The process is likened to a composer who composes music inch by

5. *God, History and Historians: An Anthology of Modern Christian Views of History*, ed. C. T. McIntire (New York, 1977), pp. 7f.
6. *Ibid.*, pp. 6f.
7. Sir Herbert Butterfield, *Christianity and History* (London, 1949), p. 94.

inch as the orchestra plays, and so can give a different turn to the piece whenever the human musicians play wrong notes.[8] The analogy is a vivid one, even if it may mislead in suggesting that the wrong notes themselves are beyond the composer's control. Progress towards some postulated human goal is dismissed as an explanation of the historical process. 'History is not like a train, the sole purpose of which is to get to its destination. . .'[9] The progress that has taken place in the acquisition of greater knowledge has been part of the providential order, and implies no transformation of human nature.[1] So hostile is the book to seeing goals in the future that it shows little trace of eschatology. The deficiency however is made good in an essay published nine years later, where it is stressed that history is based on God's promise for the future.[2] *Christianity and History* itself does place to the fore another characteristic element in a providential framework, belief in divine judgments. The events of 1918, 1933 or 1945, or of all of these together, are explained as a judgment on the militarism of Prussia.[3] Acts of mercy are less in evidence, although it is commented, for instance, that the Norman Conquest of England shows that heaven often gives men a chance to redeem the effects even of their own violence and to turn the evil they have done into later good.[4] *Christianity and History* therefore presents something of a full-blooded version of the Christian understanding of history.

Sir Herbert contrasts his providential interpretation with what can be established by 'technical' historians. Research can discover what happened in the past; interpretations like a providential view, a liberal view or a Marxist view can then be superimposed.[5] Such an account, it has here been suggested, fails to recognize the extent to which research is shaped by a point of view.[6] But in his later writings Sir Herbert analyses 'technical history', the ordinary work of the historian, more closely. It is the result of two different ways

8. *Ibid.*, p. 95.
9. *Ibid.*, p. 67.
1. *Ibid.*, p. 97.
2. Sir Herbert Butterfield, 'God in History' (1958), *God, History and Historians*, ed. McIntire, pp. 202–04.
3. Butterfield, *Christianity and History*, pp. 49f.
4. *Ibid.*, p. 50.
5. *Ibid.*, p. 23.
6. *Cf.* above, pp. 5–8.

of looking at historical events, the 'biographical' and the 'historical' ways, which can co-exist with the providential approach.

> If you go on a journey, and at the end of it I ask: Why are you here now? you may answer: 'Because I wanted to come'; or you may say: 'Because a railway-train carried me here'; or you may say: 'Because it is the will of God'; and all these things may be true at the same time – true on different levels.[7]

The 'biographical' way treats human beings as responsible for making the decisions that create history; the 'historical' way treats events as reducible to laws about the broad movements of the historical process. Both approaches are necessary. The Christian, Sir Herbert goes on, will want to use both because on the one hand he wants to affirm human moral responsibility and on the other he recognizes tendencies at work which the people involved do not create.[8] The two ways that are contrasted are what have here been called the idealist and the positivist philosophies of historiography. Sir Herbert stands with Chladenius: the two methods must be united within an overall providential perspective.

The year when *Christianity and History* appeared also witnessed the publication of *Faith and History* by Reinhold Niebuhr, Professor of Christian Ethics at Union Theological Seminary, New York. Niebuhr, like his older contemporary Karl Barth, with whom he is often classed as a neo-orthodox theologian, had arrived at a rejection of attempts to assimilate Christianity to modern culture. The Christian faith, he argues, makes an analysis of the human condition totally different from that habitual for modern man, just as it once broke with the conceptions of classical antiquity. The classical view, that man is confined to a world of recurrent cycles unless his reason penetrates to the eternal world, makes history ultimately meaningless. The modern view, that man is capable of mastering his own destiny and so ensuring progress, overestimates the extent of human freedom. The Christian view is that man inhabits an ambiguous world in which he is both constrained by the same laws as the natural world and able to overcome them in spontaneous acts of spiritual independence. Human history is a compound of necessity and freedom.

> To the degree that men are not free, their actions, both

7. Butterfield, 'God in History', *God, History and Historians*, ed. McIntire, p. 195.
8. *Ibid.*, p. 199.

> individual and collective, may be predicted with something of the assurance with which a natural scientist charts the recurrences of nature. In so far as they are free, causal sequences in history reach a height and complexity in which the full understanding of the character of an event would require the knowledge of the secret motive of the agent for action.[9]

History, that is to say, is of a character which entails simultaneous scrutiny along positivist and idealist lines. Niebuhr also concludes that a historian's viewpoint must colour his account of the past.[1] Although he is concerned only in passing with how to study man in history, Niebuhr's doctrine of the human condition leads him to a position virtually identical to the one outlined in chapter seven.

Overarching human history in Niebuhr's thought as much as in other Christian conceptions is providence. God controls history, yet he is not fully known within it. Providence stamps its quality of mystery on the historical process, Niebuhr argues, and so explains why the tension of necessity and freedom is not resolved.[2] The great problem of a providential view, the question of suffering, is met by pointing to the life, death and resurrection of Jesus as the divine remedy for the evil that flows from human freedom.

> Thus the suffering of the guiltless, which is the primary problem of life for those who look at history from the standpoint of their own virtues, is made into the ultimate answer of history for those who look at it from the standpoint of the problematic character of all human virtue.[3]

Yet if some elements of a providential frame of meaning are prominent in Niebuhr, the most characteristic elements are strangely nebulous. Creation is interpreted as symbol rather than event, so that the starting-point of history is nullified.[4] Hence history is seen less as linear than as unitary. Similarly eschatology is treated not as what comes at the end of time, but as a signpost to the eternal that can transfigure any historical moment.[5] High expectations of the

9. Reinhold Niebuhr, *Faith and History: A Comparison of Christian and Modern Views of History* (London, 1949), pp. 62f.
1. *Ibid.*, pp. 131ff.
2. *Ibid.*, pp. 42, 116.
3. *Ibid.*, p. 161.
4. *Ibid.*, p. 37.
5. *Ibid.*, pp. 267f.

future are therefore presented as the property more of modern culture than of the Christian faith.[6] Divine judgments in the course of history are reduced to the operation of the criminal law and occasional instances of resistance to tyranny.[7] Traces of providence are so obscure, according to Niebuhr, that we cannot justifiably talk of a 'Christian philosophy of history.'[8] Thus Niebuhr offers a providential understanding of history, but exaggerates its mysteriousness to the extent of blurring the outline of Christian beliefs.

Alongside those who have written about history within a providential frame of meaning, there have been a few who have criticized their efforts from a Christian standpoint. Prominent among them was C. S. Lewis, the literary critic and master of Christian apologetic. Lewis published in 1950 a pungent article in which he (confusingly) labelled as 'historicism' any attempt to lay bare the inner meaning of the historical process. Christian 'historicists' who look for divine judgments in history are censured on two grounds. First, to read all calamities as judgments is to claim without justification to be as inspired as the prophets who so read certain Old Testament calamities. Secondly, passages in Scripture such as the book of Job, Isaiah's picture of the suffering servant and Jesus' answers about the disaster at Siloam are rebuffs to understanding suffering as punishment.[9] To these points, however, it can be replied that no Christian perspective on history would wish to treat *all* calamities as instances of divine judgment. Only cases where the evidence invites that interpretation, such as Butterfield's instance of German militarism, will be treated in that way. Nor will the Christian analyst wish to claim that the inspiration of a prophet eliminates for him the hiddenness of God. The Old Testament prophets saw with clarity what God revealed; we can only discern provisionally what history suggests. And while none of the biblical passages that Lewis cites prohibits the reading of some disasters as acts of judgment, Jesus' explanation of the tower of Siloam points the other way.[1] Lewis goes on to deny that we can extract the meaning of history from the fragmentary evidence of the bit of the past that is left to us.[2] But that is to pass over the biblical

6. *Ibid.*, p. 152.
7. *Ibid.*, p. 146.
8. *Ibid.*, p. 155.
9. C. S. Lewis, 'Historicism', *God, History and Historians*, ed. McIntire, p. 227.
1. *Cf.* above, p. 49.
2. Lewis, 'Historicism', *God, History and Historians*, ed. McIntire, pp. 230–37.

teaching that the work of Jesus is the key to the historical process. That is why the long tradition of Christian historical thought has existed. Strangely enough, the explanation of Lewis's position lies in the influence over him of historicism – a version of the historicism discussed in chapter five. He wishes to restrict the portion of history that can be understood to our present experience, the '*Now*'.[3] That is to urge, with romantic theorists of the early nineteenth century, that the eternal can be intuited only in the particular, by the individual, without regard to the broader sweep of history. Lewis was drawn, perhaps by the romantic assumptions of the literary world, to modify a Christian view of history in a historicist direction.

Others have modified a Christian view more consciously. Norman Sykes, Dixie Professor of Ecclesiastical History at Cambridge, whose great service to scholarship was the favourable reinterpretation of the eighteenth-century Church of England, received the publication of Collingwood's *The Idea of History* with enthusiasm. He accepted its claims to demonstrate that history is not a science because it is concerned with the self-determining activity of unique human beings. From this premise he inferred, for instance, that any search for the Jesus of history is a scientistic misconception.[4] The conclusion, however, was wholly dependent on the historicist analysis that he had embraced. The opposite deviation, towards the idea of progress, has been more common among professing Christians in the English-speaking nations and has probably been more damaging to a Christian worldview. Shirley Jackson Case, an American early church historian, published a work entitled *The Christian Philosophy of History* in 1943 which was a twentieth-century echo of Turgot:

> History to date is also reassuring. Even the casual observer realizes the tremendous spread of moral and spiritual interests over the earth during the last two thousand years. A gradually enlarging circle of mankind has learned to cherish ways of living that exemplify honesty, justice, and brotherly kindness.[5]

Meanwhile the holocaust of Auschwitz was at its height. Modernism in theology, which largely consisted in an attempt to take over the

3. *Ibid.*, pp. 237ff.
4. Norman Sykes, 'Some Current Conceptions of Historiography and their Significance for Christian Apologetic', *The Journal of Theological Studies*, 50 (1949), pp. 27f., 32.
5. Shirley J. Case, *The Christian Philosophy of History* (Chicago, 1943), p. 217.

idea of progress as a Christian theme, was suffering revenge at the hands of history. Case also accepts the positivist implications of the theme of progress. History, he says, is a form of science that pays attention to events only at a natural level. He therefore dismisses the possibility of belief in 'the capricious intervention of the Deity'.[6] Capitulation to positivism is total. This is a particularly vivid instance of how a Christian view of history can be sacrificed to one of its competitors.

The risk of allowing a Christian view of history to be over-influenced by current alternatives is ever-present. A desire to engage in dialogue with exponents of contemporary thought is imperative for the vitality and propagation of Christianity. But the dialogue can all too easily degenerate into an acceptance of the premises of contemporary thought. Conventional wisdom is transient, not eternal. 'Has not God made foolish the wisdom of the world?'[7] Historicism and the idea of progress are not the only pitfalls. There is a need to guard against the attractions of a worldview blending the Christian conception with elements of the cyclical view. The study of comparative religion can lead to proposals for such a blend, whether in the manner of Arnold Toynbee or according to some other formula.[8] There is also a pressing need to guard against creating a conflation of Christianity and Marxism. The fashion for liberation theology in the style of the Peruvian Gustavo Gutiérrez is one of the tendencies encouraging attempts to fuse a Christian view of history with a Marxist view, and especially a Western Marxist view influenced by the Frankfurt school.[9] The Christian understanding of history is in no need of supplementation. It must be recognized, on the other hand, that neglected strands in Christian thought about history can be illuminated once more by contact with other schools of opinion, especially those historically derived from it. The stimulus given by Ernst Bloch, a member of the Frankfurt school, to Jürgen Moltmann's valuable stress on the importance of hope in Christian theology is a case in point.[1] But such service will be to draw attention to what is already there in the structure of Christian thought rather

6. *Ibid.*, p. 205.
7. 1 Corinthians 1: 20.
8. On Toynbee, *cf.* above, pp. 38f.
9. Gustavo Gutiérrez, *A Theology of Liberation* (1971: London, 1974). On the Frankfurt school, *cf.* above, p. 132.
1. Jürgen Moltmann, *Theology of Hope* (London, 1967), p. 16.

than to add to it: for in a strong sense the Christian view of history, a view centred on Jesus Christ, is given. The source documents about Jesus Christ, the Bible, provide the continuing norm for any Christian perspective on history.

CHRISTIAN HISTORIOGRAPHY

A historian, as much as a person in any other walk of life, can adopt a Christian outlook on history. But can a Christian who has to write about the past, whether as a professional, an amateur or a student, put his vision of the historical process into his writing? It is certain that he will not wish to treat providence, in the words of Buckle, as 'the draff and offal of a bye-gone age'.[2] There are, however, risks in trying to write history from a Christian perspective. In 1839 the Rev. J. D. Schomberg, Master of Stoke Grammar School, Leicestershire, published a work entitled: *The Theocratic Philosophy of English History, being an attempt to impress upon history its true genius and real character, and to present it, not as a disjointed series of facts, but as one grand whole, exhibiting the progress of the social system, tending under the conduct of its Divine Author, by gradual and almost imperceptible advances to its completion*. The large claims made by Schomberg appear to come to grief on the admission that the pattern has been 'impressed' on history and that it is 'almost imperceptible'. Such bombast invites ridicule. A few years later the novelist George Eliot criticized another Christian minister for offering 'an evangelical edition of history with the inconvenient facts omitted'.[3] The Christian historian can all too easily fall into the twin traps of describing over-boldly the outworking of the divine will and of ignoring details that do not readily fit into the resulting scheme. He must recognize his own limitations. The Christian historian cannot write history in the manner, say, of the writer of the Second Book of Kings. He lacks the inspiration that gave the biblical historians their special insight. The first lesson that the Christian historian must learn is humility.

Yet it is possible for him to bring together his writing and his vision of the historical drama. He can make his account of the past

2. H. T. Buckle, *Introduction to the History of Civilization in England* (1857), ed. J. M. Robertson (London, n.d.), p. 901.
3. George Eliot, 'Evangelical Teaching: Dr Cumming' (1855), *Essays of George Eliot*, ed. Thomas Pinney (London, 1963), p. 161.

consistent with a providential understanding of history. He can write in conformity with his convictions that God is guiding the whole historical process; that hope is justified by the end God has in view, an end already assured by the work of Jesus; and that God sometimes takes a more direct part in events to dispense judgment and mercy. He can say, for instance, that when good surprisingly emerges from evil, God is evidently at work. That is not to deny that human beings are responsible for such events, but it is to contend that God is active in and through human affairs. Why, taking Baxter's example, was the Restoration of 1660 achieved peacefully? The Christian historian will want to give circumstances their due: the virtual power vacuum after the death of Oliver Cromwell called for an authority with claims to legitimacy if anarchy was to be avoided. The Christian historian will want to recognize the role of individuals: much of the credit for the smooth transition must go to General Monk. But he will also wish to acknowledge, like Baxter, God's merciful part in the process. The historian should take providence into account.

It might be objected that this is simple to announce as a principle, but extremely difficult to put into practice. Yet it has not ceased to be common in church history, where the hand of God is regularly discerned in the spread of the early church or the Evangelical Revival. Nor is it impractical in fields that we might suppose to be further from God's immediate action. In economic history, for example, the characteristic divine tactic of bringing good out of evil can frequently be recognized. The recurrent plagues of the fourteenth century were certainly a horrifying experience, but they seem to have prepared the way for a marked increase in the standard of living of English labourers. Again, the acceleration of the British rate of inflation in the mid-1970s brought a needed – but perhaps too little heeded – rebuke to post-war materialism. History in general can be conceived by the historian within a providential frame of meaning.

There then arises the vexed question of the historian and moral judgments. If the historian can write on Christian premises, should he express praise and blame? The classic case in favour of making moral judgments was worked out by Acton. It is morally irresponsible, he argued, to refrain from condemning what is morally wrong. The wrongdoer must not be whitewashed by the historian:

> The strong man with the dagger is followed by the weaker man with the sponge. First, the criminal who slays; then the sophist who defends the slayer.[4]

Acton pushed his view to an extreme. He wanted to formulate a historical blacklist by grading figures according to the worst deed committed by each.[5] Sir Herbert Butterfield takes the opposite point of view:

> I can condemn myself after self-examination, but in the case of others I can never know what allowance has to be made for conditions . . .[6]

The historian has the opportunity for exercising Christian charity, according to Sir Herbert, and must reflect that, 'There but for the grace of God go I'. He should not condemn. Both cases appeal to the Christian historian. He is attracted by a call to uphold moral standards and also by an appeal to exercise forgiveness. He is drawn in opposite directions.

The solution to his dilemma is suggested by the Christian analysis of the human condition outlined in the last chapter. Man can justly be compared with God, but also with dust. He is capable of spontaneous action, yet a creature affected by the rest of the created world. He enjoys the freedom that entails moral responsibility, but is deeply affected by his natural surroundings and human companions. The historian will therefore wish to write in the knowledge that human actions are subject to a moral law, which, as Acton put it in his inaugural lecture, is 'written on the tablets of eternity'.[7] Yet the historian will be aware that his fallible judgment cannot accurately estimate what 'allowance has to be made for conditions' in any particular case. His history will suggest neither that wrongdoing is a permissible option nor that the historian is the final arbiter of right and wrong. Just as he will want to write in a way consistent with his confidence that providence is at work yet mysterious, so he will want to describe human beings in the past as morally responsible agents yet leave their ultimate judgment to God.

4. Lord Acton, *Lectures on the French Revolution* (London, 1910), p. 92.
5. Sir Herbert Butterfield, Review of D. McElrath, *Lord Acton: The Decisive Decade, 1864–1874*, *The Historical Journal*, 15 (1972), p. 822.
6. Butterfield, *Christianity and History*, p. 45.
7. Lord Acton, *Lectures on Modern History* (London, 1906), p. 27.

A practical problem confronts the Christian historian at this stage. If he makes plain his religious commitment in his writing, will he not be excluding it from general notice and certainly from academic attention? The canons of ordinary historical scholarship have not permitted references to God for nearly 200 years. It is therefore entirely understandable that a providential framework for history is seldom thought acceptable outside the pulpit. One solution to the problem is that of Sir Herbert Butterfield. His distinction between technical and providential history encourages the historian to create separate compartments for his historical studies on the one hand and his personal interpretation of history on the other. Any such distinction, however, tends to obscure the extent to which all historical studies are necessarily moulded by the historian's point of view. Academic history cannot be preserved immune from the convictions of its practitioners. If a historian tries to minimize the effect of his personal views on his history, the effect is merely to increase the effect of other influences on what he writes – the assumptions of his time, his place, his profession. The consequences for a Christian outlook on history are serious. If a Christian historian tries to write without a thought for providence, he is likely to succumb to some alternative view or blend of views that happens to be in fashion. He will probably grow accustomed to the current assumptions of the academic world, positivist, historicist, Marxist or whatever. His Christian understanding of history will decay. It is far better to make no attempt to compartmentalize. Faith and history should be brought together, not separated out. Faith, after all, should be excluded from no part of life. A believer should not be a Christian and a historian but a Christian historian.

The difficulty that what he writes is likely to be ignored outside the community of faith therefore remains. Historiography that draws attention to traces of providence is unacceptable to the world at large. But the Christian historian is helped in his problem by the nature of written history. We have seen that, as history is a form of argumentation, the historian uses the methods of rhetoric.[8] He is writing not for himself but for an audience – the general public, a particular group or perhaps a university tutor. His arguments have to be framed so as to persuade his audience of the validity of his case. If a Christian historian is writing for the religious community,

8. *Cf.* above, pp. 14f.

there is no problem about the acceptability of providential history. If he is trying to show his readers the truth of the Christian faith, he will probably wish not only to write within a providential framework but also to offer a justification for it. If, however, he is writing for the general public or a university tutor, he must not put obstacles in the way of communicating with his audience. To describe an event as an expression of divine mercy, for instance, would be to surprise and perhaps to annoy his readers. They would be likely to dismiss the Christian historian's case about human responsibility for an event along with his comments on divine participation. He must therefore prune what he writes of overt Christian references. The mention of divine mercy, for example, would have to be omitted. His history must be adjusted according to the audience that he expects. The rhetorical nature of historiography suggests that a providential framework should be more explicit in some pieces of writing than in others.

This may appear an admission that in the last analysis there is a gulf between technical history, equally valid for historians of all persuasions, and providential history, on which the Christian meaning of history has been imposed. That is not, however, so. Even when a piece of history has been shorn of specific Christian allusions, the Christian vision of history can still have shaped its composition. The task can be conceived from the beginning as an investigation of the historical process under God's control although no reference is eventually made to his activity. The final version will still be entirely consistent with the Christian view of history. What is written will be a distinctively Christian product, but the Christian content will be implicit rather than explicit. If the same piece of history is needed for a Christian audience or to vindicate a Christian position, reference to providence can readily be restored. The Christian historian can discern God at work in the past without necessarily writing of him there. This approach is nothing other than the Christian attitude to living carried over into historical work. In ordinary life, believers do not always make Christian claims explicit at all times. They do so when it is appropriate, whether within the Christian community or in apologetic and evangelism. Similarly, the Christian historian is not obliged to tell the whole truth as he sees it in every piece of historical writing. He can write of providence or not according to his judgment of the composition of his audience. So long as his account accords with the Christian vision of the historical process, he will be fulfilling his vocation.

There is sometimes a need for the providential framework of history to be portrayed without reserve. For the church, it provides the encouragement of knowing that hitherto the Lord has helped his people. For the world outside the church, it has a defensive and an offensive role. History on Christian premises has the apologetic task of revealing as credible the belief that God stands behind and acts within the historical process. It also serves the evangelistic task of proclaiming Jesus Christ as the one whose victorious work assures us that God will bring history to a triumphant close. Christian history brings hope. But how are people to hear the message of hope without a historian? God's ways in the affairs of men need to be illuminated. There is a continuing call for Christian historians. The task is not a novel one, for there is a tradition of Christian historical thought and practice second to none. That tradition is itself responsible for generating the alternative ways of viewing and writing history that dominate the modern world. But historiography can be distinctively Christian. Allied with a philosophy of historiography that makes sense of the historian's work, it can operate within a Christian frame of meaning that does justice to the complexities of the world.

Booklist

This booklist is intended to provide ideas for further reading in the areas covered by this book. The material is arranged broadly according to the chapter headings in eight sections. Most, but not all, the items listed here are referred to in the text. All of them are in English. The list is, of course, highly selective.

1. WHAT IS HISTORY?

THE HISTORY OF HISTORIOGRAPHY

1. James W. Thompson and B. J. Holm, *A History of Historical Writing*, 2 vols (New York: Macmillan, 1942).
   The most useful compendium, containing valuable references.
2. Sir Moses I Finley, 'Myth, Memory and History', *The Use and Abuse of History* (London: Chatto and Windus, 1975).
   Perceptive essay on the origins and limits of historical consciousness in ancient Greece.
3. Arnaldo D. Momigliano, *Studies in Historiography* (London: Weidenfeld and Nicolson, 1966).
4. Arnaldo D. Momigliano, *Essays in Ancient and Modern Historiography* (Oxford: Blackwell, 1977).
   Two collections of closely argued and thoroughly annotated essays by a scholar of broad European cultural background.
5. Denys Hay, *Annalists and Historians: western historiography from the eighth to the eighteenth centuries* (London: Methuen, 1977).
   Recent general survey.
6. Sir Richard W. Southern, 'Aspects of the European Tradition of Historical Writing: 1. The Classical Tradition from Einhard to Geoffrey of Monmouth', *Transactions of the Royal Historical Society*, 5th Series, 20 (1970).
   Study of the uses of the classical historiographical inheritance following the Carolingian Renaissance.
7. Peter Burke, *The Renaissance Sense of the Past* (London: Edward Arnold, 1969).
   Collection of extracts from Renaissance writers with useful introductions.
8. George Huppert, *The Idea of Perfect History: historical erudition and historical philosophy in Renaissance France* (Urbana: University of Illinois Press, 1970).

Study of adoption of critical methods of the law and humanist attitudes by the late 16th cent. French historians.

9. David C. Douglas, *English Scholars, 1660-1730* (London: Eyre and Spottiswoode, 2nd edn, 1951).
   Study of the antiquarianism that withered with the emergence of full-blown Enlightenment attitudes.
10. Joseph M. Levine, 'Ancients, Moderns and History: the continuity of English historical writing in the later seventeenth century', *Studies in Change and Revolution: aspects of English intellectual history, 1640-1800*, ed. Paul J. Korshin (Menston, W. Yorks.: Scolar Press, 1972).
    Essay stressing that techniques of historiography began to move away from Renaissance norms only at the end of the 17th cent.
11. Sir Herbert Butterfield, *Man on his Past: the study of the history of historical scholarship* (Cambridge: C.U.P., 1955).
    Examines main currents of historiography from the late 18th cent. to Acton, discussing development of critical technique.
12. Pieter Geyl, *Debates with Historians* (London: Fontana, 1962).
    Essays by distinguished Dutch scholar on historians since Ranke.
13. George G. Iggers, *New Directions in European Historiography* (Middletown, Connecticut: Wesleyan University Press, 1975).
    Study of main post-war developments, including section on western European Marxist historiography.
14. Traian Stoianovich, *French Historical Method: the 'Annales' paradigm* (Ithaca, New York: Cornell University Press, 1976).
    Study of the 'functional-structural' approach to historiography propagated through the influential journal 'Annales'.

SURVEYS OF PHILOSOPHIES OF HISTORY

1. Fritz Stern, ed., *The Varieties of History: from Voltaire to the present* (London: Macmillan, 1956).
   Collection of extracts, including some on historical method as well as on schools of historical thought.
2. Patrick L. Gardiner, ed., *Theories of History* (Glencoe, Illinois: Free Press, 1959).
   Collection of extracts from philosophers of history from Vico to Collingwood, together with section on historical method.
3. Alban G. Widgery, *Interpretations of History: Confucius to Toynbee* (London: Allen and Unwin, 1961).
   Comprehensive survey of patterns attributed to history.
4. Frank E. Manuel, *Shapes of Philosophical History* (London: Allen and Unwin, 1965).
   Survey of patterns attributed to history; less comprehensive than no. 3, but more illuminating.

5. Ronald H. Nash, ed., *Ideas of History* (New York: E. P. Dutton, 1969).
Another collection of extracts.

2. CYCLICAL HISTORY

1. Mircea Eliade, *The Myth of the Eternal Return* (London: Routledge and Kegan Paul, 1955).
Translation of an important, but not universally endorsed, analysis by a French scholar of theories of cyclical time in archaic cultures.
2. John T. Marcus, 'Time and the Sense of History: West and East', *Comparative Studies in Society and History*, 3 (1961).
Brief survey of Chinese and Indian views of history.
3. William G. Beasley and Edwin G. Pulleyblank, ed., *Historians of China and Japan* (London: O.U.P., 1961).
Essays by leading scholars of Far Eastern historiography
4. Arthur F. Wright, 'On the Uses of Generalization in the Study of Chinese History', *Generalization in the Writing of History*, ed. Louis Gottschalk (Chicago: Chicago University Press, 1963).
On both traditional Chinese historiography and modern historians of China.
5. Robert C. Dentan, ed., *The Idea of History in the Ancient Near East* (New Haven: Yale University Press, 1955).
Collection of essays on historical thought of ancient cultures, including specially valuable one on Mesopotamia.
6. Harry Levin, *The Myth of the Golden Age in the Renaissance* (London: Faber, 1970).
Study of one of the most pervasive features of cyclical thought in western civilization.
7. Peter Burke, 'Tradition and Experience: the idea of decline from Bruni to Gibbon', *Edward Gibbon and the Decline and Fall of the Roman Empire*, ed. Glen W. Bowersock, John Clive and S. R. Graubard (Cambridge, Massachusetts: Harvard University Press, 1977).
Essay revealing variety in theories of decline over four centuries.
8. Oswald Spengler, *The Decline of the West* (1918, 1922), ed. Helmut Werner (London: Allen and Unwin, 1961 edn).
Abbreviated translation of Spengler's work that envisaged the decay of western civilization as the downturn of a cultural cycle.
9. Henry S. Hughes, *Oswald Spengler: a critical estimate* (New York: Scribner's, 1952).
Penetrating study of Spengler.
10. Arnold J. Toynbee, *A Study of History* (London: O.U.P., 1934-59).
Massive analysis in eleven volumes of the rise and fall of civilizations in a rhythmic pattern.

11. Edward T. Gargan, ed., *The Intent of Toynbee's History: a co-operative appraisal* (Chicago: Loyola University Press, 1961).
Collection of fairly sympathetic essays on Toynbee's work.

3. CHRISTIAN HISTORY

1. Burr C. Brundage, 'The Birth of Clio: a résumé and interpretation of ancient Near Eastern Historiography', *Teachers of History: essays in honor of Lawrence Bradford Packard*, ed. Henry S. Hughes (Ithaca, New York: Cornell University Press, 1954).
Essay placing Old Testament history in the background of the ancient world.
2. Christopher R. North, *The Old Testament Interpretation of History* (London: Epworth, 1946).
Useful, though perhaps now slightly dated, introduction to the subject.
3. Richard J. Bauckham, 'The Rise of Apocalyptic', *Themelios*, 3 (1978).
Illuminating survey of recent literature on the theme.
4. Constantinos A. Patrides, *The Grand Design of God: the literary form of the Christian view of history* (London: Routledge and Kegan Paul, 1972).
Primarily a study of literature expressing a Christian understanding of history, but also a mine of bibliographical information.
5. Roland H. Bainton, 'Patristic Christianity', *The Idea of History in the Ancient Near East*, ed. Robert C. Dentan (New Haven: Yale University Press, 1955).
Succinct chapter in the book listed in section 2, no. 5.
6. Robert L.P. Milburn, *Early Christian Interpretations of History* (London: A. and C. Black, 1954).
Survey of Church Fathers.
7. Lloyd G. Patterson, *God and History in Early Christian Thought: a study of themes from Justin Martyr to Gregory the Great* (London: A. and C. Black, 1967).
Alternative to no. 6.
8. Augustine of Hippo, *Concerning the City of God against the Pagans*, trans. Henry Bettenson (Harmondsworth: Penguin, 1972).
The most recent and accessible edition of the most famous theology of history.
9. Robert A. Markus, *Saeculum: history and society in the theology of St Augustine* (Cambridge: C.U.P., 1970).
Outstanding study of Augustine's historical thought.
10. Theodor E. Mommsen, 'St Augustine and the Christian Idea of Progress', *Journal of the History of Ideas*, 12 (1951).

Reconstructs Augustine's intention to show that he was combating the idea of this-worldly progress.

11. Robert W. Hanning, *The Vision of History in Early Britain: from Gildas to Geoffrey of Monmouth* (New York: Columbia University Press, 1966).
    Study of the largely Christian ideas behind early mediaeval historiography.
12. Marjorie Reeves, *The Influence of Prophecy in the Later Middle Ages: a study in Joachimism* (Oxford: O.U.P., 1969).
    Detailed study of identity and popularity of the ideas of Joachim of Fiore.
13. John M. Headley, *Luther's View of Church History* (New Haven: Yale University Press, 1963).
    Standard book on the subject.
14. Sir Walter Ralegh, *The History of the World*, ed. Constantinos A. Patrides (London: Macmillan, 1971).
    This edition contains an introduction pointing out Ralegh's place in the tradition of Christian historiography.
15. Constantinos A. Patrides, *Milton and the Christian Tradition* (Oxford: Clarendon Press, 1966).
    Chapter eight is on Milton and the Christian view of history.
16. Jacques-Bénigne Bossuet, *Discourse on Universal History*, ed. Orest Ranum (Chicago: University of Chicago Press, 1976).
    Good translation of classic Catholic view of divine purpose in history.
17. W. Owen Chadwick, *From Bossuet to Newman: the idea of doctrinal development* (Cambridge: C.U.P., 1957).
    Brilliant study of Catholic thought on the historical dimension of doctrine.
18. John D. Walsh, 'Joseph Milner's Evangelical Church History', *The Journal of Ecclesiastical History*, 10 (1959).
    Able assessment of evangelical Anglican church historian.

4. THE IDEA OF PROGRESS

1. John B. Bury, *The Idea of Progress: an inquiry into its origin and growth* (London: Macmillan, 1920).
   The classic study which has been the starting-point for subsequent research.
2. Sidney B. Fay, 'The Idea of Progress', *The American Historical Review*, 52 (1947).
   Brief and lucid account of the idea.
3. Ronald V. Sampson, *Progress in the Age of Reason: the seventeenth century to the present day* (London: Heinemann, 1956).
   Capable study.

4. Sidney Pollard, *The Idea of Progress: history and society* (London: C. A. Watts, 1968).
   Survey and statement of the idea as a substitute for theism in providing a rationale for morality.
5. John H. Plumb, 'The Historian's Dilemma', *Crisis in the Humanities*, ed. John H. Plumb (Harmondsworth: Penguin, 1964).
6. John H. Plumb, *The Death of the Past* (London: Macmillan, 1969).
   No. 5 contains the germ of no. 6, which argues that the past has always been used as a sanction for the present; that critical history has destroyed such a use of the past; but that the historian must show how progress can be achieved by the use of reason.
7. Georges Sorel, *The Illusions of Progress* (1908: Berkeley, California: University of California Press, 1969 edn).
   Vigorous critique of the idea of progress.
8. John Baillie, *The Belief in Progress* (London: O.U.P., 1950).
   Critique by Christian theologian.
9. Nathan Rotenstreich, 'The Idea of Historical Progress and its Assumptions', *History and Theory*, 10 (1971).
   Highly abstract statement of the central objections to the idea of progress from a theistic standpoint.
10. Eric R. Dodds, 'The Ancient Concept of Progress', *The Ancient Concept of Progress and Other Essays on Greek Literature and Belief* (Oxford: Clarendon Press, 1973).
    Thorough study demonstrating weakness and transience of elements of the idea of progress in the ancient world.
11. Charles Frankel, *The Faith of Reason* (New York: King's Crown and Columbia University Press, 1948).
    Penetrating general study of the idea of progress in the 18th cent.
12. Ernest L. Tuveson, *Millennium and Utopia: a study in the background of the idea of progress* (Berkeley, California: University of California Press, 1949).
    Study of aspects of the way in which the Enlightenment view of history was the Christian view secularized.
13. Ronald S. Crane, 'Anglican Apologetics and the Idea of Progress, 1699-1745', *The Idea of the Humanities and Other Essays Critical and Historical* (Chicago: University of Chicago Press, 1967), 1.
    Analysis of Christian roots in England of a belief in general and indefinite progress.
14. Henry Vyverberg, *Historical Pessimism in the French Enlightenment* (Cambridge, Massachusetts: Harvard University Press, 1958).
    By exploring the strength of the belief in cultural decline, the author cautions us against exaggerating the extent of Enlightenment assumptions of progress.
15. Andrew Skinner, 'Natural History in the Age of Adam Smith' *Political Studies*, 15 (1967).

Analysis of the historical thought of the Scottish Enlightenment revealing the premises of the idea of progress.

16. Frank E. Manuel, *The Prophets of Paris* (Cambridge, Massachusetts: Harvard University Press, 1962).
    Lively study of the French tradition of thought about human progress from Turgot through Saint-Simon to Comte.
17. Donald G. Charlton, *Positivist Thought in France during the Second Empire, 1857-1870* (Oxford: Clarendon Press, 1959).
    Detailed study pointing out some of the inconsistencies of Comte and his successors.
18. Donald G. Charlton, *Secular Religions in France, 1815-1870* (London: For University of Hull by O.U.P., 1963).
    Wider study than no. 17, analysing 'The Cult of History and Progress' in chapters seven and eight.
19. *Ideas and Beliefs of the Victorians: an historic revaluation of the Victorian age* (London: Sylvan Press, 1949).
    Section one, 'The Theory of Progress', includes some sparkling essays – especially that by G. M. Trevelyan on Macaulay.
20. John W. Burrow, *Evolution and Society: a study in Victorian social theory* (Cambridge: C.U.P., 1966).
    Examination of transformation of the idea of progress in response to impact of historicist modes of thinking.
21. Sir Herbert Butterfield, *The Whig Interpretation of History* (London: G. Bell and Sons, 1931).
    Scrutiny of the effect of the assumption of progress on historians.
22. Lionel Kochan, *Acton on History* (London: Deutsch, 1954).
    Reconstruction of Lord Acton's view of history bringing out its identification of providence with progress.
23. Francis S. Marvin, ed., *Progress and History* (London: O.U.P., 1916).
    Collection of essays edited by British Comtist claiming to illustrate 'the main lines of evolution' in various departments of life.

5. HISTORICISM

1. Calvin G. Rand, 'Two Meanings of Historicism in the Writings of Dilthey, Troeltsch and Meinecke', *Journal of the History of Ideas*, 25 (1964).
   Illuminating analysis of the nature of historicism.
2. *The New Science of Giambattista Vico*, ed. Max H. Fisch and Thomas G. Bergin (Ithaca, New York: Cornell University Press, 1948).
   Translation of Vico's seminal work.
3. Arnaldo D. Momigliano, 'Vico's *Scienza Nuova*: Roman *Bestioni* and Roman *Eroi*', *Essays in Ancient and Modern Historiography*

(Oxford: Blackwell, 1977).
Explains Vico's intention of defending the dichotomy of the sacred and the profane in Christian historical thought.

4. Giorgio Tagliacozzo, ed., *Giambattista Vico: an international symposium* (Baltimore: The Johns Hopkins Press, 1969).
Collection of essays by distinguished contributors embracing extensive discussion of relation of subsequent historicist thinkers to Vico.
5. Johann Gottfried von Herder, *Reflections on the Philosophy of the History of Mankind* (1784–91: Chicago: Chicago University Press, 1968).
Source of many of the ideas in the mainstream of historicism.
6. Sir Isaiah Berlin, *Vico and Herder: two studies in the history of ideas* (London: Hogarth Press, 1976).
Impressive analyses of Vico and Herder.
7. Peter H. Reill, 'History and Hermeneutics in the "Aufklärung": the thought of Johann Christoph Gatterer', *The Journal of Modern History*, 45 (1973).
An instance of the emergence of a historicist view.
8. Peter H. Reill, *The German Enlightenment and the Rise of Historicism* (Berkeley, California: University of California Press, 1975).
Important analysis of the roots of historicism.
9. George G. Iggers, *The German Conception of History: the national tradition of historical thought from Herder to the present* (Middletown, Connecticut: Wesleyan University Press, 1968).
Illuminating and comprehensive study of historicist mainstream.
10. Leopold von Ranke, *The Theory and Practice of History*, ed. George G. Iggers (Indianapolis: Bobbs-Merrill, 1973).
Extracts from Ranke, together with Von Humboldt's programmatic essay, 'On the Historian's Task'. The introduction is a revealing study of Ranke.
11. Duncan Forbes, *The Liberal Anglican Idea of History* (Cambridge: C.U.P., 1952).
Study of early 19th cent. English historians, including Thomas Arnold, who fell under the influence of Niebuhr.
12. Hugh R. Trevor-Roper, *The Romantic Movement and the Study of History* (London: Athlone Press, 1969).
Brief study focusing on the influence of Sir Walter Scott.
13. Hans P. Rickman, ed., *W. Dilthey: selected writings* (Cambridge: C.U.P., 1976).
Collection of extracts with introduction bringing out the significance of Dilthey.
14. Benedetto Croce, *History: its theory and practice*, ed. Douglas Ainslie (New York: Russell and Russell, 1960).

Statement of views of idiosyncratic but important Italian thinker influenced by a speculative interpretation of Hegelianism.

15. Robin G. Collingwood, *The Idea of History* (London: O.U.P., 1946).
    Posthumously published papers of the Oxford thinker steeped in the historicist tradition.
16. Michael Krausz, ed., *Critical Essays on the Philosophy of R. G. Collingwood* (London: O.U.P., 1972).
    Contains two essays on Collingwood's historical thought and extensive bibliography.

6. MARXIST HISTORY

1. Karl Marx, Frederick Engels and V. I. Lenin, *On Historical Materialism: a collection* (Moscow: Progress Publishers, 1972).
   Collection of texts by the founders of Marxist-Leninism. Includes 'The German Ideology' (1846), the most significant text on history.
2. Karl Marx, 'The Eighteenth Brumaire of Louis Bonaparte', Karl Marx and Frederick Engels, *Selected Works* (Moscow: Foreign Languages Publishing House, 1951 *etc.*).
   Best instance of how Marx actually practised the writing of history – a study of the French revolution of 1848.
3. Helmut Fleischer, *Marxism and History* (London: Allen Lane, The Penguin Press, 1973).
   Rather abstract elucidation of the theory of history in Marx's writings.
4. William H. Shaw, *Marx's Theory of History* (London: Hutchinson, 1978).
   Careful study of Marx's view of production as the motive force of history.
5. Melvin Rader, *Marx's Interpretation of History* (Oxford: O.U.P., 1979). Forthcoming.
6. Georgy V. Plekhanov, *The Development of the Monist View of History* (1895: Moscow: Foreign Languages Publishing House, 1956).
   Elaboration of Marxist historical theory in reply to critics.
7. Perry Anderson, *Considerations on Western Marxism* (London: New Left Books, 1976).
   Revealing analysis of development of Marxist thought in western Europe since the 1890s.
8. Martin Jay, *The Dialectical Imagination: a history of the Frankfurt School and the Institute for Social Research, 1923–1950* (London: Heinemann, 1973).
   Study of significant phase in Marxist thought.
9. Maurice C. Cornforth, *Dialectical Materialism: an introduction: 2. Historical Materialism* (London: Lawrence and Wishart, 1953).

Statement by British theorist of mainstream Marxist understanding of the historical process.

10. Vladislav Kelle and Matvei Kovalson, *Historical Materialism: an outline of Marxist theory of society* (Moscow: Progress Publishers, 1973).
    Contemporary Russian Marxist view of the historical process.
11. Geoffrey Ellis, 'The "Marxist Interpretation" of the French Revolution', *The English Historical Review*, 93 (1978).
    Case study of Marxist historical analysis.
12. Edward P. Thompson, *The Poverty of Theory and Other Essays* (London: Merlin Press, 1978).
    The main essay forms a critique of contemporary Marxist theories of historical technique.
13. Harry B. Acton, *The Illusion of the Epoch: Marxism-Leninism as a philosophical creed* (London: Cohen and West, 1955).
    Includes clear critical account of historical materialism as a positivist misconception.
14. Sir Karl R. Popper, *The Poverty of Historicism* (London: Routledge and Kegan Paul, 1958).
    Well-known trenchant attack on Hegel and Marx as (supposed) determinists.
15. Gordon Leff, *The Tyranny of Concepts: a critique of Marxism* (London: Merlin Press, 1969 edn).
    Critique of Marxist theory of history by a historian.
16. David Lyon, *Karl Marx* (Tring, Hertfordshire: Lion, 1979).
    Appraisal of the development of the thought of Marx by a Christian.

7. THE PHILOSOPHY OF HISTORIOGRAPHY

1. Hans Meyerhoff, ed., *The Philosophy of History in our Time: an anthology* (New York: Doubleday, 1959).
    Well selected essays including extract from Berlin (no. 13) on moral judgments.
2. Patrick L. Gardiner, ed., *The Philosophy of History* (Oxford: Clarendon Press, 1974).
    Excellent collection of essays including Hempel (no. 18) on general laws. Includes valuable bibliography.
3. Patrick L. Gardiner, 'The Concept of Man as presupposed by the Historical Studies', *The Proper Study: Royal Institute of Philosophy Lectures*, ed. Godfrey N. A. Vesey, 4 (1971).
    Illuminating study of the contrast between the idealist and the positivist positions.
4. William H. Walsh, *An Introduction to Philosophy of History* (London: Hutchinson, 1967 edn).

Invaluable review of idealist and positivist positions, and an attempt to hold a mediating position.

5. Burleigh T. Wilkins, *Hegel's Philosophy of History* (Ithaca, New York: Cornell University Press, 1974).
   Sympathetic study revealing that Hegel was engaging with the issues that still occupy the philosophy of historiography.
6. Raymond Aron, *Introduction to the Philosophy of History: an essay on the limits of objectivity* (London: Weidenfeld and Nicolson, 1961).
   Translation of a masterly French attempt to synthesize an idealist position derived from Dilthey with a positivist position derived from Weber.
7. Theodor W. Adorno *et al.*, *The Positivist Dispute in German Sociology* (London: Heinemann, 1976).
   Papers in which idealists and positivists disagree, applying as much to history as to sociology.
8. Alan Bullock, 'The Historian's Purpose: history and metahistory', *History Today* (Feb. 1951).
   Rejection of the view that history should aim to establish general propositions in the manner of traditional philosophy of history or of sociology.
9. Edward H. Carr, *What is History?* (London: Macmillan, 1961).
   Analysis of issues in philosophy of historiography at once popular and profound.
10. Geoffrey R. Elton, *The Practice of History* (Sydney: Sydney University Press, 1967).
    Manifesto for the self-sufficiency of history, much concerned to rebut no. 9.
11. Hugh R. Trevor-Roper, *The Past and the Present: history and sociology* (London: London School of Economics, 1969).
    Lecture contending that history, while using scientific technique, is not itself a science.
12. William H. Dray, *Philosophy of History* (Englewood Cliffs, New Jersey: Prentice-Hall, 1964).
    Review of issues in philosophy of historiography from anti-positivist standpoint, together with critical assessment of certain philosophies of history.
13. Sir Isaiah Berlin, *Historical Inevitability* (London: O.U.P., 1954).
    Eloquent denunciation of theories of historical inevitability, positivist and Marxist.
14. Paul O. Kristeller, 'Some Problems of Historical Knowledge', *The Journal of Philosophy*, 58 (1961).
    Approach to many of the traditional problems, especially those of the historian of ideas, from an idealist standpoint.
15. Michael Oakeshott, 'The Activity of being an Historian', *Rationalism in Politics and Other Essays* (London: Methuen, 1962).

Written from the standpoint of a distinctive form of absolute idealism.

16. Thomas McCarthy, *The Critical Theory of Jürgen Habermas* (London: Hutchinson, 1978).
    Demanding but rewarding study that illuminates the thought of the leading contemporary exponent of an idealist approach to the disciplines concerned with man.
17. Theodore Abel, 'The Operation called *Verstehen*', *The American Journal of Sociology*, 54 (1948).
    On the limits of historical intuition from a broadly positivist viewpoint.
18. Carl G. Hempel, 'The Function of General Laws in History', *The Journal of Philosophy*, 39 (1942).
    Classic claim that history may be conceived as using the methodology of the natural sciences.
19. Michael M. Postan, *Fact and Relevance: essays on historical method* (Cambridge: C.U.P., 1971).
    Series of lucid statements and exemplifications of the avowedly positivist view that human studies can be undertaken wholly by the methodology of the natural sciences.
20. Burleigh T. Wilkins, *Has History Any Meaning?* (Hassocks, Sussex: Harvester, 1978).
    Study of methodology of Sir Karl Popper.

8. THE MEANING OF HISTORY

RECENT STATEMENTS OF CHRISTIAN HISTORICAL THOUGHT

1. Sir Herbert Butterfield, *Christianity and History* (London: G. Bell and Sons, 1949).
   Classic discussion by distinguished historian.
2. Sir Herbert Butterfield, *History and Human Relations* (London: Collins, 1951).
   Collection of essays supplementary to no. 1, including 'The Christian and Historical Study'.
3. Sir Herbert Butterfield, 'God in History', *Steps to Christian Understanding*, ed. Richard J. W. Bevan (London: O.U.P., 1958).
   Brief statement of a providential view of history.
4. C. Thomas McIntire, ed., *Writings on Christianity and History: Herbert Butterfield* (New York: O.U.P., 1979).
5. Michael Hobart, 'History and Religion in the Thought of Herbert Butterfield', *Journal of the History of Ideas*, 32 (1971).
   Appreciation and critique.
6. Reinhold Niebuhr, *Faith and History: a comparison of Christian and modern views of history* (London: Nisbet, 1949).

Statement by American neo-orthodox theologian contrasting Christian view especially with the idea of progress.

7. Hugh F. Kearney, 'Christianity and the Study of History', *The Downside Review*, 67 (1949).
   Plea for Roman Catholic historians to omit providence from their historical understanding. Followed by anonymous note upholding against Kearney a more traditional Catholic view.
8. Kenneth S. Latourette, 'The Christian Understanding of History', *The American Historical Review*, 54 (1949).
   Thoughts on the practice of history by Baptist church historian.
9. Norman Sykes, 'Some Current Conceptions of Historiography and their Significance for Christian Apologetic', *The Journal of Theological Studies*, 50 (1949).
   Welcomes Collingwood's historical thought (section 5, no. 15) as ally of Christianity.
10. Eric Voegelin, *Order and History*, 4 vols (Baton Rouge: Louisiana State University Press, 1956–75).
    Schematic analysis of the panorama of ancient history by Lutheran theorist.
11. H. Christopher Dawson, *The Dynamics of World History*, ed. John J. Mulley (London: Sheed and Ward, 1957).
    Collection of valuable essays by Roman Catholic thinker on Christianity and culture.
12. M. C. Smit, 'The Divine Mystery in History', *Free University Quarterly* (Amsterdam), 6 (1958/1959).
    Wrestles with the problem of how far a Christian historian can discern the workings of providence.
13. Clive S. Lewis, 'Historicism', *They asked for a Paper: papers and addresses* (London: Bles, 1962).
    Critique of all claims to discern patterns in history, and especially Christian claims.
14. John W. Montgomery, *The Shape of the Past: a Christian response to secular philosophies of history* (Ann Arbor, Michigan: Edwards Brothers, 1962).
    Wide-ranging survey of philosophy of history and related matters by American evangelical scholar.
15. Henri-Irénée Marrou, *The Meaning of History* (Baltimore: Helicon, 1966).
    Translation of work by French Catholic historian, which, despite its title, is primarily about technique.
16. Henri-Irénée Marrou, *Time and Timeliness* (New York: Sheed and Ward, 1969).
    A historian's theology of history.
17. Van A. Harvey, *The Historian and the Believer* (London: S.C.M., 1967).

Thorough study of the role of historical method in theology, valuable for its analysis of different standpoints.

18. Daniel P. Fuller, *Easter Faith and History* (London: Tyndale Press, 1968).
    Study of the theological problem of the relation of faith and history by American evangelical scholar.
19. Willem den Boer, 'Graeco-Roman Historiography in its Relation to Biblical and Modern Thinking', *History and Theory*, 7 (1968).
    Translated rather unevenly from Dutch, this essay, apparently the only writing in English by an able Dutch Reformed historian who writes within a providential framework, argues that biblical historians were unique in the ancient world in seeing events as prefigurings of the future.
20. Gordon H. Clark, *Historiography: secular and religious* (Nutley, New Jersey: Craig Press, 1971).
    Although occasionally misleading (as over Vico and Hegel), this survey includes much cogent discussion of theorists of history, historians and theologians from an evangelical viewpoint.
21. George Marsden and Frank Roberts, ed., *A Christian View of History?* (Grand Rapids, Michigan: Eerdmans, 1975).
    Collection of essays favouring the writing of a distinctive Christian history.
22. C. Thomas McIntire, ed., *God, History and Historians: modern Christian views of history* (New York: O.U.P., 1977).
    Useful anthology of recent Christian statements.
23. Eric W. Ives, *God in History* (Tring, Hertfordshire: Lion, 1979).
    Examination by a historian of the evidence for Christianity and of Christian practice in the early modern period.

Index